Affinities

Affinities

Potent Connections in Personal Life

Jennifer Mason

polity

First published in 2018 by Polity Press

Polity Press
65 Bridge Street
Cambridge CB2 1UR, UK

Polity Press
101 Station Landing
Suite 300
Medford, MA 02155, USA

ISBN-13: 978-0-7456-6463-7
ISBN-13: 978-0-7456-6464-4(pb)

A catalogue record for this book is available from the British Library.

Typeset in 10.5 on 12 pt Plantin by
Servis Filmsetting Ltd, Stockport, Cheshire
Printed and bound in Great Britain by CPI Group (UK) Ltd, St Ives PLC

The publisher has used its best endeavours to ensure that the URLs for external websites referred to in this book are correct and active at the time of going to press. However, the publisher has no responsibility for the websites and can make no guarantee that a site will remain live or that the content is or will remain appropriate.

Every effort has been made to trace all copyright holders, but if any have been inadvertently overlooked the publisher will be pleased to include any necessary credits in any subsequent reprint or edition.

For further information on Polity, visit our website: www.politybooks.com

'Those who don't believe in magic will never find it'
(Roald Dahl, *The Minpins*)

Contents

Expanded Contents

Acknowledgements

In researching and writing *Affinities* I have drawn upon and debated with the work of all kinds of fascinating thinkers, researchers, artists and writers, many of whom are cited in the book. Although I do not know all of them personally, I wanted to start by saying a general thank you for their willingness to put exciting ideas, thoughts and work out there for the rest of us to benefit from and engage with.

I am also very grateful to the Economic and Social Research Council, and to the Leverhulme Trust, for funding a range of projects which have fed into my thinking about affinities, and on which the book draws. I am especially grateful to all of the people who participated in those research projects, generously sharing their time and experiences with me and my colleagues.

I owe an enormous debt of gratitude to all of my colleagues past and present in the Morgan Centre for Research into Everyday Lives at the University of Manchester. The Morgan Centre was established in 2005, and it is no coincidence that it was around that time I began thinking about affinities. Collaboration and an irrepressible desire to think differently are at the very heart of the Morgan Centre, and these create a special atmosphere which encourages and nourishes all those involved. Being part of all this has given me the most wonderful and intellectually generous set of colleagues it is possible to imagine, as well as many exciting and stimulating times through conferences and events over the years. I consider myself very fortunate to be part of the vibrant conversations and associations that are the Morgan Centre.

I feel especially blessed to have worked with or been close to particular people who I know have shifted and shaped how I think about affinities, and lots else besides. In this regard I would especially like to thank Carol Smart, Becky Tipper and Katherine Davies, all of whom – in their inimitably different ways – have inspired and influenced my thinking and writing about affinities. Very special thanks to Andrew Jones who has lived with this book and its themes for as long as I have. It simply would not have come to fruition without his insights, encouragement, clarity of thought and endlessly generous support. Finally, thank you to Rosa and Joe for always having been both a grounding and an inspiration.

Introduction: Affinities as an Invitation to Think Differently

Why does a woman who discovers relatives she never knew she had, feel so moved when she recognises a family resemblance with them? What does it mean when a life is changed through the serendipity of a chance encounter? How is it possible to have an affinity with a place? What is happening when someone feels almost literally transported to another place or time by a chance encounter with a smell or a texture or a song? In each of these cases, some kind of potent connection is being made, and experienced viscerally and personally. In this book I want to suggest these kinds of connections are *affinities*, and to explore what they are and how they seem to matter so much. Affinities *do* matter, and I suggest that taking them seriously and exploring them opens up new and exciting possibilities for conceptualising living in the world.

I am going to argue that affinities are potent connections that rise up and matter. They are encounters where it is possible to identify a spark or a charge of connection that makes personal life charismatic, or enchants, or even toxifies it. Affinities are those connections that feel 'kindred' in some way, or make things kindred, whether or not they involve a family or kinship link as conventionally defined, and indeed we shall see that affinities can take shape between elements other than people too. Crucially, affinities are personal connections that have *potency*. They can be affinities of opposition, alterity or negativity, just as much as affinities of resemblance, empathy and closeness. They can involve ephemeral and ethereal yet somehow defining and elemental connections, and even epiphanal ones. They may feel *of us*, in ways that seem inscribed or seared into us and yet they also seem to live beyond us and can feel capricious, anarchic, otherworldly and even lyrical and poetic. Affinities involve fascination, wondering and puzzlement, often about their very potency and ineffability.

The *potency* of the connections is the point, and that is where I want the focus of the book to be. Let me make it clear straight away therefore that this is not a book about kinship systems, where 'affines' are formally conceptualised as a specific category or order of kin (usually seen as kin by marriage). Indeed it is not a book about kinship in that sense at all, although I am interested in connections that *feel kindred* in some way. Neither is it a book that uses affinity as a device to study *people* who are strongly attracted to *certain things, or pleasures, or behaviours,* or indeed to *other people.* Both of these examples involve seeing affinities as to do with the fixed points that they connect (people, kinsfolk, pleasures, behaviours, things), and make the assumption that it is these fixed points, and possible correlations or patterns in them, that are of interest. Such an approach might tell us that young men of a particular social class are strongly attracted to online gaming for example.

My approach to affinities, however, is to understand them as *connective charges and energies* that are of interest in themselves and not because of what they connect. It is the character and potency of the connections that I want to explore, more than the points that they put in relation. Central to my arguments about affinities is that they constitute animate or living connections, and hence I focus a great deal on concepts like *flows, forces and energies.* Always something is thought to be moving, flowing, seeking, encountering, making and even forcing connection. Affinities are essentially *living,* and they are lived through multidimensional encounters and sensations in personal life.

Given that affinities are *lived,* they are also, ironically perhaps, *parochial.* I use the term parochial here not in the pejorative sense that has come to characterise it in recent years as the petty or insubstantial, but in a stronger, active and experiential sense to mean the medium and means through which we encounter the world. My reasoning is that our activity of living is always done locally (locally to ourselves) through the medium, as it were, of our own personal 'parish'. I had been thinking about parochialism and its connection with the concept of personal life in this way for some time, when I came across Robert Macfarlane's wonderful interpretation of Patrick Kavanagh's 'The Parish and the Universe', in his introduction to Nan Shepherd's *The Living Mountain.* Following Kavanagh, Macfarlane suggests that the parochial is 'not a perimeter but *an aperture*: a space through which the world [can] be seen' (Macfarlane, 2011: xv, my emphasis). This idea of an aperture on the world echoes the argument I want to make that the parochial is not an insubstantial quality of existence, nor is it a fixed locale, but instead – and in keeping with the concept of personal life (Smart, 2007) – it is nexus, medium, mode and locus for our engagement with the world and, as such, it can sometimes channel potent connections, or affinities. It is how affinities can feel powerfully and simultaneously *of us*, and *beyond us*.

Perceiving and apprehending affinities in these kinds of ways means we need to allow ourselves to think differently and openly, even or especially when we feel confined by conventional disciplinary orientations. It is in this sense that I want to suggest that affinities, as I develop them in this book, constitute an invitation to think and theorise differently. They invite us to imagine connections, charges and energies that cannot be contained within, or done justice by, existing sociological modes of thought. They tantalise and beckon us to think more boldly, freely and poetically about how we understand living in the world.

The book is therefore written as an invitation, a beckoning, a suggestion of an orientation, rather than as a treatise or a frame-work. I do not 'cover' all possible 'types' of affinity (indeed I do not deal in 'types' of affinity at all). Instead, I take you on a journey through examples and illustrations of what affinities can involve, woven together with an alternating and cumulative argument about how we might understand their potencies. I want to encourage you to imagine and attune to affinities as potent connective charges and energies. I want to tantalise and beckon you to imagine and then reimagine affinities in your own fields, and in your own personal lives as well for that matter. In the pages that follow I show what happens when we shift our lenses and lexicons to be able to capture or attune to affinities that I argue come alive in *sensations*. I go on to suggest that understanding affinities means we need to be able to apprehend energies, forces, flows and charges which can take shape as *ineffable kinship*, or *ecological connection*, or the *'socio-atmospherics'* of personal life. The three parts of the book – part 1, 'Sensations of Living'; part 2, 'Ineffable Kinship'; and part 3, 'Ecologies and Socio-Atmospherics' – correspond to these sets of ideas and they constitute layers in the cumulative argument. Thereafter, I conclude the book with a discussion of 'Affinities in Time', arguing that the allure and enigma of *time* is crucial in all this, but that we need to see beyond conventional linear understandings of temporality to be able to appreciate in what ways. In the conclusion I also return to consider the possible implications, for sociology in particular, of accepting the invitation of affinities to think differently.

To do all this I have adopted a somewhat unconventional approach to writing and compiling the book, which is inspired by 'facet methodology' – an approach developed by colleagues and myself at the University of Manchester (Mason, 2011). The main premise of facet methodology is that we can use 'flashes of insight' gained through an exploration of strategically and artistically chosen *facets* of a problem – rather than attempting (and usually failing) to describe and document all dimensions of the problem in its entirety. The argument is that these 'artfully' chosen facets can offer strongly resonant and evocative forms of understanding and insight.

What this means for the book is that I have structured each of the three main parts to allow me to present a carefully chosen range of facets, whilst embedding these in a cumulative argument about affinities. Each part of the book is structured in the same way, beginning with an introduction that asks why the concepts developed in that part might be useful. Each then takes the reader on a journey through a set of 'facets' – in part 1 these are 'facets of sensation'; in part 2 they are 'facets of ineffable kinship'; and in part 3 they are 'facets of ecologies and socio-atmospherics'. The facets are drawn from a range of sources that I have chosen because they express or illustrate something important or resonant about the energies of affinity. These sources include the arts and literature, current affairs, broadcast radio, poetry, music, academic research, and various forms of creative and autobiographical writing. Each facet, in a sense, is a stand-alone piece, and some of them contain analysis and commentary to feed into the argument about affinities. And yet it is best for the facets to be read together and in sequence, because there are threads that link them, and because they have been chosen to illuminate distinctive and important aspects of affinities. In each part of the book the facets are then followed by a 'layering' of the argument about affinities, which draws insights from the facets in that part of the book, and also engages with relevant literature, debate and theorising. Ideas and themes bubble up and are reinforced cumulatively throughout the book in these layers of argument. The conclusion then adds the fourth and final layer, in its focus on 'affinities in time'.

For ease of reading, facets and the layerings of the argument are presented in different fonts.

PART ONE

Sensations of Living

Why Sensations?

We sense others. We know what they are like and who they are by seeing, touching, smelling, hearing and generally experiencing the sensations of them, at the same time as they are experiencing the sensations of us. We know what it feels like to be with and apart from them and in that sense our relations generate sensations. We know how they *are* with us (their manner of being with us, of interacting with us, their character and demeanour with us and so on) in these ways. More than that, we do not even have to be physically with others in the moment to experience the sensations of them, and of being with or connected to them, because sensations can be manifest in memory and imagination, just as longing or dread about the company of another can be experienced in sensory-kinaesthetic ways. We can conjure up as well as remember the sensations of others and how they are with us. Such sensations can form part of the weight of grief for example, felt as sensations of the mind, soul, head and chest. Contrary to popular assumption, online and 'virtual' interactions are also full of sensations, often bringing faces to faces quite literally in direct interactions with one's own and others' faces and bodies, words (spoken or created and experienced in text and symbols), language, sound and noises, immediate environments – and all this viewed on our screens, physically felt, sensed and executed through our bodies, including our fingers as we stroke and tap our devices, aurally heard and encountered in our earphones (see, for example, Jamieson, 2013; Morgan, 2009: 106–7; Wilding, 2006). It is in these ways that the experience of living routinely involves tuning into its sensory-kinaesthetics.

Of course, once we start to think about it, all life is lived in and through these sensory-kinaesthetic registers – even the so-called

'virtual' – but they are not usually factored into sociological understandings of relationships. Except perhaps sometimes in the sphere
of romantic relationships and sexual attraction (and even there the
focus is more usually on appearance as an individual characteristic
or a personal preference), most analyses of relationships and relating
are curiously drained of any sensations, to the extent that a scholar
of relationships might be forgiven for thinking that sensations are not
involved at all. Yet in everyday life it is well known that sensations
are important: for example, whether or not we experience touch, or
face-to-face contact in our personal relations with various others, and
what it feels like; whether certain interactions are experienced as full
of noise or silence, movement or stasis; whether we sense a good vibe
between people or an atmosphere that you could 'cut with a knife';
the capacity of a particular smell or a piece of music to evoke particular occasions in our relationships with others, or to virtually *transport*
us to them. These kinds of examples point to the constitutive role of
sensations in social life and interactions, as well as the need for those
who wish to study and explain these things – like sociologists – to
engage in a sensory-kinaesthetic attunement.

   Part of the problem with sensations is probably that sociologists
and others do not quite know what to do with them when it comes
to analysing relationships, even though as people who live in the
world and have their own relationships, they must understand their
importance at some level. So even though there is increasing interest in the anthropology of the senses and environmental philosophy
(for example, Abram, 1997; Classen, 1992, 2012; Howes, 1991;
Howes and Classen, 2014; Pink, 2015), or the sociology of the senses
(Lyon and Back, 2012; Mason and Davies, 2009; Riach and Warren,
2015; Vannini et al., 2011; or the journal *The Senses and Society*,
established in 2006) or indeed the sociology of the body or embodiment (for example, Burkitt, 2010; Crossley, 2006; or the journal
Body and Society, established in 1995), these do not have a great
deal to say about sensations in relationships. For the most part they
prefer to keep the level of analysis at either the 'self' or 'society' or
'culture'. If we look more specifically from the perspective of the
families, relationships and intimacies field, we have seen an interesting 'cultural turn' away from more abstract structuralist approaches,
with a greater focus on relationships as everyday practices which
can include exploring the role of feelings (as in emotions), embodiment, or of things and objects (for example, Gabb, 2008; Gillis,
1997; Morgan, 1996; Smart, 2007). And there have been interesting developments in interpersonal dynamics and the psychology of

'affect', which explicitly wants to draw emotion into the frame (for example, Brennan, 2004; Wetherell, 2012). But notwithstanding these, and with some notable exceptions (for example, Davies, 2015; Widerberg, 2010), *relationships* still are often analysed without much or any attention to sensations that might characterise or constitute them, and indeed often without recourse to a sensory-kinaesthetic register of any sort. Alternatively 'the sensory' is often analysed without much or any attention to relationships or to the mutualities and dynamics of sensations. As a consequence, it is still perfectly respectable to conceptualise a 'relationship' as a rather abstract thing that has little or nothing to do with sensation, which is, I think, a pity. In opposition to this, I am going to argue in this part of the book that sensations constitute a 'core seam' in our relationships with others (see also Mason, 2008), rather than simply our way of perceiving them, or a kind of adjunct to them (for example, as we might think of 'relationships *and the* senses').

My use of the term 'sensation' is quite deliberate, and yet requires certain caveats. 'Sensation' is defined in the *Oxford Dictionary of English* as 'a physical feeling or perception resulting from something that happens to or comes into contact with the body' (ODE, 2005). I am loosening and taking liberties with that definition somewhat, so that for me 'sensations' encompass the idea that they are not only felt, perceived and experienced in 'the body', but also that they emanate and flow in things that happen, and things coming into contact. Furthermore, it is an important part of the argument I develop in the book that we think generously and innovatively about what those 'things' that happen or come into contact might be. So instead of sensations being the felt effect of external stimuli, perceived or received via bodily receptors or mental faculties, I will argue that they flow through and are *generated in encounters*. This is crucial in my argument, and requires a more open and interactive conceptualisation than is sometimes applied to the idea of 'the senses' in the social and human sciences. What is more, in using the concept of sensation I want to gain a distance from the conceptualisation of particular senses as individual and mutually distinct, either from each other, or as separable from the experience of living in, moving within, relating with and apprehending the world. I am following Merleau-Ponty (2002 [1945], 2004 [1948]), Benjamin (1999), and in particular Ingold (2000, 2011) in this approach, but I shall also draw other ideas and insights into the frame.

Once we start to take sensations seriously, as I try to do in this part of the book, something else happens however. If my starting point was a desire to 'inject' sensations into the lacking-in-sensations study of interpersonal relationships, I quickly realised that sensations will not be contained in such a framework, and neither will the affinities they express. The energies and sensations of affinities operate not only within but way beyond and outside of interpersonal relationships, and this part of the book is thus a gateway to a much wider appreciation of affinities in the book as a whole. The major premise of this part of the book is that affinities are lived, made up of, and made potent through and in sensations. We might usefully see sensations as part of the habitat of affinities, or as an essential element in the atmospherics that can create affinities. And at the same time the visceral, moving and affecting nature of sensations is an important clue to understanding the potency of affinities. But we cannot appreciate and apprehend all of this unless we are prepared to tune into the sensory-kinaesthetics of the world around us.

What follows is a selection of facets, which are designed to illustrate and help to explore some of the ways that sensations are implicated in affinities, and in constituting them as more or less potent. In writing the facets I have consciously tried out a sensory-kinaesthetic attunement, directing this to a range of encounters and materials that help to draw to light the centrality of sensations in interpersonal relationships. This involves writing differently and variously across the facets. I have chosen to include facets with the aim of creating insights into sensations and the part they play in affinities, rather than representing a particular range or making any claims about propensities and patterns. The aim is to enable you to see what sensations can be in the world and maybe, hopefully, to inspire you to wonder about sensations and affinities that touch you, and to use this kind of attunement in your own field. After the facets, I draw together some of the threads and engage with wider literature and debate, so that I can take forward some propositions and ideas about affinities – in the process moving beyond the confines of interpersonal relationships – into the next part of the book.

Facets of Sensation

❦

1. Ashes, ghosts and the 'sense of presence'

My father died a year ago. I have his ashes in a large green plastic canister, alongside my mother's, which are in a mud-brown coloured canister, under a desk in the room where I work and write. The canisters have been labelled administratively, simply and clearly, by someone whose job was to ensure or to reassure that there was no mix up; to convey a clinical sense of certainty about what or who the canisters contained. The canisters are functionally shaped in ways that would be readily stackable on shelves, with the labels showing for ease of retrieval, and they have a surprising heft given how slight and frail both of my parents were when they died.

I don't look very often at the contents of the canisters, but I know what is there. A startlingly large quantity of stuff; a mixture of fine dust and more coarse-grained gravelly bits. It doesn't exactly look like ash, or ashes as we come to pluralise them under these circumstances. It looks more like builders' dust. I can see it in my 'mind's eye', feel it in my mind's fingers, sniff it with my mind's nose – my 'sensory imagination' (Mason and Davies, 2009) – without having to unscrew the lid and look, and I can feel its texture without actually ever having had the nerve to plunge my hand in and ferret about it in, although I know one day I will, and I have often anticipated lifting out a handful and scattering it somewhere meaningful. I can smell it or, more precisely, I can smell the curious absence of any smell at all, as some of the finer dust rises into the air and enters my nostrils, like a chalky grey vapour that hits my olfactory senses with a form of substance, but not of odour. All this without needing to take the lid off every time. What sensory-kinaesthetic stuff this is!

It is a form of stuff that raises uncertain and awkward questions because in many ways I do not trust it. What is it, this dusty, grainy, gravelly stuff? What are the bits? Are they bone, teeth, bits of coffin? Why aren't there some really big lumps, if it really is what is left behind in the incinerator when the heat has died down? If the stuff is ash – as they would have us believe – why doesn't it smell of smoke or incin-eration, or of anything for that matter? How was it gathered? Was it tipped or swept into this functional plastic container, or vacuumed, or scooped by someone's bare or gloved hand? Did any get dropped on the floor, or brushed off onto someone's clothes? Did it make anyone sneeze? Was it sieved into finely graded grains like the McDougalls finer flour used to be, to get rid of the big lumps, or the odd tooth or bit of vertebra, the odd molten filling. What happened to those big lumps? Were other bits, dust and debris from the floor or the incinera-tor, other people's ashes, swept up along with it, in a subtle subversion of the individuality and certainty of the label on the canister? Was it topped up with some spare dust or ash because my small, frail dad (big man of previous years) and his wicker coffin hadn't generated a convincing enough mass or volume? Of course I can't actually ask such questions of the undertaker, partly because to do so is to chal-lenge or doubt the carefully constructed line between the sacred and the profane that we have all been heeding and negotiating, in keep-ing with Western death and burial rituals (Hallam and Hockey, 2001). Ashes are sacred and revered in the material culture of death, and worse than questioning the undertaker's professional practice would be the sense that I was disrespecting the memory of my father.

But I do not entirely trust the ashes. Sometimes, for no apparent reason, my sensory imagination will conjure up the grainy grittiness of this dusty stuff when I am doing something quite other, alone or in company, and I will find myself contemplating its peculiar yet mun-dane nature and the questions about sensory dis/belief that it raises. My dad (only once dead) was burned up, and this is what is left. How can I be expected to believe that? It isn't that I don't believe he was burned or that ashes were produced. It is the implication that *this* scentless, gravelly dust can in any sense be what was left behind that is the problem, both because I do not trust it, and also because its odd sensory-kinaesthetic qualities, and the formal sterility of its packaging, are completely at odds with the mass of sensory-kinaesthetic goings on that were my dad.

The gravelly dust has enormous power which is difficult to reconcile either with the sensory-kinaesthetic textures of what it seems to be, or with the idea that my dad has simply gone, or with all the other sensations of him that are vying for my attention; because at the same time, and at other times, there are all the other kinds of sensory memories and animations of him. The sound of his voice, his intonation, his turns of phrase, his ways of laughing, the sounds he made when he was anxious and confused and that I cannot bear to remember, but which assert themselves into my soul and assail my consciousness and my dreams nonetheless. His smell, that I tried to preserve by keeping one of his jumpers tightly wrapped in a plastic bag, ready to take out and smell from time to time. As with any living person, his smells were combinations and minglings of good smells and less good smells. As well as that, I can feel/hear/see/smell the touch of his hand. I realise that most of the hand-holding I did with my dad was in the early stages of my life and then (after a long gap) towards the end of his – and these hand-holding times were sensorily different but now powerfully combine with a cavalier disregard of time.

I know that I can cut across the years in a moment, traversing them, telescoping them, calling up or encountering situations and atmospheres from a lifetime; my sensory memory is very agile in that sense. I can hold in one moment my shock at seeing my ninety-four-year-old dad when his hair had been cut in a brutal short-back-and-sides by a well-meaning hairdresser who didn't find a way to discover his coiffuring preferences, with the sensations of 'styling' Dad's hair when I was a child (he was tolerant of all kinds of outlandish hairdos). Both are here with me now creating a nearly tangible absent/presence and I can *feel* the hairstyling moments (his fine grey hair, his warmth and movement, his bodily tolerance and compliance, the velvety armchair where I perched behind him to do my childhood styling). I can *smell* them too ('his smell', the lightest touch of Brylcreem on his hair), and I can *hear* them (the feel and sounds of laughter – his and mine), and I *feel involved in* them – I am there and here, with him and without him, all at the same time. And also here with me are the gravelly ashes and the uniform individuality of their packaging with the promise it is intended to convey, and that I don't trust.

And as I reflect on all this, I think that perhaps these moments come together not just because memory is agile across the years, but also because these sensory-kinaesthetic forces have their own agility and potency, so that in combination these memories and forces produce something that is more like an *encounter* than a memory. Certainly, these moments and times *feel* more like encounters than memories, in their capacity to assert themselves almost tangibly without or despite being conjured, and to create sensory-kinaesthetic perceptions in the here and now, where things I have not consciously remembered rub shoulders with sometimes jarring sensations from different times.

I think my experience of my dad's ashes in amongst this melee of sensations is 'awkward', in the way the poet and essayist Mary Cappello uses that term (Cappello, 2007), because ashes themselves are awkward to encounter, and because they sit awkwardly with the living, breathing, sensory memory of the person. Cappello has a similarly awkward encounter with the death certificate of her mother's partner – her own 'beloved father and friend' – whilst on a mission to purge her life of clutter and tidy out her filing cabinet. She says:

> Is the awkwardness of a death certificate obvious? I don't think so. What's awkward about it is that it can't be expected, the fact of it, of finding it in a folder, a stumbling block in the process of a clearing of the decks. It's awkward for the way it makes you wonder how you will come to fit within its squares; awkward for how it makes death by 'natural causes' something to aspire to. It's awkward in its redaction of a person to a list of wheres and whens. It's full of information, and it's full of gaps. The death certificate makes *me* awkward as it plays its certitude against my confusion. It claims to know what happened to Sidney, whereas I do not. . . . A friend's sympathy letter seems light *and* full; the death certificate seems empty *and* heavy. And full. And empty. It's trying so hard with its serial numbers, and seals, its approvals and affirmations, its clockwork and authenticating signatures, its decipherable grid, to be correct in its assertion that this person was not buried alive. (Cappello, 2007: 23)

For Cappello there was an awkwardness in the coexistence of the certitude of the death certificate, which she cannot entirely believe or trust, with the sheer 'force of being' of Sidney and 'all that was attributable to him and to no one else', leading her to ask whether 'rival awkwardnesses necessarily co-exist' (Cappello, 2007: 24). I like this notion of rival awkwardnesses necessarily coexisting – indeed awkwardness being a normal state of affairs – because it suggests that we should not expect the experience of interpersonal forces of being to be consensual or singularly categorical, even if sociologists and others sometimes want to see it that way.

I think we get used to remembering those who have died in these kinds of searing and agile sensory-kinaesthetic encounters. For those of us who have experienced the death of another we have known intimately, this weaving of sensory memory – or encounters – into life becomes simply part of the everyday experience of living. So too, to

paraphrase Cappello, does the discomfort of the necessary coexistence of these vivid sensory-kinaesthetic encounters with the palpable
sterility and empty-heaviness of the material paraphernalia of death
– the death certificate, the administratively labelled canister of ashes,
the oddly smell-free builders' dust – which create their own ordinary
ambivalences in our lives.

In all this with my dad and his ashes, I have never felt the sense of
his presence being manifest or asserting itself in a more extra-sensory
or supernatural way. Actually I would like to have done, and with
my mum too, although both have 'visited me' as you might say, in
dreams. However Gillian and Kate Bennett, in a fascinating study of
'the presence of the dead', have pointed out that 'feeling a presence'
of a dead person in everyday life is actually very common amongst
people who have suffered a close bereavement – they made a particular study of widows – and a study by Hallam et al. notes a similar
phenomenon in 'the continuing presence' of dead spouses (Bennett
and Bennett, 2000; Hallam et al., 1999: 149; and see also MacKian,
2012, for an important analysis of the re-enchantment of everyday
life and the significance of everyday spirituality).

Bennett and Bennett detail different types of everyday experiences,
including a sense of being watched, hearing a voice – for example calling your name – the manifestation and sensing of odours of a dead
person, and seeing the dead person – fully animated – or feeling their
touch and warmth, for example alongside you in bed. These experiences ranged from the 'classic ineffable "feeling" that he is there, to
clear sensory experiences' (Bennett and Bennett, 2000: 143–4). I think
it is both interesting and important to note the centrality of intimate
relational sensations in these apparently intangible or extra-sensory
experiences, and the potency of the connections that were being
made. The extra-sensory is clearly full of sensations.

Bennett and Bennett argue that the numbers known to have experienced such presences are likely to be significantly underestimated in
a society where the dominant discourse about such things is that they
are illusory, or they are ways of coping with grief, or they are 'symp-
toms of broken hearts and minds in chaos' (Bennett and Bennett,
2000: 139). In such a context it is difficult as a widow for example to
tell others about your experiences, for fear of being thought 'crazy' or
unable to accept your partner's death and move on. They suspect that
this societal scepticism or disapproval is, at least in part, at the root
of the tendency they noted for people to switch between 'materialist' and 'supernaturalist' discourses, or the 'language of reality' and
'the language of illusion' in their accounts – the former emphasising

the material realities, which are presumably more likely to be eviden-
tially convincing – 'he *was* there', 'I was fully awake' – and the latter
the more ethereal ones – 'it was as if he was there', or 'I don't know
whether I was dreaming or not' (Bennett and Bennett, 2000: 151–2).
They suggest that choices and switching of language might be to do
with producing a satisfying narrative structure, or decisions about
appropriate language for the audience.

And yet I wonder whether there isn't something tantalising and
exciting, something potent, in the very ineffability and acknowledgement of something outside our comprehension that the switching of
language and the air of uncertainty in these accounts speak of. In a
way, in everyday life experience, just as in the telling of the stories,
there is a *delicious speculation* being lived and voiced here; a knowing and a not knowing, a wondering, a fully sensory experiencing of
something that *must* be extra-sensory – *was I asleep or awake? was
I dreaming? what kind of connection was I part of?* There is a playing across or a hovering over the boundaries between tangibility and
intangibility – what we might call an in/tangibility – in process here.
And of course let us not forget that the idea that dreams are 'only
dreams' – products of one's own neural activities, rather than magical
and ethereal sets of relations with the other-worldly – is a fairly recent
Western invention and one that I suspect many people do not fully
subscribe to. And as many commentators have noted, notwithstanding the legacies of the Enlightenment and the dominance of scientific
discourses, 'there is a persistent fascination with what is loosely conceptualised as an "other worldly domain" at the level of everyday
experience and in media representations' (Hallam et al., 1999: 165;
see also MacKian, 2012).

People know what they know and what they experience about the
'other-worldly', and I think what they know and experience is full
of fascinating ineffabilities and impossibilities. The searing emotional
and sensory-kinaesthetic intensity and power of such affinities with
the absent presence of the dead come from the absolute and felt
knowledge that these in/tangibilities cannot be self-invented whether
in a dream or otherwise, and that they emanate from, or are mani-
festations of, a communing with an other-world that is somewhere
beyond one's own wishful thinking and capacities to conjure. That
idea that these are not simply conjurings of the bereaved is supported
by Hallam et al:

> Continued relationships between widow and husband are not static,
> fixed in time and based solely on the nature of interaction in life. Rather,

they are dynamic relationships within which survivors develop new forms of interactions and, as their life changes, they craft new relationships with the living and with the dead. . . . It is not simply the case, however, that the living are retaining bonds with the dead ... the dead may also seek to continue their social presences, some, even imposing themselves where they are not wanted. (Hallam et al., 1999: 155–6)

It is interesting that the studies by Bennett and Bennett, Hallam et al. and MacKian, in their different ways, all point out that social science has been so busy asserting its right to be seen as a rational science, that it finds it has little space to take on board the ethereal and the other-worldly in any other way than to see it as a socially constructed belief system.

2. 'Grandma's Hands' by Bill Withers (version by Gil Scott-Heron)

If you don't already know it, you should listen to this song – the Gil Scott-Heron version. Bill Withers wrote 'Grandma's Hands', a bluesy soul song, about his African-American maternal grandmother who had been born into slavery, and his memories of her clapping and singing to gospel songs in church, as well as dispensing advice and discipline to her young grandson. 'Grandma's hands clapped to church on Sunday mornings' it rhythmically begins, and you will be hooked and want to hear the rest, to move in time to the music, to hear how it is that a young adult man is singing about his grandma.

Gil Scott-Heron was one of many artists who covered the song, and he clearly made a strong connection with the lyric as well as the song itself, producing a powerful version. Gil Scott-Heron was brought up until the age of twelve by his maternal grandmother, Lillie Scott. She was an important figure in his life, and she gets a mention in many of his songs and poetry, and he often referred to her in his live shows. Although in some ways the song is not literally about her hands and their sensations and rhythm, in other ways that is exactly what it is about. He sings of a grandma whose hands 'used to ache sometimes and swell'. These are hands that evoke gender, class, ethnic and religious dynamics of the American South, in just a few phrases like these, and in the sounds and rhythms of the music.

I saw Gil Scott-Heron perform live several times, before his death in

2011, and my memory (which may possibly be embellished by nostalgia) is that he performed this song on every occasion and always talked about his grandma, Lillie Scott.

3. The sensations of others: children's perspectives

Becky: What's your uncle like?
Sam: He's really loud. And he does things like, he goes to the top of that big rock, and he'll go up and shout 'that's the nicest fresh air I've ever had' or something like that! And he like screamed it and everyone looked at him, it was really embarrassing. *Really, really* embarrassing [laughing].

It is fascinating to listen to what children say when they are asked about who matters to them, and to observe them when they are talking. Research that has done this, my own included, has tended to focus on the 'who' part of the question, and to argue that a wide range of relationships matter to children, beyond parents, siblings and friends. Studies have highlighted the importance of wider kin, especially grandparents, cousins, aunts and uncles, as well as those who children regard as like-family even though they are not formally related. Often, children are not clear about what their formal or genealogical connection with relatives is in any case, but that does not stop them feeling they are family. Also, we know that others such as teachers or neighbours can be important, as can those who are definitely '*not*-friends' but are annoying or difficult presences in children's lives nonetheless. And of course relatives can be annoying, difficult and problematic for children too. Crucially we also know that many of those regarded by children as friends, family, neighbours, acquaintances, as well as *not*-friends, are animals (Mason and Tipper, 2008a, 2008b; Tipper, 2011).

But the sociological enthusiasm for categorising kin relationships, either genealogically or in terms of degrees of significance (such categorisation itself defied, actually, by the fluidity and inventiveness of children's kinship constructions), misses a dimension in children's perspectives on those who matter in their lives; namely, what they articulate about what others *are like*, and the way that their accounts of their relationships with them are full of sensations. Becky Tipper and I found out about this in our research study 'Children Creating

Kinship'[1] with children aged seven to twelve in the UK. One of the things we talked with children about in the study was what those who mattered to them *were like*. I think at the time we probably phrased it in that way to make sure the children found our line of enquiry easy to understand and to talk about, but in retrospect I am very glad that we did. Had we been speaking with adults about kinship we might, perhaps, have asked people the 'significance' of particular 'relationships' with others instead, thus immediately (and unhelpfully) introducing two abstractions – 'significance', 'relationships' – into the question which might have led us to miss the extent to which sensations are right in there in the mix of things when people are doing kinship.

We were fascinated to discover that the children found it easy to articulate what others were like and how they related to them, and that they did this by providing evocative insights that oozed sensations and imagination. There was a visceral physicality, both in how the children were expressing themselves, and in what they were expressing. Indeed, if you listen to and watch children communicating about who matters to them, you will find it can involve movement, mime, expression, comedy, song, pulling faces, gesticulation, variance of voice, volume and intonation, grunting, clapping and other noises, touch, and you might just get showered in spit as well. Children become very animated when talking about others and this animation takes full sensory-kinaesthetic form. From discussions about snot and earwax to wee and poo, or the precise timbre and cadence of a grandmother's voice or a pet dog's bark, children's experiences of their connections with others are acted out in ways that are full of life, energy and physicality (Mason and Tipper, 2008a, 2008b).

In our study, and in these animated ways, children gave us clear insights into what they felt people and animals who mattered to them *were like*, and especially what they *were like to be with* – just as Sam did with the story of his embarrassing uncle shouting from on top of a rock at the beginning of this facet. Often their answers were quite brief and succinct, and many involved – as did Sam's – an anecdote given as an example, often with a clear point in the tale, and sometimes a twist – which might be about humour, or embarrassment, or awkwardness, or fear, or disgust, or warmth, or 'weirdness', and so on.

What was especially interesting was the range of phenomena – always closely observed – that the children chose to present as defining of others and their doings with them. These included how people or animals looked and sounded for example, as well as how they moved, what they *did* physically (rather than for a living, which was never spontaneously mentioned). They also included aspects of character, mood, outlook and ways of relating to others. Here are some other examples.

> *Sam also told us about others in his family:*
> Sam: Everyone gets on fine, but it's really funny when we meet, cause we've got my grandpa and my other grandpa and one of them is like really, really quiet . . . I can't really describe him – a hermit! And then we've got my other grandpa who's like screaming and singing and shouting! It's really funny. But they get on. And one of my grandmas, she still goes out with like young boys! [laughs] I don't think she goes out with anyone her own age! She never meets us with them, unless like they're really nice. But she's like *mad*, she goes on for hours and hours and hours like [in funny, warbling voice] 'ooh I met this lad and he's *really* nice!' [laughs]

> *Tamsin told us about her cousin and her boyfriend:*
> Tamsin: But he's *like* part of this family.
> Becky: OK. Have you known him a while?
> Tamsin: No. When we went there [a family wedding], that's when we all just known him, but he let us do owt to him! He let us like pull the hat on his head and let go [miming pulling the elastic of a party hat].
> Becky: Oh, like ping it?
> Tamsin: [Laughing] Yes, but he just started laughing and he just let us do it! He was nice. I think he is the best boyfriend that she has had, because all the other ones were really miserable.
> Becky: Right OK. And what is she like, Michelle?
> Tamsin: She puts lots of makeup on! She's really nice to talk to, she is really cuddly

> *Lara told us about Ronald the dog, and his friends:*
> Lara: Ronald doesn't really play with other dogs, because he's interested in us. He's mostly interested in guarding my brother. He likes my brother. He's really friendly, he doesn't bite, he just licks, and to children he doesn't know he jumps up, but no-one minds because he'll just lick, not bite. He's calm. My grandma took him to school one day and he was sitting really calmly, and when he saw me he started running around the place on his lead! And then when my brother came out, he went even more mad! Ronald's funny! Sometimes he just lies down and [speaking softly] you just stroke him. But after he's been in water his head goes all curly, like mine! My baby cousin Clarisse smiles and claps every time she sees him.

It is important to notice the *relational* nature of these children's comments and gestures. They are not just talking about how others look or sound, or what they do, in the sense of personal attributes or individual states; instead they are describing interactions in which they and others are involved, and what we get to learn about in full and multi-sensory registers is the *relational characters* of and exchanges between those who are featured in the stories, including the narrators.

It is possible to tease out a number of themes from the children's accounts, which seem to operate as different kinds of sensory-kinaesthetic registers through which others are known interactively, remembered and indeed judged.

Looks

The children's accounts often centred on the question of looks, in various senses of the term.

> Becky: What is your gran like?
> Chloe: She's kind and she has white hair.

> William: Auntie Cynthia, at Liam and Louise's wedding, we were like giggling about Uncle Tom and how stern he was looking, and his mysterious looks [demonstrates 'mysterious look': gazing around wide-eyed]. [Laughs]

As Chalfen (2010) and Brighenti (2010) have both pointed out, the idea of 'looking' can involve both active and passive orientations simultaneously. So for example one can look at something or someone in a certain way, but equally people and animals can have 'a look' about them. How things look, and how looking is done, are mutually implicated, in the sensory-kinaesthetics of interaction. This can involve exchanges of looks between confidants or enemies (knowing looks, amused looks, angry looks), or giving off a particular kind of look (a stern look as in William's Uncle Tom, or a friendly look, for example). Conversely, it can involve reading certain things about others from how they look, and how much we like or do not like how they look. In this sense, the concept of looks is more active or agentic than the idea of 'appearance', which is very passive, and only involves part of the processes involved in looking. Children also talk about consciously creating looks, for example by making or pulling faces.

> Becky: [Laughs] Do you mind having your picture taken?
> Jasmine: I'm not bothered. But sometimes I'm a bit stuck for what faces I should do. You see with my friend I'd be like that [pulls a silly face] or something, but if it's like my auntie I would be like [makes a blank, scared face], I wouldn't know what to do.

Becky: Because you can't mess about as much?
Jasmine: Yes because I wouldn't know if my auntie would shout at me.

In just a few words and gestures, Jasmine's example about the sensibilities of face pulling is very revealing about how she *is* with her friend and, by comparison her aunt, and how they *are* with her. And although she is talking about pulling faces, her example implies other kinds of sensory-kinaesthetic interaction – shouting in particular, which is something that was important for many of the children.

Malik: He's a relative of my granddad's. He's got yellow eyes. I think he doesn't get a very early night. I don't like him because he's loud and I don't like him because I feel like he's like a bad person. I don't know why but just like having yellow eyes and stuff like that I feel like he does something bad or something. You know like what a mercenary does like gets paid for just doing something and then running away. I feel like that's why his eyes are all yellow. But then it might be because he always rubs his eyes at night.

Malik struggles to put his finger on what he finds troubling about this relative, but the combination of loudness and looks – the yellow eyes in particular – is what he lights upon to characterise his sense of unease and his suspicion that this man is not to be trusted, and may be a bad person, even someone as bad as a mercenary. He hedges his bets slightly by saying the yellow eyes might be because he gets tired and rubs his eyes, although he does not have a similarly innocuous explanation for the man's loudness. But Malik returned to these aspects at several points in his interview, making it clear that this person is an uneasy presence in his life.

Voices, volume and imitation

Malik referred to granddad's relative being 'loud', and indeed he spoke with detail and precision about all the people in his life in terms of their relative loudness (which he experienced as bad) and quietness (which he experienced as mostly good). Although other children did not have quite such a comprehensive volume-scale for categorising others as did Malik, the qualities and volume of voices and bodily noises were important. Loudness or quietness, timbre and intonation along with what voices and sounds – human and animal – communicated about sternness, affection, comedy, silliness, or scariness, were profound in the children's experience of and relationships with others.

Becky: What is Auntie Esther like?

Jake: She's nice, every time I go, she goes [imitating an indulgent, affectionate voice] 'Give us a big hug!' She does it all the time.

Bethany: This year's teacher is the *worst* teacher that you could possibly
get in the whole school. He's just non-stop shouting all the time. He's
been there since my mum was there! On the first day it was like, 'you
are the *worst* class I've had!' and it was just like, god it's our first day,
give us a break!

Rilla: I get on fine with my grandma, but she has this dog and she really
shouts at it, so whenever we go there it makes me really jump. When
it's not barking or anything it's OK but you know it sort of leaps up to
you and tries to lick you and stuff so I don't really like dogs that much.
And it really barks the place down, it really, *really* barks. *Seriously*
barks. It like echoes in the room! [Laughter] My grandma has like this
cage thing and it doesn't help the barking really, it just makes him bark
even more and he goes [growling and scrabbling] gruwfff, like that
cause he tries to get out. [Laughter]

Jemma: My granddad he's got a new wife and I don't see them much,
but I don't really care because after like 10 minutes of her speaking,
you get *so bored* and you feel like you want to stop the conversation!
Her voice is really annoying.

Malik, Bethany, Rilla and Jemma's comments, in talking about shouting and annoying voices and loud dogs, all speak of a lack of control
in their interactions with certain others. Bethany *feels* the injustice of
her noisy teacher's premature judgement on the class, and his use of
shouting (across the generations as it turns out) to assert himself in
their company. And Jemma's comments conjure up a picture of reluc-
tant children being almost physically pinned down by the droning and
tedious voice of a not too loveable step-grandma. Children also sometimes found people's voices amusing, or ludicrous, or posh, or affected.
A strong theme in their accounts was the 'putting on' of voices.

Bronagh: My grandma doesn't approve of lesbians and gay people
and my mum says to her 'well Mum what would you do if I got a
girlfriend?', and she says [putting on a haughty posh voice] 'I'd think
it was very naughty and disgusting, but I'd accept her as one of the
family.'

Jake: Every time I go there he goes [imitates in a comedic deep, 'James
Earl Jones' voice] 'Well hello!' That's what he does. And my granddad's silly – every time I go he goes, instead of 'look who it is', he goes
'look who it isn't' [imitating granddad's comedic voice]

Jasmine: [speaking of her brother] We fight a lot . . . but he is nice. He's
very funny, like entertaining. He's not like funny as in what he says,

just funny as in how he acts. He's just silly, yeah. I mean he's just like doing really funny faces, not like [sticks her tongue out in a silly face], but when he's saying hello he'll go, 'helloooo' [whispering, with one eyebrow raised]. And he does this funny thing, he goes [in deep raspy voice] 'oh yes'. It's *really* like funny just like how he does it, he's so funny. [Deep raspy voice] 'Oh yes'!

William: Sometimes when Uncle Gary rings and I've picked up the phone he sounds really mysterious, he goes [in comedic, rising intonation] 'hellooo?' and he does really mysterious voices and I'll go 'who is that?' and he's like 'oh it's Uncle Gary!' 'oh hi Uncle Gary, I'll put you onto my dad'.

Reuben: There's someone at school I really can't stand, cause he always goes up to me and goes [sing song baby voice] 'my fwend!' He'll go like [miming giving an embrace] 'my fwend!'. That's annoying! [Laughs]

The children did many such impersonations of others with whom they had good, bad, difficult, casual or cloying relationships, and it is clear that these animations and imitations are not simply performed for interviews, but are part of the everyday more-than-verbal jousting and knock-about that is children's kinship. It is significant that the expression 's/he goes' rather than 's/he *says*' enables children to convey a fuller sensory-kinaesthetic experience of these interactions, including voices, gestures and more, than they could by reducing it to the verbal content of speech.

The putting on of voices and gestures in interactions, and in recounting them through imitations and further interactions, not only animates scenarios in ways that can be enlivening or engaging, but also has the capacity to mock or undermine others, as well as to irritate and annoy them. Sometimes impersonation and imitation clearly speak of children's relative powerlessness in certain interchanges with others – they are used to being shouted at, spoken sternly to, or being on the receiving end of others' pomposity and prejudice – and being able to imitate people afterwards is a limited way of going against the grain of the power dynamics. The capacity to imitate, mock or undermine is therefore also a valuable good, and just as the experience of voice and sound can serve to emphasise aspects of the social hierarchy, it can also help children to subvert them.

Size, height, weight, growing

Size and height, and the whole question of being small and physically growing, are topics close to children's hearts. As an adult it is easy to forget the extraordinary ordinariness and daily transaction with the question of growing that children experience, even though we can be awestruck and delighted as adults when we are in the presence of children's growing – 'my haven't you grown!' I say 'question' here, because growth does not always happen as desired or planned for children, and can be a matter of longing, fear or denial. Of course adults also expand and contract, grow and shrink, and although these changes are undoubtedly noticed and perceived, body mass and height are rarely seen as an acceptable and polite topic of social exchange (except under certain circumstances, pregnancy for example). But there is an ordinary regularity in the way the question of growing, mass and height infuses children's experiences and their accounts of relating with others.

> Joel: I think my cousin's about the same age as me. It's hard to tell cause he's about up here on me [indicates level of his nose]. I'm like [looking down at level of cousin's height] 'Hello!' [laughs]
>
> Miriam: I didn't get to meet them [branch of the family] until I was about 4, then I met everybody.
>
> Becky: Do you remember that?
>
> Miriam: Yeah I remember it. I was scared, they were [awed voice, wide eyes] *too big*! They were like giants. I ran upstairs and hid under my bed for about 5 minutes! [Laughter]
>
> Jessica: She got knocked over and killed, when she was a little kitten. I saw her get knocked over. I went and I picked her up and I took her to my mum.
>
> Becky: Oh, what was that like? How did you feel about it?
>
> Jessica: Well I didn't really like it because she felt really light.

Jessica's story is not about growing per se, although there is a sense in which the lack of substance in the body of the dead kitten is shocking in its physical revelation that the kitten had not had the chance in life to grow heavy. But Jessica was probably familiar with the weight of the living kitten, having held it many times, so the fact of its lightness may not have been a revelation in itself. I think what is unsettling for her is the almost weightless *dead* weight of the kitten in her hands. A dead weight is always a shock of course – the lack of movement or animation marking a sudden shift in a relationship with a living-breathing being to a dead-still one. But a light, almost-not-there dead weight is perhaps doubly shocking because of its sudden contrast with the energies and heft of life that was the kitten moments before.

Play fighting and real fighting

Children often engage in, experience, or observe, physical fighting with others, and their accounts reflect this, as in the following examples.

> Lara: We *used* to be best friends, but now Nadia hasn't really got any friends because her mum and dad split up, they got back together then they split up again, and she keeps getting friends but then frightening them away like because she always smacks me and pushes me and pulls my hair and that. I said 'that's why you're not my first best friend' and she smacked me and I said 'nor my second!' [laugh] The only friend *she's* got is her brother and her half-cousin.
>
> Matthew: Sometimes if I annoy him [the family dog] too much he tries to have a bite at me. We don't really get on.
>
> Becky: What do you do to annoy him?
>
> Matthew: Just tease him with his favourite toys or lie on him or get him to scratch me. And he gets annoyed. He's done it to mum *sometimes* and he has done it once to Joseph, but he hasn't done it to dad before. He's done the most to me though. I don't think he likes me that much.
>
> Kieran: My Uncle Jasper tries to give me Ear Twisters and Chinese Burns and Laughing Fingers. Do you know what a Laughing Finger is? He squashes your finger like that [demonstrates lightly on his own finger]. It hurts. And he's really fat and he's mean. If we do something wrong by accident and he sees it, he'll just get Jamie and slap him! Because he's the one who's always the naughtiest. But I'm normally hiding under the cover, flat. I'm like this [demonstrates staying really still], acting like a statue. And then he walks out the room and I get back up.
>
> Aaron: It's *OK*. It's just I don't want him [cousin] to grow up and when he's older, like punch and kick everybody, or anything like that. At the moment he's not punching, he's not *proper* punching. He's actually a weakling. He cries a lot. But then he just gets up and, his kicks are *massive* for a little kid, for a kid. When he plays football he *blasts* the ball off.

Aaron has a sophisticated set of concerns about his cousin's propensity to punch and kick, especially as these relate to size and to growing up, and the shifting balance between 'play' fighting and 'the real thing'. Just like growing, physical fighting is an extraordinary ordinariness in children's lives, as is the fine and shifting line between play fighting and aggression or oppression, which the children in our study were closely tuned in to.

Bodily proximity with others

Children's physical proximity with others generates intimate sensory-kinaesthetic knowledge which can feel positive, funny or difficult.

> Tamsin: My grandma's a really nice lady, nice and cuddly. Because like when we are watching horror films, or we're watching things that are very scary, that my sister wants to watch because she's old enough, but like *I* don't want to watch but I just have to watch because I don't like going upstairs and it scares me. So I don't mind watching it as long as she's there and my grandma sits on the sofa right up in the corner and I lay down there and she puts her arms around me and I just hold her hand. And I feel safer because I know that she's there. She's a really cuddly person. *Really* cuddly. Uncle Wayne's another cuddly one. He will give me a cuddle when I see him, but sometimes he's got a hairy chin and it hurts! It's like with my dad I tell him to shave every time it hurts, so I can test it when I'm giving him a kiss.

> April: When Sable's running [family dog], his ears are like going at the back, and it's like [demonstrates flapping ears with her hands] [laughter]

> Harvey: So he's like going flap, flap, flap, flap, flap, flap, flap! Because he's going [panting and bobbing his head up and down like a dog running]!

> April: He's really fast.

> Jasmine: Granddad is weird but he likes me the best. He gives me hugs and I will say 'thank you', and he goes like that [demonstrating granddad approaching and trying to hug/kiss her] and he is just a bit blurrggh.

> Claire: He [granddad] lives on his own now, because his wife died, and his house is a tip and it's not really, he's a bit . . . [pulls disgusted face], I don't really see him often. I don't want to.

Relational traces and bodily inscriptions

Injuries of various sorts – including scars, burns, broken bones, the drawing of blood – are ways in which children's relations with others become inscribed into flesh and bone, as well as memory and storytelling.

> Rosie: There is another thing what reminds me of Ant [brother], that burn mark! [Lifts leg to show a scar on her foot]. My mum went out to dinner and so Anthony made some dinner for me and Poppy and it was fish fingers and chips and he didn't have any oven gloves on and he picked the tray out of the oven, dropped it and one of the fish fingers went on that foot.

Becky: Oh my gosh, that's quite a burn. Wow.
Rosie: Yes it's very deep. I screamed!

Colleen: When I was a bridesmaid my Auntie Jeannette pulled my arm
    out my socket the week before. She was throwing me around and my
    arm got pulled out of the socket! And it had to get pushed back in
    and it was a couple of days before the wedding! I was crying at the
    time. But I wasn't *shouting* my head off like I normally do when I hurt
    myself, when the doctor was pushing it back. But my arms are fine
    now. I forget which one it is because there isn't a scar.

Overall, we can see a literal physicality and sensory-kinaesthetic
engagement in the way the children in our study understood, imagined, judged, related to, interacted with, remembered, told stories
about and impersonated others. It is not possible to somehow separate the senses and physicality from the relationships or characters in
these children's accounts and performances – the one is always the
other. The loudness of someone's voice, for example, is important
because of its physical force, the level of decibels and its cultural
meanings and associations. But it is also important because it is a core
part of the relating that is going on, and of the characters of those
who are in relation. These dynamics are crucial in the way affinities become more or less potent – whether as, for example, sources
of love, embarrassment, hilarity, disgust, or a shifting or ambivalent
combination of these things. The imitations, impersonations, actings
out and animations of others and of interactive scenarios are ways in
which the characters in children's lives get made and become known,
and affinities get settled, unsettled and resettled.

I do not think that children's experiences of sensations are so different from those of adults. It is certainly the case that recent research
on children's and young people's lives and relationships has had a
strong sensory focus (Davies, 2015; Wilson et al., 2012), and also that
adults' memories of their childhoods are full of sensory detail (James,
2013: 101; Widerberg, 2010). This might suggest that childhood is
an acutely sensory-kinaesthetic time, although equally it points to
adults' capacity for potent sensory imagination and memory. Certainly
our sensory-kinaesthetic relational contexts may change over time,
especially for example in the sense that Western cultural ideals of
adulthood rarely incorporate physical play, which is seen as the preserve (and sometimes the right) of childhood. But then we should
remember that adults have more accumulated layers of history and
potentially more sensory-kinaesthetic encounters than children, by
virtue of having been around longer. And although that might mean
that particular encounters have to work harder at standing out in

memory or experience from the masses that make up an adult life-time, or that new encounters and discoveries happen less often and thus are less remarked upon, it would not mean sensations were any less important or involved in interactions and relationships. I am not convinced by the narrative of lament that suggests we somehow lose our childhood capacities for a sensory-kinaesthetic appreciation of the world and our relationships as we grow up, or that adult lives are somehow less full of sensation.

I think therefore we would be wrong to assume that children have a more direct or innate connection with sensations than do adults. We should be careful not to underestimate adults' capacity for these kinds of engagement and inventiveness – even if adults have less socio-cultural licence to express or articulate it – just as we need to take care that we do not simplistically assume children to be pre-social or not-yet-fully-social beings who are somehow closer to a more primal sensory existence (Tipper, 2011). Neither, incidentally, should we underestimate the relational worldliness and experience of children, because aren't children's relationships and their immersion in them just as real and 'of the world' as those of adults?

4. The sensory-kinaesthetic intimacies of violence

Certain relations of violence involve a deep sensory-kinaesthetic intimacy. We know that the rhetoric of smart bombs, drone warfare and clinical manoeuvres is designed precisely to distance perpetrators of violence from their victims, and to break a connection that would otherwise be troubling. One of the things that is removed is the visceral experience of violent encounters, and the intimacy of relationship created by them, that would otherwise be there. Researchers conducting psychological experiments have explored the extent to which breaking that connection (amongst other things) enables people to perform violent acts that they might not otherwise countenance (for example, the infamous and flawed Milgram 'obedience to authority' experiment [Milgram, 1974] and the variation on the moral 'trolley problem' by Navarrete et al., 2012). I am interested here in the intimacy of connection created in violent interpersonal encounters between strangers, or those who barely knew each other beforehand. The point is that interpersonal violence means those involved come to know physical and sensory-kinaesthetic things about each other.

Consider, for example, autobiographical and literary accounts of interrogation and torture, such as those of Maziar Bahari, the *Newsweek* journalist incarcerated and tortured in Iran in 2009, and Gillian Slovo's novel *Red Dust*, about the South African Truth and Reconciliation Commission. Both involve narratives of torture, and in both cases the accounts of violence and abuse include something that one might call a sensory-kinaesthetic intimacy. Bahari, for example, begins his book thus:

> I could smell him before I saw him. His scent was a mixture of sweat and rosewater, and it reminded me of my youth. (Bahari, 2011: xi)

'Rosewater', as he goes on to refer to his interrogator (whose name he never knows during his incarceration), comes alive in the book as a deeply flawed, erratic, brutal and ignorant character, with a sensory and physical presence that is almost overwhelming at times. Bahari only has sight of Rosewater on the first and last day of his incarceration – he is forced to wear a blindfold for all interrogations and can only steal glimpsed views beneath it, of the floor and sometimes Rosewater's slipper clad feet. But Rosewater's smell is omnipresent, along with the sounds he makes, the feel of his spit on Bahari's face, and his touch – frequently violent and slapping, punching and kicking Bahari's head and body, but sometimes a gentle touch on the arm or a massage of the shoulders. The sheer physical proximity and sensory-kinaesthetic engagement that occur in the encounters between them are striking:

> I sensed him quickly crossing the room. His face was near mine. 'Are you deaf? I'm asking you a question!' he screamed into my ear. This wasn't the scenario I had been picturing. I felt a trickle of sweat slide down my side, and I tried to steady my voice. 'I'm sorry. I don't understand'. . . . Rosewater moved away from me but remained in the room. I could smell his stench. 'I don't understand,' I whispered. (Bahari, 2011: 177)

Slovo's character, Alex Mpondo, in a 'courtroom' style scene where he is questioning his former interrogator and torturer as part of the South African Truth and Reconciliation process, feels overcome by the sudden and unexpected surfacing of the sensory memory of their earlier encounter:

> he could smell the rankness of his own terror and its physical manifestations – his soiled trousers, the urine trickling down his leg, his foul breath as the bag was pulled away. . . . Now it came flooding back,

his taking the hand that Hendricks offered to him, taking it eagerly, the pupil wanting to please his master, allowing Dirk Hendricks to pull him gently up, to smooth his hair, to say softly: *go wash now*, as he patted Alex's shoulder. Like a father – and Alex his compliant son. 'It was better between us after that', said the Dirk Hendricks opposite, joined now to the one that Alex had known. 'Remember? You needed fresh air so I took you for a drive.' (Slovo, 2000: 192–3)

In both of these extracts the intimacy is accompanied by revulsion and horror – for Bahari in the proximity and disgusting physicality of his torturer, and for the character Mpondo in a deeply sensory memory that assails him in the different circumstances of the Truth and Reconciliation Commission proceedings, where the tables are turned on interrogator and interrogatee. One of the things that is so difficult to bear in these accounts is that the extraordinarily violent circumstances produced such deeply intimate interpersonal physical and sensory-kinaesthetic knowledge of the other – an affinity of opposition.

5. Becky Tipper's creaturely 'moments of being'

Becky Tipper, who I collaborated with in our study of children's kinship, also conducted a fascinating and separate study of human–animal relations in a suburban neighbourhood in northern England. She explored a range of 'creaturely encounters' between humans, non-human animals and places – including encounters with wildlife, pets and 'pests' in public parks, private gardens, and a range of other public and private places in the neighbourhood (Tipper, 2012).

In her article 'Moments of Being and Ordinary Human–Animal Encounters', Tipper recounts two examples from her ethnographic data. The first is of a woman, Sandy, who had discovered a moth cocoon and looked after it until it had hatched. Sandy tells a detailed story about this, and then comes a magical part – a 'tiny moment' – where she released the moth into the dark. Tipper lyrically recounts how Sandy spoke in hushed tones 'as if even the telling of it must be handled with care' (Tipper, 2013: 15), of how the moth felt delicate on her finger, and how – perhaps sensing the moon – 'it suddenly began to just vibrate. It just quivered, and then in seconds, it took off' (Tipper, 2013: 15). Sandy is in awe of the moth's non-human capacity simply to fly without tutoring, and also of its possible affinity with the moon, and the capacity of the moth to be there, quivering, in one second, and gone the next. She rounds off her story with a joke that it was then 'probably eaten by a bat', but the overall tone of the narrative that Tipper recounts is one of reverence, with Sandy experiencing 'a profound sense of wonder, amazement and connection with the nonhuman; an awakening to something beyond the "cotton wool" of ordinary life' (Tipper, 2013: 15).

Tipper's other story in the article is of Fiona, who, on a trip to China, witnesses some boys plucking feathers from a live dove, and is horrified and reminded of similar incidents of boys doing 'the most appalling things to animals' at school. What Tipper wants to draw out of this is the empathy that Fiona felt with the animals – a kind of visceral empathy with their agonies, like that described in Acampora's concept of 'corporal compassion' (Acampora, 2006). Speaking of her empathy, Fiona said 'you . . . obviously don't feel it *for* them . . . but . . . something makes you *realize how it must feel*. And you couldn't possibly do that to an animal' (Tipper, 2013: 15, emphasis in original).

Tipper's examples are full of sensory-kinaesthetic – and in the case of Sandy perhaps extra-sensory – evocation. The experiences are sensed, felt, lived, experienced, and recounted as such. She analyses these and similar stories from her research by applying Virginia Woolf's concept of 'moments of being' to her own data, and especially these examples where 'people find connection, common ground or authentic understanding with animals' (Tipper, 2013: 14). She situates her discussion against the background of John Berger's claim that there is an 'abyss of non-comprehension' between humans and animals, and instead she argues that sometimes interspecies encounters occur as vital, vivid, profound and revelatory moments of wonder, connection and realisation, just as she argues they do in these two cases. Importantly, these are real, sensory-kinaesthetic, encounters – affinities – where human and animal come up against each other, rather than an intersection of abstract or cognitive contemplations of the categories 'human' and 'animal'.

> In such moments of being, humans might indeed appreciate 'what it is like' to be a creature: people may experience interspecies 'fellowship' or intimacy: the suffering of an animal might be *felt* viscerally in one's own body; and such moments might blur or collapse ordinary boundaries and binaries (between self and other, between human and animal) beyond recognition. But perhaps, such experiences are always only ever momentary – brief and startling (and sometimes alarming) glimpses into creaturely lives. (Tipper, 2013: 16)

Tipper points out that one of these experiences, Sandy's, was magical in a rather uplifting and delightful way, while Fiona's experience was more crushing and upsetting. Both, however, seem to illustrate what she refers to as a sense of 'wonderment'. She sees this as a combination of feeling awe-inspired, with the less passive activity of wondering, and I think too – although it is implicit in her argument – that the sensory encounter is at the heart of this. 'Wonderment', for Tipper, is not so much a recognition of the significance of animal otherness, although it may involve that, but instead it is a condition in which people are 'actively and reflexively engaged in musing and speculating on its nature'. For Tipper, what is important is the active nature of these acts or moments of wonderment, and she also makes a strong argument to the effect that this is not just something philosophers do, but it is part of humans' everyday relations with creatures – thus making the dual points that this is a democratic and everyday activity, and that it is grounded in lived, sensory experience rather than armchair theorising. Importantly, she argues, this 'complex meditation on the species boundary' involves both appreciating and having a brief insight into the amazing otherness of creatures, and at the same time 'reinscribing a sense of the species boundary as firm and unbreachable' (Tipper, 2012: 211). In a sense it is a sudden or sharp empathetic glimpse into a creaturely world. She suggests, it may be the very knowledge that we can never truly know animals, but that we can sometimes have these species-crossing encounters, these 'shocks' (Tipper, 2013: 14) or epiphanies, that create a sense of magic and wonderment.

6. Meat, 'food-animals' and Rhoda Wilkie's 'sentient commodities'

I have not eaten meat for over thirty years, but I can still clearly remember the taste of all kinds of meat, and I don't doubt that I could recognise them all in a blind taste test. You might say I have a gustatory memory of meat. But I can also remember the way the textures and sinews turned in my mouth and against my tongue, and were cut by my teeth, and swallowed. I can remember the feel-taste of the fleshy juiciness of some meats, or the dry and delicate flakiness of others, and the disgusting tangle of gristle that made me gag. I can remember a vaguely guilty pleasure in the texture and taste of rare meat. This is all without longing for another taste of meat, and it is *despite*, and not *because*, of the very many sensory-kinaesthetic encounters with the meat of others that I continue to have – barbecue smells wafting in the street; meat consumed in close proximity; the pallid blood streaked haunches hanging in the street as the delivery wagon unloads outside the butcher's; cat food levered from the tin, hitting my nostrils and leaking onto my fingers; the half-eaten mouse on the kitchen floor. For sure, all of these experiences and more are likely to keep the memories – good and bad – fresh, but the memory of meat in the mouth and pervading the senses seems to have its own deeply ingrained and self-perpetuating intensity. I have chosen not to eat it for thirty years, but I can see there is a potency in that historical affinity between me and meat.

I would argue that for many people, eating, handling and cooking meat will be their most frequent and also perhaps their closest affinity with animals, although they may not think of it as such. Their encounters with animals-as-meat will be variably sticky, moist, tasty, odorous, disgusted, labour-intensive, leisured, pleasurable and ceremonial, but invariably they will be deeply intimate and sensory-kinaesthetic. What can be more intimate than touching, slicing, crafting, enveloping, chewing, savouring, ingesting, and absorbing? How can you get closer (in a literal rather than emotional sense) to animals-as-meat than that?

Of course, for the twenty-first-century Western meat eater, there is usually a considerable disconnect between the sensory-kinaesthetic realities of a living animal and the pleasurable (or unpleasurable) sensations of meat. Most people are not usually involved in killing and butchering animals, and rarely do people know or get to meet the particular living animal (I mean the individual character as opposed to the type of animal) that they are consuming at any one time. Nor do people know how many individual animals they have ever consumed (parts of), or how many animal killings they have in some way had the benefit of. Indeed, it is often not apparent how many individual animal deaths have produced one single meal or mouthful. This disconnect still prevails notwithstanding the interest in small-scale 'hobby farming', the impetus (partly fuelled by health scares around BSE and the like) to know and document the provenance of meat, the increasingly 'free-range' approach of TV celebrity chefs who are enthusiastic to raise and kill their own animals, and the tenacity of the hunting minority. Because it is not customary or usual to consume creatures while they are living, meat is taken to be the flesh or body parts of an animal that has been killed.

This means that most people do not *know* – in a visceral, personified or associative sense – their meat as live animal, even though they know intellectually that meat comes from a formerly alive animal (although it is interesting that many young children do not realise this, and are not encouraged to do so). Indeed, it is usually assumed that it is in large part this de-personification of animal flesh, and the disconnect from the unpleasantness involved in turning live animal into meat, that explains how so many people can eat it. If people had to kill their meat, so the argument goes, then most would become vegetarian.

But those who work with food-animals, often getting to know them quite well in close physical contact over a period of time, or those involved directly in their slaughter, do not have the same access as the rest of us to easy methods of de-personification or to the disconnect between the live animal and the meat product. Rhoda Wilkie has explored the challenges such workers face. Her book *Livestock/Deadstock* is an insightful ethnographic study of a range of types of agricultural worker who work with food-animals at various stages from birth to slaughter. She is interested in how workers interact with food-animals, and especially how they might manage the everyday processes of being and working with animals who are destined for slaughter and who need to be regarded as meat in the making. Her focus is on people's 'practical relations with livestock' (Wilkie, 2010: 3), and although she does not directly tease out for specific analysis the sensory and kinaesthetic aspects, they are core elements in those practical relations.

She did her research in Scotland with farmers, stockmen, mart workers, hobby farmers, veterinary staff and abattoir workers. She found that livestock workers develop different degrees of 'affinities and aloofness' with the animals they work with (Wilkie, 2010: 129) – importantly, she says, they do not always and uniformly regard them as non-sentient products or commodities. She says that in order to understand human–livestock attachments and interactions it is important to grasp both the particular 'career path' of the animal from birth to slaughter, and the points at which humans in different work roles play a part in that, for how long, how physically closely, and to what ends. As she puts it:

> producers can form a range of emotional affinities to and aloofness from their animals. That livestock cannot always be reduced to, or totally defined by, their productive roles facilitates a more multifaceted appreciation of these animals. Such insights, though fleeting at times, can and

do occur during fairly routine or exceptional human–livestock interactions of a positive or negative nature. . . . Animals can be located and
relocated along a status continuum that ranges from commodity to
companion, whereby the same animal may at times be seen by the same
worker, or by a different worker, as a tool of the trade, a work colleague,
a friend or even a pet. (Wilkie, 2010: 130–1)

Thus she talks about how the regular handling or milking of animals
can foster a closeness with them, and the difficulties and ambivalences
that can attend the processes of rearing orphan lambs who, in the
words of one of her farm stock managers, ' "get attached to *ye*, and
they get attached to *yer* kids, and things like that, and trying to get
rid *o* them, it's difficult" ' (Wilkie, 2010: 115, emphasis in original).
The stock manager's words here indicate the mutuality in these physical relationships, where the lamb is not just a passive, characterless
thing, but an active being with its own ideas and relational orientations. They also indicate that this is not simply a two-way exchange
between stock manager and lamb, but that children's relationships
both with animals and parents are implicated too, as children become
physically and emotionally close to the lambs, and parents have to
work out their stance on this: the subtext being that the stock manager has the difficult task of socialising his farming children into a
more 'appropriate' orientation to food-animals.

    As well as getting emotionally close to animals, those who work
physically closely with them cannot help but notice their particular
characters and get to know them as individuals. In a sense they are
forced to confront the particular life forces and energies of animals
who have unique characters. A commercial stockman told her: ' "Out
of the cows we have, some of them you could go up to in the field
every day and . . . scratch their backs, and they'll stand and obviously enjoy it" ' (Wilkie, 2010: 130). But others might dislike being
handled or wanted the freedom of the field, and the workers knew
the preferences and predilections of the different individuals. Wilkie
says that breeding animals, who are kept alive for longer and have
more sustained physical contact with workers, are treated more as
individuals than animals for slaughter. She also reports that as well as
sustained physical contact, the intensity (physical, sensory, emotional)
of the contact has an impact, such as in the case of this commercial
farmer: ' "there's four out there that I know quite well, because I've
sat up with them in the middle of the night or I've had to physically
feed them or I've had to inflict quite a bit of pain on them so that they
[could] get better" ' (Wilkie, 2010: 139).

Unsurprisingly, workers who had formed a relationship with animals through close physical contact preferred not to be involved in killing them, and sent them to abattoirs for that part of the meat production process. One farmer described sending two lambs who had been hand reared for slaughter, and the guilt she felt at the trusting way they followed her into the trailer to be taken to their deaths. People were much happier once the animals had been turned into packs and cuts of meat no longer recognisable as the living characters of their provenance, without contemplating too deeply the stages that came in between, although it was important to them to maintain belief in the ideology of humane slaughter.

Nevertheless, Wilkie did talk to people who worked in the slaughterhouse and, although those workers by definition could not disengage from the realities of slaughter, and had not built a prior relationship with the animals, still some of the same themes of sensory-kinaesthetic relationality were reflected. This was not least in that, for example, facing the live animal and firing the shot that 'stunned' him or her was the least popular role in a system where 'the killing act is made nebulous' in the assembly line style division of labour (Wilkie, 2010: 164). She cites a slaughterman thus:

> 'Shooting the animal. I can do it. I don't like doing it. A lot o guys are the same. A lot o guys can't do it because you have to face the animal and shoot it at point-blank range'. The significance of being face to face with the animal was captured in a 'moon-eyes' look, which, he explained, was a 'sad, longing, unsure, looking-for-comfort [look]. You see that walking towards you and you've got to shoot it'. Before it is shot, the animal is a living thing, he said. But once the animal had been shot, it became a 'unit' for him, 'like a tin o beans'. (Wilkie, 2010: 163)

If we had doubted it, the importance of sensations in relationships (and indeed of 'looks' as discussed in earlier facets) is plain to see here, as the slaughterman describes a moon-eyed 'sad, longing, unsure, looking-for-comfort' *look* walking towards him, and that he has to shoot. It is as though the animal's whole being and relationality with the slaughterman are expressed in that look that is both active and passive: describing the animal and passing between the characters involved.

Wilkie rejects the easy assumption that livestock are entirely 'de-anthropomorphized' (Arluke and Sanders, 1996: 169), and simply seen as objects, commodities or tools by people who work with them in a hands-on capacity. On the contrary, her argument suggests that people cannot and do not resist connecting with the lifefulness and characterfulness of animals, and these affinities acquire their potency in the sensory-kinaesthetics of human and food-animal relations. Wilkie uses the term 'sentient commodity to draw attention to the ambiguous and dynamic status of livestock and the fine perceptual line workers have to negotiate in terms of seeing animals as both economic commodities and sentient beings' (Wilkie, 2010: 182). What is especially interesting, I think, is Wilkie's argument that many agricultural workers work with food-animals precisely because they like being with them: they enjoy the closeness of their company.

Layering the Argument: Sensations of Affinity

The facets that I have discussed are illustrations of encounters involving potent connections that rise up and matter in some way, and where it is possible to identify a spark or a charge that intensifies, enchants or indeed toxifies the ordinary. These sparks or connective charges, I want to argue, are affinities. With all the facets in this section I have wanted to show how it is that sensations are central in what makes these connections and associations *potent*; and thus in what makes them affinities. Each facet offers an example or version of sensory-kinaesthetic attunement to a particular set of encounters, and this of course brings the sensations of those encounters into focus so that we can observe and consider them. This is necessary, because I am arguing that sensations are part of what is in play – part of the atmospherics or the ether in which life is done and experienced, and in which affinities arise. It is important to emphasise that I am not suggesting that sensations represent a 'type' of affinity.

In this section I want to gather up some of the threads and to consider what we can learn from this kind of sensory-kinaesthetic attunement across these different facets. What might such an attunement lead us to apprehend? More specifically, what does this approach, and this focus on sensations, enable us to see and to say about affinities and how might this work as an invitation to think differently? How might we meaningfully engage with wider literature and debate in this process? This is part of a process of layering the argument about affinities that begins here with sensations, and continues throughout the book.

Life is full of sensory-kinaesthetics

The most obvious thread to gather in first from the facets is that being attuned to sensations helps us to recognise that relationships, interactions and the *living of personal life is full of sensory-kinaesthetics*; living is conducted in these registers, and once we start to be attuned to this, we cannot fail but to see it, or more appropriately to apprehend it with all our senses. The facets have shown encounters and situations that are full of sensations. That includes virtual interactions, and we should note that it is not just our interactions but also our memories and our imaginations that are fully imbued with sensations. Memory, from this perspective, is another form of perception, and of sensory encountering. My ideas about the role of sensations in characters, and in interactions, partly although not entirely reflect Merleau-Ponty's argument that we experience and perceive the world as mindful bodies, and that in 'perceiving as we do with our body, the body is a natural self and, as it were, the subject of perception' (Merleau-Ponty, 2002 [1945]: 239). I like the idea that bodily perception is one of the things that is going on in the experience of living, and what I have said about how we know others clearly echoes some of Merleau-Ponty's thinking:

> Other human beings are never pure spirit for me: I only know them through their glances, their gestures, their speech – in other words, through their bodies. . . . I cannot detach someone from their silhouette, the tone of their voice and its accent. If I see them for even a moment, I can reconnect with them instantaneously and far more thoroughly than if I were to go through a list of everything I know about them from experience or hearsay. (Merleau-Ponty, 2004 [1948]: 62)

Importantly, just as Merleau-Ponty says humans are not 'pure spirit', we should remember they are not 'pure bodies' either.

The ubiquity and weight of sensations in everyday interactions and relationships – indeed the idea that these are made up of, not just embellished by, the sensory-kinaesthetic – run counter to a set of ideas that are sometimes assumed to characterise Western societies; the first is that we have somehow lost touch with 'the sensuous' and with our sensory appreciation, perception and experience of the world, and in fact that the history of Western civilisation has been a history of such losses. David Abram's fascinating ecological polemic, *The Spell of the Sensuous*, whilst celebrating the sensuous, nevertheless has this assumption of loss or deficit at its heart. Abram makes an impassioned and eloquent argument for a renewed sensory perception and appreciation of ourselves as mindful bodies in reciprocity with our 'natural world'. Drawing on Merleau-Ponty's concept of 'the perceived world' in particular, he argues that Western philosophical thought, science, religion and forms of language have invented the concept of the human being as a rational mind distinct from its physical body, separate from its environment (which is reduced to context or resource for human livelihood), and superior to all other forms of animate nature. The very construction of abstract, non-sensuous and disembodied concepts like 'mind' and 'psyche' or indeed 'soul', and the arrogance of assumed human intellectual and moral superiority, work to distance human cognition and perception from the sensuous, as well as divesting the 'natural world' of the possibility of its own generative sensory qualities (Abram, 1997).

Abram's argument is convincing in many ways, and especially perhaps in its emphasis on the animate and sensuous energies of the environment and non-human lives – 'it is not all about us humans' you can almost hear him say – and his bid to destabilise the arrogance of assumed human superiority:

> It is all too easy for us to forget our carnal inherence in a more-than-human matrix of sensations and sensibilities. . . . To shut ourselves off from these other voices, to continue by our lifestyles to condemn these other sensibilities, is to rob our own senses of their integrity, and to rob our minds of their coherence. We are human only in contact, and conviviality, with what is not human. (Abram, 1997: 22)

Yet his argument does play into a deficit model of the loss of sensory-kinaesthetic connection, so that he finds contemporary Western society wanting in this respect. There are sound political and historical reasons for making these arguments, and what he says chimes with a new interest amongst social geographers for example in more-than-human worlds. But a by-product of his approach is that it deflects attention from exploring the different ways that sensations actually do infuse and express everyday lives and relationships – even in the West – and also the extent to which people do know this and do have a sensory-kinaesthetic appreciation of their own and others' experiences of living and (as I shall explore later in the book) of their environments.

A more dominant version of the idea of the Western loss of connection with the sensuous is one that, contra Abram, sees this as evidence of a higher intellect or level of development: the capacity to operate a rational mind, apparently freed from the exigencies of one's body and no longer in thrall to one's senses, is seen as emblematic of 'civilisation' and evolutionary ideas of development. In this version, the 'closer-to-nature' status of so-called 'primitive', tribal, native or indigenous peoples and indeed of non-humans is constructed as evidence of their inferiority, and part of the justification for all kinds of abominations, dominations and appropriations by self-styled superior or more 'advanced' peoples. Abram of course wants to reverse this moral ordering, and to celebrate the sensuous connections that tribal peoples have with 'non-human nature'.

The idea that some groups are closer to or more associated with the bodily and that this is evidence of inferior social status/social standing has echoes in the dynamics of power and inequality within contemporary Western societies too. For example we can see this perhaps in the disempowering way in which children are more closely associated with or defined by their sensations, or women with bodily processes and substances (menstruation, menopause, pregnancy, lactation, and dealing with children's and others' bodily substances) (Grosz, 1994), or working class people with 'their appearance, their bearing and their adornment' being seen as 'a kind of join-the-dots pathologization' (Lawler, 2014: 149), or animals in their assumed non-sentient and non-characterful simple physicality. These are all powerful discourses, that can be and are put to use in micro- and macro-dynamics of power relations. But they are not only built on a false premise about the supposed superiority of a kind of a-sensual existence, but also about the supposed receding or non-essential place of sensory-kinaesthetics in everyday interactions and relationships more generally. It is important here, I think, not to be gullible in accepting the rhetoric, or the discursive constructions and narratives about the distancing of the sensory-kinaesthetic, and thus failing to see what is staring us in the face, prodding us in the arm, and whispering in our ears about sensations in interactions and relationships.

Sensations are multiple and atmospheric, emanating in encounters

A sensory-kinaesthetic attunement also shows us that, if it is vital to recognise that relationships and interactions are full of sensations, it is equally important to understand that those *sensations are always multiple*, and I mean a number of related things by that. To begin with I mean that sensations are not simply derived from single sensory stimuli, or perceived through singular sensory receptors, for example, of sight, touch, smell. It is helpful here to reiterate the difference in definitions of 'senses' and 'sensations'.

Sensation: a physical feeling or perception resulting from something that happens to or comes into contact with the body

Sense: a faculty by which the body perceives an external stimulus (ODE, 2005)

In my version of sensations, different senses and kinaesthetics are rolled together in the mutual and relational experience of sensations. This is easy to appreciate when we consider what it is to encounter the sensations of others, for example Wilkie's slaughterman experiencing that 'look' 'walking towards' him, that we can imagine contained a whole range of sensory-kinaesthetics at the time, as well as in subsequent remembering and telling. But we can also appreciate this multiple nature of sensations in apparently inanimate things, like my father's ashes for example: his ashes are the touch and feel of them at the same time as they are the smell (or non-smell, or odourless sensation in the nostrils) of them, and the look of them (how they look and how I see them), and the heft, density and texture of them, and the sound of them (their silence, or the sounds I can imagine them making if I scattered them, or the swish-thud they make if the canister is tipped), and hence also the movement of them. And they are also a whole other set of in/tangible sensations of his alive and no-longer-alive textures, ways of being and relating – and their attendant discordances in time and confrontations with the meaning of death. Ashes are also at the same time an extra-sensory wondering (What stuff is this? What essence? What spirit or sensory-kinaesthetic qualities emanate from it or are somehow anchored to it?). And they are an awkward in/tangible presence.

The idea of in/tangibility – a kind of liminal hovering across and transcending of the boundaries of tangibility and intangibility – and the questions and intrigue that raises about what things are, what we are, what sensations are, is a core theme to grasp in relation to the potency of affinities. It has an allure and an attraction – a sense of delicious speculation – and it also makes clear that sensations also include all those extra-sensory, magical, ghostly and dreamlike experiences that are so potent in the 'sense of presence' we saw in the work of Bennett and Bennett, or Hallam et al., on widowhood. These ethereal and 'extra-sensory' relationalities between the living and the dead are multiply sensory, and are fully part of what I want us to understand by 'sensations'. Ethereal-relational sensations express something about the ineffable and other-worldly nature of affinities, and about things that will not settle into place for 'rational' or categorical explanation. Yet they are a familiar part of everyday life, and of people's narratives and explanations, so that they are in a sense ordinary and commonplace, yet extraordinary and remarkable all at the same time. In order to perceive them, we need to appreciate and take seriously what people experience as ineffable, in/tangible, ethereal and elemental.

Even as we sociologists may be busy forgetting this multiple and in/tangible nature of sensations in our professional work, it is readily manifest in life experience. Anyone who has experienced being 'transported' to somewhere or some-when in their past by a piece of music, a taste, a sight or a smell, knows that what is conjured in the sensory memory is never just a single-sense experience (if such a thing could be imagined) like a sight or a sound, but instead an *atmosphere* of multiple sensations. Sometimes but not always such atmospheres are of searing intensity, but whether or not that is the case they are powerfully felt and experienced – assaulting the senses and occupying both the air and memory, as though in a new encounter – and cannot be apportioned neatly to different and separate senses; indeed, sometimes it is hard to discern which constellations of senses are involved. Proust famously wrote in *À la Recherche du Temps Perdu* of being transported in this way by the taste and smell of a madeleine cake dunked in a cup of tea, something he had not done since childhood until that moment. This sensory experience called up involuntary memories for him that felt quite overwhelming, of atmospherics, characters, auras, emotions and the *feel* of a time in his childhood. Proust interestingly speculated on circumstances under which the senses of taste and smell might act powerfully to produce such multiple sensations in involuntary memory:

> when from a long-distant past nothing subsists, after the people are dead, after the things are broken and scattered, taste and smell alone, more fragile but more enduring, more unsubstantial, more persistent, more faithful, remain poised a long time, like souls, remembering, waiting, hoping, amid the ruins of all the rest; and bear unflinchingly, in the tiny and almost impalpable drop of their essence, the vast structure of recollection. (Proust, 1996: 51)

But of course the experience of consuming the dunked madeleine cake involved other senses as well as taste and smell (sight, touch, sound), and certainly the memories called up were of multiple sensations, so I do not think Proust's fascinating observations quite warranted the flurry of attention into the supposed mechanically singular powers of 'odour-invoked memory' that they initiated (for example, Chu and Downes, 2000). The fact also that transportations such as Proust's *take us to* atmospheres and places that *contain* characters and relationships, but are not solely or singularly *about* them, should alert us to aspects of the limitations in the concept of relationship that are revealed when sensations are taken seriously. And that these kinds of experiences of being unexpectedly transported to the full atmospherics of a somewhere or some-when are not the conscious result of an individual's memory work (trying to remember for example) or self-invention, just as one cannot conjure the 'sense of a presence', also leads to my next point.

The argument I have made so far is that sensations are multiple in ways that involve perception, feeling and experience. But it is important to add that they also *emanate* (and circulate and reverberate) – from and in others, and environments, situations, atmospheres, things and indefinable sources. In saying this I do not wish to suggest that sensations are simply the felt-effects of our sensory receptors picking up signals that come from external sources, in some sort of passive one-way process. But it is important also to counter the opposite idea that sensations are entirely formed and given shape through human or cultural interpretation and meaning systems, in an active one-way process that runs the other way, according all agency and generative capacity to human perceivers. This latter view would see sensations as always already interpreted, and always the result of actively enquiring human perception. The idea that sensations *emanate* is an important counter to this, suggesting that sensations have capacities of force and flow.

My arguments here are influenced by Ingold's ideas about perception of the environment (Ingold, 2000), although I do not think he uses the concept of emanation and probably would not especially like it; but there is something in his argument that fits with my own and that I want to elaborate on. Ingold draws on, amongst others, Merleau-Ponty's ideas about mindful, experiencing bodies, and on Gibson's notion of a 'perceptual system', to question the assumed distinction between: an external environment / a sensory gateway (in faculties of sight, hearing and so on) / and a meaning-making or interpreting mind. For Ingold, these cannot be separate entities, as he explains when reflecting on the processes of looking, listening and touching:

Questions about the meaning of light, as of sound, are surely wrongly posed if they force us to choose between regarding light and sound as either physical or mental phenomena. They are wrongly posed because they continue to regard the organs of sense as gateways between an external, physical world and an internal world of mind. . . . It is my contention that there is no such interface between eye and mind . . . the process of vision consists in a never-ending, two-way process of engagement between the perceiver and his or her environment. (Ingold, 2000: 257–8)

Therefore, he goes on to say:

Looking, listening and touching . . . are not separate activities, they are just different facets of the same activity: that of the whole organism in its environment. (Ingold, 2000: 259–60)

This idea of a 'whole organism' moving and living in its environment, in a 'never-ending, two-way process of engagement', conjures the kind of relational dynamic engagement and interactive involvement that I want to convey with the concept of sensations, and it also suggests an ecological disposition, which I shall discuss in part 3 of the book. In summary then, to say that sensations are multiple and emanating is to say, first, that they are felt, perceived and experienced in ways that do not separate senses, or mind and body. Secondly, that they emanate (and circulate, and reverberate), operating in a multi-way dynamic, and as forces, flows, energies and atmospherics, sometimes feeling ethereal or mystical. And thirdly, that they happen in encounters.

Sensations *as* sensations: not representations, adjuncts or qualities

A third point that comes from a sensory-kinaesthetic attunement in the facets is that *sensations are manifest and of interest in themselves*; they do not simply stand for or tell us about or express something else. Neither do they lose their significance once a something else that they are supposed to represent is understood. They are not simply an adjunct to, or a version, type or quality of something else. My conceptualisation of sensations removes the requirement for us to see them always as the result of human or socio-cultural processing, or as signs and symbols of other things, and I think that is important because they lose their essence and integrity in those interpretations.

Whilst we can of course see that senses can be imbued with cultural meaning, and that this may vary at different times and in different cultures (which may differently label or value the oral, aural, or visual, or tactile for example), I think we miss that relational, visceral and emanating essence of sensations if we move quickly towards abstracted interpretations. Again, I agree with Ingold's line of reasoning, although I would perhaps be less dismissive of the 'anthropology of the senses' than he, when he says:

> The anthropology of the senses – as presented in the work of scholars such as Howes and Classen – seems determined to leave lived, sensory experience behind in the search for what it stands for, namely the incorporeal 'ideas' and 'beliefs' of a culture. (Ingold, 2000: 284)

I agree strongly that it is vital to see sensations for what they are, in and of themselves, rather than seeing them as standing for, or telling us about (symbolically or otherwise), something else – such as an abstract notion of the concept of relationship, or indeed of culture. As I have suggested, relationships in the living are not abstracted things, somehow separate from their sensations. I think we need to be openly attuned, as I have suggested, to sensations, if we are not to lose sight of them or relegate them to the position of adjunct or representation; and that means putting sensations centre stage.

And sensations *are* centre stage, as I have argued, in those potent connections that I am calling affinities. Sensations – as I have conceptualised them – are part of what makes some connections rise up and become potent, in the living and the telling – with poignancy, power, energy and force. These are affinities, but of course affinities are not confined to interpersonal relationships, and neither are sensations. Focusing on sensations takes us beyond that somewhat limiting frame because sensations are generated in a much wider range of encounters than those we might see as interpersonal relationships or interactions, and affinities can be sparked in all kinds of encounter. One needs only to consider the sensory, kinaesthetic and affective force that engagement with music can give rise to (see DeNora, 2000), or the powerful sensations that are generated through atmospheres or environments, or the 'other-worldly', to understand that it would be nonsensical to try to squeeze all of these through the filter of interpersonal relationships. Once we start exploring 'relationships' with a sensory-kinaesthetic sensibility, we find all kinds of other irrepressible questions start to vie for our attention which may apparently have little or nothing to do with 'relationships', and the concept of interpersonal relationship starts to seem too limiting and restrictive for where we want to go. Starting with sensations leads us perhaps most notably to environments or ecologies (and we have seen this is important in the work of Ingold), and to atmospherics, and I will explore these as the book progresses.

The need to recognise sensations as sensations, and to allow them to loosen the grip of conventional or habitual modes of conceptualising and theorising, is one reason why I am not trying to fit sensations into well-known existing approaches that might be thought to have some relevance. We need an attunement that will recognise *a charge*, and most approaches are not designed to do that. So, for example, I do not see sensations as confined to or simply an adjunct of *'practices'* (as emotional or sensory practices might be seen to be) – an approach which has had great influence, very positively, in the families and relationships field, as well as outside it (Morgan, 1996). But although practices may be involved in interactions and relationships, their theoretical formulation and especially the connection with 'doing' is very human-centric and tied to the concept of a social actor, and does not foreground sensations or necessarily help us to apprehend those situations where forces and flows, and more diffuse emanations and atmospheres, create potency. Indeed, in some ways it occludes these in wanting to bring what is going on back to the concept of practices.

There is a similar problem with approaches that emphasise *'embodiment'* or *'the body'*, some of which developed in light of Merleau-Ponty's arguments about the perception of mindful bodies, but many of which do not seem to hold onto the significance of his refusal to separate mind/body. As Ingold has suggested:

> Formerly placed with the organism on the side of biology, the body has now reappeared as a 'subject' on the side of culture. Far from collapsing the Cartesian dualism of subject and object, this move actually serves to reproduce it. (Ingold, 2000: 170)

I agree with Ingold and although, on the face of it, approaches foregrounding embodiment should be sympathetic to sensations as I have conceptualised them, I find that the direction such studies have taken very often distances the proposed subject of analysis (the body, the social body, sexuality, the self, culture) from fleshy, sensory-kinaesthetic, experiential sensations that are needed to understand affinities. Synnott's important work on the 'body social' for example sees its subject as the 'study of self as embodied' and thus directs attention away from sensations in and of themselves (Synnott, 1993).

And Classen makes the point that much of the work on sexuality and embodiment is highly theoretical and abstracted, and, ironically, does not engage with the sense of touch (Classen, 2012). Other work on embodiment which is more sensory and 'fleshy' (for example, Riach and Warren, 2015) can still have the effect of enhancing the conceptual status of corporeality, at the expense of that fusion of mind, sensation, emanation and atmospherics that I am seeking to pursue. There is undoubtedly considerable merit in these approaches for many purposes, but if we are to understand affinities, I find many of them to be too socially or culturally or corporeally constructivist, too human-centric, or too categorical.

So we can see that approaches that see sensations as an adjunct to relationships on the one hand, and those approaches that we might think of as centring the concepts of practices or embodiment on the other, will not tend to lead to putting sensations centre stage *as sensations* in the way that I think is necessary for understanding affinities. Although a great deal of interesting and useful work has been done under these rubrics, their reluctance to see sensations as sensations in their own right means that they do not naturally lead us towards the conceptual tools we need to recognise the kind of *charge* that makes affinities potent.

Some versions of 'affect theory' are potentially more fruitful, and especially Kathleen Stewart's book *Ordinary Affects*, which she suggests:

> tries to provoke attention to the forces that come into view as habit or shock, resonance or impact. *Something* throws itself together in a moment as an event and a sensation; a something both animated and inhabitable. (Stewart, 2007: 1)

Stewart's desire to apprehend and take notice of *somethings* that throw themselves together in these ways has parallels with my argument that we should be willing to notice (and, as sociologists, to be engaged by) the potencies that constitute affinities, and that we should understand sensations to be central in this. She goes on to say:

> Ordinary affects are the varied, surging capacities to affect and to be affected that give everyday life the quality of a continual motion of relations, scenes, contingencies and emergences. They're things that happen. They happen in impulses, sensations, expectations, daydreams, encounters and habits of relating, in strategies and their failures, in forms of persuasion, contagion, and compulsion, in modes of attention, attachment and agency, and in publics and social worlds of all kinds

that catch people up in something that feels like some*thing*. (Stewart, 2007: 2)

I think this kind of conceptual and methodological openness, together with the willingness to hold in focus not only sensations but phenomena like impulses, daydreams and encounters, is powerful and important. This is the kind of thinking which it is useful to bring to understanding affinities, and I shall continue to engage with Stewart's ideas throughout the book.

However, I do not adopt an 'affect theory' approach more generally, partly because that sense of 'capacity to affect and be affected' that underpins such an approach does not define or give enough analytical purchase on affinities; in some ways it is too confining, and in others it is too broad. Indeed, sometimes it seems as though 'affect' applies to everything – that there is nothing that is not affect – and this can dilute its explanatory potential. Also though, in the rise and rise of affect theory over the last decades, a high level of abstraction and theoretical obfuscation has come to characterise some of the approaches and debates. This has had the unfortunate and ironic effect in some quarters of taking discussion away from those very sensations that I want to keep centre stage (see Wetherell, 2012, for an excellent overview of affect; see also Clough and Halley, 2007; Gregg and Seigworth, 2010).

A sensory-kinaesthetic attunement reveals *characters*

A fourth thread that I want to gather from the facets is that a sensory-kinaesthetic appreciation or attunement helps us to understand *how we come to know, and to be, the characters in our lives*. I am using the term 'characters' in a loosely dramaturgical or literary way, to think about those beings who have some part in our lives (including ourselves) as they might if the living of our personal lives were a play or a novel. In doing this I am keen to develop the idea of *relational characters*, in favour of more familiar sociological concepts of self and identity, not least because it is clear that particular characters figure centrally in affinities at particular times. Consider for example Gil Scott-Heron's grandma's hands, alive with 'clapping to church', no longer alive but reanimated and celebrated in the sounds, lyrics and music of song; or my dad or Mary Cappello's Sidney, both awkwardly manifest for Mary and I in sensory-kinaesthetic remains; or the particular characters discussed, enacted and mimicked in the

children's stories about who matters to them; or the violent intimacies of Bahari's and Mpondo's torturers; or the moth, the dove and
the wicked boys evoked for Becky Tipper; or the lambs who trust-
ingly followed Rhoda Wilkie's farmer into the trailer that would lead
to their deaths, and who continued to play on her conscience; or the
'moon-eyed' look that Wilkie's slaughterman sees 'walking towards'
him and has to shoot. These are all examples of characters-in-relation,
who have parts in the lives in question; parts which have a potency
that in many ways emanates from, and is expressed, perceived and
recounted in a brimming sensory-kinaesthetic parochiality.

This sensory-kinaesthetic parochiality of particular characters-
in-relation is important because I think that affinities are not
experienced as types of relationship or ties-in-general (for example between grandmother and grandson), even though sociologists
might want to generalise about the processes involved. But we do
not simply inhabit categories of person, group or relationship type,
or find ourselves socially constructed into them, even though we can
sometimes identify ways in which such things are socio-culturally
imbued. Affinities are experienced as particular potent connections
with specific others who are characters with appearances, smells,
voices, gestures, physicality, habits (disgusting and otherwise), ways
of being in the world, traits, political and moral orientations and of
course their own personal socio-cultural relational histories. It is this
particularity of character, and the role of characters-in-relation, as
they might be seen to function in a novelist's story or a playwright's
plot, or in the visceral and immediate parochiality of our lives, that I
think is all too easy to miss in the impulse to create general categories.

Like Gil Scott-Heron in his evocation of his grandma, creative
writers, poets, novelists and students of literature know all about the
importance of character. But sociologists, deflected perhaps by their
greater concern with categories, practices, discourses, assemblages,
and the construction of identities, selves and so on, can overlook the
ways in which lives are peopled, animaled (I have made that word
up) and animated by relationships between particular characters. Yet
what distinct characters are like, interactively, in their full sensory-
kinaesthetic glory (remember the children using expressions like 'he's
like going . . .', 'she goes . . .' as they gesticulated and acted out their
stories and imitations of the full sensory-kinaesthetics of others' ways
of *being*), and how they relate to others in their environments, is crucial in how affinities take shape, and in what they are made of.

Others whom we have known closely for many years, as well as
those whom we encounter briefly, can equally become characters in

our lives, and I would argue that sensations are central in how that happens and manifests itself. We know already that we and others can gain moral reputations as, for example, trustworthy, difficult, unreliable, generous, capricious, well behaved or naughty and so on. And we know that such reputations are formed, constituted, established and sometimes disrupted in cumulative sets of interactions, in particular and changing socio-cultural and familial contexts, and that these may take place over many years. Such reputations can be narrated, remembered, forgotten and denied, both in stories that may be passed down generations, and in family secrets too (Finch and Mason, 1993, 2000; Smart, 2007, 2011). However, sensations have been underplayed in these analyses – often in favour of a non-sensory analysis of biographies and practices – and yet the insights from the facets (and indeed from studies of, for example, family photographs, genealogical documents and autobiographical memory) suggest that the sensations are likely to be central (Kramer, 2011; Kuhn, 1995; Mason, 2008; Smart, 2007, 2011; Widerberg, 2010); one might even go so far as to say that they are a large part of what such biographies are made of. Often these kinds of empirical analyses are not written or 'read' for what they say about the sensations but once we are ready to be tuned in, it is easy to see how such data are saturated with them. That includes situations of apparent sensory 'absence' or impairment – for example anosmia (lack of sense of smell), or blindness and deafness, where a sensory-kinaesthetic reading reveals that characters are still formed and encountered through sensations and a relational sensory-kinaesthetics (Hull, 1997; Ingold, 2000: ch. 14; Philpott and Boak, 2014; Wright, 1990). As Ingold has commented, 'Blind and deaf people, like everyone else, sense the world with their whole body' (Ingold, 2000: 270). The relational characters and interactions and encounters in our lives may shift and change in the face of sensory changes such as gradual loss of hearing or sight, but relational characters would only ever be considered a-sensory if one was using a deficit-model to approach the question (Schillmeier, 2006).

In terms of the emergence of characters in briefer or less sustained and intimate encounters, Morgan has interestingly suggested that sensory-kinaesthetic knowledge (this is my term; Morgan calls it embodied knowledge) of the other might actually be particularly important as a characteristic of *acquaintanceship*, where we do not have detailed biographical knowledge of the other as we would with an intimate (Morgan, 2009). Sensory-kinaesthetic knowledge ensures the sufficient degree of 'non-substitutability' to distinguish an acquaintance from a stranger in that we recognise them and know some embodied things about them. This might include, for example, 'knowing the face' but not recalling the name – Morgan makes the important point that 'this reference to the face is frequently a shorthand term for a whole collection of embodied characteristics, including tone of voice, physical presence and context' (Morgan, 2009: 101). I agree, and can certainly recognise the important role of the sensory-kinaesthetic in acquaintanceship, alongside even more fleeting forms of encounter which can engender or involve characters such as those described by Wilkie and Tipper in the facets; these also, incidentally, point to the role of chance, happenstance, serendipity or vicissitude in encounters with, and the emergence of, characters in the living of personal lives.

In a sense, Morgan's argument about the sensory-kinaesthetic and acquaintances is that, in the absence of more sustained knowledge that might come with the interweaving of the biographies of intimates over time, this is all we have to go on. And yet I wonder if this is not something of a deficit model, which might by implication – and perhaps unnecessarily – somewhat underplay the role of sensations in more incontrovertibly intimate relationships. It also risks reducing what I think is a sensory-kinaesthetic *relationality* (in the encounters of acquaintanceship, intimacy and otherwise) to a more individualised and static notion of 'embodied characteristics'. 'Sensations' has a more multi-directional and open character, implying that these sensory-kinaesthetic phenomena both emanate and are perceived, operating as flows, forces and energies. I shall return to this point.

Before leaving the concept of character for now, I should explain that I am using it differently here from a more Goffmanesque approach where the interest is in the role or performance and in how the person, or *the self*, is constituted – in and through roles and performances that are played and made in situations. Goffman's interest is in the role, or mask, or performance, and from his perspective this is not simply a mask that is donned by some form of separate and essential person, but instead 'to be a person . . . is to perform being a person' (Lawler, 2014: 121).

However, I am not using the concept of character to try to expound on the nature of the self, or the person, or performativity, so much as to argue that characters are *those who play a part in something*. I want to keep open what that something is, by seeing it as the relational living of life, rather than any more restrictive notion of, for example, a sequence of performances, or a more self-conscious *narration* of the self, or narrative identity in Ricoeur's sense (Ricoeur, 1991). This is because, as I shall come to show, I do not think the various energies, forces, potencies and connections – affinities, in fact – can be folded into or seen as emanating from a narrated self or identity, even though such narrations may indeed be part of living. Indeed, I do not want to make any assumptions about the nature of the self or the essence of the person, dramaturgical or otherwise, or to pursue an argument that requires us to see character as mask or performance, or living as a narrative. It is not that I strongly disagree with such ideas, so much as that I want to do something different with the dramaturgical or literary analogy, and that is to understand what a character is by looking in an open rather than closed way from the perspective of the relational living of life (rather the narration of a self). Characters then are those sensory-kinaesthetic beings who play some relational part – which might be central, epiphanal, or peripheral – in that living; they are those who have *something to do with* that story, some spark of interest or contingency for it, as would characters who appear in a novel or a play.

Affinities are charged with the energies of fascination, wondering and discordance

The facets involved many examples of people wondering – but also remembering, conjuring, and animating, in ways that were full of sensations. Tipper's examples of 'wonderment' about human–animal relationships were especially interesting, not least because many discussions of such relationships focus on the ways humans categorise or classify animals, and whether there are contradictions in those classifications, in quite a static fashion, rather than the more active focus on wonder*ing* as a wide-eyed and fascinated, or even willing to be amazed, activity. Similarly, we have seen the wonderings that can take place around what human ashes are, and around the absent presences and in/tangibilities of ghosts and death. Or the fascination with and imagination about the sensations of others – human and animal. Or the sensory conjurings and rememberings (and transportings) that take people to other places, times and contexts. What I am especially interested in, for affinities, is that sense of wonder*ing*, or imagin*ing*, or remember*ing*, or conjur*ing*, or animat*ing*, or transport*ing*, as *relational lines of energy and forces of affinity*. I think these kinds of *'ings'* are live wires, connective energies, creating charges – and we need to notice and attend to them.

That people are fascinated by these things is important for understanding the potency of affinities, and a strong theme in the facets is a fascination with sensory-kinaesthetic *discordance*. We can see this in, for example, the disbelief of ashes and sensations of living, the sensations of being close with food-animals and with meat, the temporal discordance between living sensory memories and non-living absences, the discordance between 'the real' and 'the ethereal' (or tangible and intangible) in the absent presence of the dead, the sensory-kinaesthetic intimacies of violence. The social scientific impulse is probably to see these as contradictions or ambivalences that need ironing out and reconciling, but I think it is possible to argue that these discordances are part of the charge and the potency of affinities, and that people do not find it odd to live with them, and indeed are often intrigued or fascinated by them. I like the term discordance because, in a musical context, it can suggest a charge and an energy – where we think of a searingly beautiful yet discordant harmony (or an agonisingly jarring one for that matter) for example. This is more suggestive of a potent quality, than an untidy or inconvenient anomaly that needs settling.

Again, I am influenced by some of Tipper's arguments here. She develops a fascinating discussion of the concept of irony and humour (sometimes 'gallows' humour) in human–animal relations. She explores the ideas of ambivalence and contradiction in how humans relate to animals – or creatures – and finds these wanting in explanatory terms. She gently suggests that the tone of many human–animal studies is too 'earnest'. For example, where pets are described as child substitutes, many 'studies allow no room for the ways people might play with and joke about these possibilities – neither fully endorsing them nor entirely rejecting them' (Tipper, 2012: 221). She suggests that the problem is that most writers in the human–animal field (for example, Arluke and Sanders, 1996; Charles and Davies, 2008) see ambivalence and contradiction as uncomfortable and problematic states, and focus on practices which they argue are designed to minimise or mask them. Examples here might be seeing pets as 'individuals' but laboratory animals as 'things' that do not warrant the same level of empathy or compassion, or seeing certain creatures – especially those it is thought necessary to 'control' – as non-individuated and categorical 'species' or 'pests', or indeed using euphemisms for killing such as 'pest' or 'control' or 'reduction' or 'management', or making a joke about one's love for a pet to deflect attention from the possibility that you prefer animals to humans. Yet although such apparent ambivalences, contradictions and denials are familiar parts of everyday life, Tipper wants us to reimagine them in a more sophisticated way, and she draws on Nigel Rapport's suggestion that we should recognise the allure and reality of 'both/ and' thinking, instead of requiring that things settle or are forced into a more tidy 'either/or' (Rapport, 1997, cited in Tipper, 2012):

> I want to argue that ambivalence itself, and irony in particular, might be understood as much more than a state of indecision or denial, and that humour might be seen as more than simply a 'coping mechanism' whereby people seek to minimise the threat of contradictory ideas. Irony – 'the tension of holding incompatible things together' – might be viewed not in terms of the imminent resolution of the tension, but rather, this tension itself might be a *pleasurable, creative frame of mind*. A state where two things might be equally true. (Tipper, 2012: 218, my emphasis)

I do not think this only applies to human–animal relations. The cases of widows 'switching' language back and forth from supernatural to material forms in the kinds of delicious speculation I have discussed, for example, are indicative of something of the same order. So, I think we should recognise that people can frequently engage in thinking that seems contradictory – thinking two conflicting things at once – and that it is not annoying indecision or a temporary conflict that will ultimately be resolved, or a device for successfully being 'in denial', but is instead a steady and sometimes charged state, a normal way of being and, as Tipper suggests, may even be part of the pleasure or the magic or indeed, the affinity.

In this part of the book I have argued that sensations are crucial in affinities – affinities are made of and in them, and we need a sensory-kinaesthetic appreciation to start to apprehend them. Affinities come alive and take shape as sensations, and it is through encounters with these emanating, circulating and reverberating sensations that we feel their potency. I explained earlier that I began the book, and specifically this part of the book, with an interest in introducing sensations into the nexus of interpersonal relationships. But already we can see that taking sensations on board necessarily shifts our thinking so that it cannot be contained – indeed it does not want to be contained – within conventional ideas of what constitutes an interpersonal relationship. Much of what sensations are about, and indeed what affinities are about, does not fit within that particular frame. The discussion of sensations is a first layering in my argument about affinities, and it edges us closer to understanding what affinities might be, and how they might constitute an invitation to think differently.

PART TWO

Ineffable Kinship

Why Ineffable Kinship?

Some of the most potent affinities feel like an ineffable kinship; *a something* that is in connection, with a charge that feels fixed, immutable and elemental. Yet although we often think we know what such affinities are, or that we know what that something that is in connection is (we might see these as self-evidently connections of blood, or genetics, or family, for example), at the same time we know that we really do not know what such connections are at all; they seem to have a sense of mystery at their very heart, which is hard to explain or put into words. The affinities that I want to explore in this second part of the book are, on the one hand, *parochial* and *quotidian*, taking shape in and generated through our own relations, known and understood from our own experiences and sensations. Yet at the same time they hint at and tantalise us with more *boundless* and *ethereal* realities of ineffable connection which insist on something that must be the very opposite of parochial, even as it is manifest in our familiar experience of living in the world. The ever present paradox between the parochial and the boundless, the ineffable and the quotidian, and the playing out of a fluctuating divide between the tangible and intangible in everyday life, is in the very essence of the affinities I will discuss in this section and is crucial in understanding their fascination and potency.

In this part of the book I am focusing on ineffable kinship because insight into this is important in the layering of my argument about affinities that began with the discussion of sensations in part 1. In the spirit of layering, sensations remain present and central in the argument here, rather than there being any sense of that part of the argument having been completed and done with. It also needs to be made clear that my aim here as elsewhere is to seek to understand the nature of the charge that makes affinities potent, rather than seeking, for example, to explicate *kinship* per se, or indeed to say that these are the main or most important points to make about kinship. This is not an attempt to 'cover' or categorise types of kinship, and indeed any reader expecting such will be disappointed, not least because there is more to kinship than the strands I will discuss here. My starting and finishing point is affinities, and I am looking for insights into them.

In identifying facets I have therefore been guided by what I think can provide flashes of insight into affinities of ineffable kinship, and I have lighted upon facets that bring into play questions that can be seen to be fascinating and troubling about family resemblance, heredity and relatedness, and where matters of affinity are central. The point as ever is to show how affinities can work and arise, rather than to say these are the only ways in which that happens. In the facets that follow we will journey through some of the haunting ethereal in/tangibility of matters of family resemblance, to a contemplation of the meaning of 'offspring' in experiences of kinship and especially bio-genetic connection – a journey which is steeped in the enigmatic potency of everyday magic and chance just as much as in the science of genetics. These are not necessarily themes that would be predicted to be bedfellows – especially perhaps genetics and magic – and yet if we are exploring *potencies of connection* rather than, for example, *types or categories of relationship*, we find them to be elementally entangled.

Family resemblance is a theme that begins to demonstrate those entanglements of affinity. There is a widespread fascination with matters of resemblance, likeness, family ways and traits. I shall argue that resemblance (and alterity) are recurrent and powerful elements in affinities, and that they come into play especially, but not only, where matters of kinship are thought to be at stake. Questions about who looks like or takes after whom, who does not, whether resemblance is inevitable, and what likeness and alterity mean, generate enormous interest on a range of levels in social life, and not just among family members. Resemblances can sometimes appear to confirm or carry or bestow a particular form of kinship (and alterity can seem to deny it), and sometimes they seem to question or 'trouble' this, or render it ineffable or even magical. People's personal, parochial, involvement with matters of resemblance can feel very profound and elemental, ranging for example from the adoptee who yearns for relatives she resembles, to the young man who neighbours say has inherited his criminal father's bad blood, to yourself when you realise you have your sister's laugh or your grandma's hands or your father's tendency to melancholy, to childhood friends who are just like twins or are 'soulmates'. Resemblances seem to matter, sometimes very profoundly, and to 'touch a nerve', yet at the same time they are often seen as trivial and humorous.

However, academic research usually sees resemblance as mattering, or being representative, idiomatic or metaphorical, only in relation to *something else*, like identity, or genes, or other metaphorical or literal substances (such as blood, flesh, skin) which are thought of as carriers of kinship, relatedness or identity (Mason, 2008). As I argued with sensations in part 1, so too with resemblances – I think we miss something crucial about their essence if we only see them as telling us about something else. For something so familiar and commonly experienced, social scientists have made surprisingly little headway in understanding what family resemblances are in and for themselves (and a lot less headway than novelists and creative writers), instead deferring to scientific 'genetic' explanations that do what they do, but persistently fail to grasp the potencies of affinity that are involved by reducing it to the idea of a genetic instruction or predisposition.

Yet resemblance is both a familiar and potent part of everyday life, and is worthy of investigation in its own right. *Everyone knows* that sisters can be 'two peas in a pod', or that a child can inherit his grandfather's mercurial character, or that resemblances can be capricious and anarchic – skipping generations only to surface unexpectedly and in surprising combinations. Resemblances engage our imaginations, our memories and our senses, as we hear a daughter emit her grandmother's laugh, or we spot a familiar but impossible-to-place gesture and movement in one of our relatives. They can feel like magical and ghostly presences or auras – even spectres. Resemblances can be laughed about, delighted in, longed for, denied, feared and even a source of horror. They are an awkward (again, borrowing Cappello's term) combination of things that are potent and things that are trivial (Cappello, 2007). They can threaten to betray uneasy secrets of conception and kinship, or to broadcast an absence of kinship where one ought to be.

Of course kinship and relatedness in themselves are matters where we can identify a longstanding societal preoccupation as well as a contemporary set of sensations and atmospherics – particularly perhaps around the question of how we understand the ways in which 'offspring' are related to others, and whether and how offspring channel kinship. Historical developments in how parenting, paternity, maternity and wider kinship are established, understood, experienced and regulated, along with associated judgements about responsibility, legitimacy and 'natural instinct', have shown these always to be contentious and highly charged matters. But what is sometimes seen as a new form geneticisation of society – emanating in part from the cultural and scientific dominance of genetics, together with the potential of evolving reproductive technologies to destabilise what might have been thought of as the biological facts of procreation and reproduction – has perhaps created an intensification in this history. I want to show how we can apprehend some of the potencies in affinities of ineffable kinship if we focus on how negotiations about and experiences of relatedness and heredity are being lived through some contemporary situations where what constitutes kinship and offspring seem to be at stake.

Some of the facets that follow therefore explore what comes into play around the dynamic and ambivalent character and sensations of resemblance, and some pursue encounters with contemporary challenges, transformations and unsettlings in how relatedness is decided, negotiated, felt and lived. I examine the sensations of encounters in these domains, as well as what seems to be in connection and how affinities can arise in them. The facets draw on a range of materials, including from literature and the arts, where arguably the fascination of resemblance, for example, has been more readily apprehended than in social science. Some of them also draw on academic research, including a study entitled 'Living Resemblances' that I conducted with Katherine Davies, Carol Smart and other colleagues.[2]

Following on from the facets I return to the layering of my argument about affinities, by considering how the insights into ineffable kinship provided by the facets invite us to think differently. In particular, my argument explores the poetics of metaphor, the frisson of ineffability and discordance, and the energies of ethereality, wondering and in/tangibility in ineffable kinship. Underlying the whole argument here is that we (as social scientists for example) would do well to be attuned to the charge and the energy that comes about in the wondering people do about what it is that is circulating and relating when heredity and kinship seem to be at stake. This is crucial in understanding both the allure and the potency of affinities of ineffable kinship that are discussed in this part of the book.

Facets of Ineffable Kinship

Resemblance
The state of resembling or being alike. A way in which two or more things are alike.
Alterity
The state of being other or different. Otherness.
Kinship
Blood relationship. A sharing of characteristics or origins.
(ODE, 2005)

1. Family resemblances in literature and art

Literature is full of family resemblances – sometimes to build characters and context, sometimes as plot devices, sometimes to create mystery and poignancy, sometimes to hint at secret kinship (for example following illegitimacy or unfaithfulness), and often to show or pose conjectures about ineffable kinship and connection glimpsed in a fleeting moment. Once you start to observe how such resemblances are handled in literature, it becomes clear that creative writers are significantly more eloquent in capturing the everyday sensations, potencies and nuances of resemblances than are social scientists, and at appreciating that these are remarkable or beguiling in and of themselves, and not simply as signifiers of something else that is more 'important'.

Consider for example Thomas Hardy's musings on both the poetics and the potencies of resemblance in his classic poem 'Heredity'. Hardy speaks in the first person of 'the family face' as an 'I' that *lives* and *moves* eternally, with complete disregard for the span of human lives, 'projecting trait and trace' in leaps and bounds across times and places (Hardy, 2007 [1917]). Hardy's poem is fascinated by resemblance as a forever living, wilful and mysterious character that paradoxically is *in* and *of* humans – in faces, traits and gestures – yet exists ethereally and ineffably elsewhere. The very character and nature of resemblance that Hardy evokes seem to insist upon a poetic appreciation.

The sensations and potencies of resemblances are also important in the work of contemporary writer and poet Jackie Kay. For example, her memoir *Red Dust Road* traces her experience (as a black adopted child of white Scottish parents) of searching for her birth parents. The memoir is a sensitive, witty and evocative tale that engages with and is fascinated by what heredity and relatedness are, and how affinities of kinship arise. Whilst the memoir certainly does not constitute an argument that 'genes' or 'biology' are all-determining – quite the reverse – it also engages honestly with the power of the sensations of resemblance, as do some of Kay's poems (see her collection *Fiere*, for example; Kay, 2011). Kay's account in *Red Dust Road* of meeting her birth half-brother in Nigeria for the first time is revealing in this respect:

> I can't get over him; just watching him order chips is a fantastic experience, just watching his mannerisms and listening to the sound of his strong Nigerian accent.
> 'This is such a big surprise', Sidney says turning to me, and taking my hand in his. I'm drinking in his face. His face has the same shape as my own, his forehead is the same. I feel a strange almost ecstatic sensation of recognition. It is nearly primitive. I could happily sniff his ears and lick his forehead. It has completely ambushed me; I wasn't expecting it at all. (Kay, 2010: 272)

Later in the book she talks of telling her much loved parents about her meeting with Sidney. Her mum is excited, but thoughtful, so Kay asks her for her reactions to the story of her encounter with her brother:

> Then she says, 'What is he to me? What relation is he to me? What am I to call him?'
> I think for a moment and say, 'He can call you his Scottish mum.'
> 'I like it. I like it', my mum says. . . .
> I show them the photograph of Sidney and me . . . 'Oh my,' my mum says, 'he's your spit. He's your double.'

'Ye can definitely see a likeness,' my dad says. 'Oh Christ, aye.' (Kay, 2010: 282)

Kay's parents' reaction to the likeness they perceive in the photo, and her decision to recount this (and indeed other examples) in her memoir, illustrate that resemblance is a *something* that matters and can strike you – ambush you even; a force to be reckoned with.

Literature also can evoke the ethereal or haunting nature of resemblances, where their capacity to strike you may be fleeting or arise only in moments of animation, and where it is simultaneously tangible and intangible. The work of contemporary Northern Irish author Maggie O'Farrell contains many such examples. Here is one from her novel *The Vanishing Act of Esme Lennox*, where a woman unexpectedly perceives a resemblance in a stranger:

> Esme reaches out and laces both her hands round one of Iris's. 'You have come to take me away', she says, in an urgent voice. 'That is why you are here.'
>   Esme is withdrawing her hands, turning her head away from her. And something about her changes, and Iris has to hold her breath because she has seen something passing over the woman's face, like a shadow cast on water. Iris stares, long after the impression has gone, long after Esme has got up and crossed the room and disappeared through one of the doors. Iris cannot believe it. In Esme's face, for a moment, she saw her father's. (O'Farrell, 2006: 55–6)

We can see that same kind of in/tangibility in the sensations of resemblance in the work of the Canadian writer Carol Shields, as for example here in her novel *Duet*:

> As Meredith grows up I look at her and think, who does she remind me of? A shaded gesture, a position struck, or something curious she might say will touch off a shock of recognition in me, but I can never think who it is she is like. . . . Last night at the table, just as she was cutting into a baked potato, she raised her eyes, exceptionally sober even for her, and answered some trivial question Martin had asked her. The space between the movement of her hand and the upward angle of her eyes opened up, and I almost had it. Then it slipped away. (Shields, 2003: 23)

Shield's extract evokes the fleeting yet striking nature of resemblances, in the sensation and 'shock of recognition', and also it connects with Hardy's notion of resemblances as traits and traces projected eternally and ineffably, cropping up and dissipating at different times and places with a logic that defies the span of individual lives. It also brings into play the idea that the sensations of resemblance can involve conjecture and wondering – not only about who resembles whom, but what resemblance is and what is the essence of the connection it manifests. Resemblances in this sense are puzzling, fascinating and engaging.

The Canadian photographer and portraitist François Brunelle has a project that plays on as well as provoking these kinds of conjecture and fascination about resemblance. It is called 'I'm Not a Look Alike' and can be viewed on his website at http://www.francoisbrunelle. com/. This details his project of more than fifteen years to photograph doppelgangers together – people who are not related but who bear an 'uncanny' resemblance to each other. His portraits are beautiful black and white images, with the doppelgangers posed together, touching each other, in similar or mirrored poses and clothing. From humble beginnings, word about the project has spread internationally over the internet, and Brunelle now reportedly receives hundreds of requests from all over the world for him to find people's doubles. It appears he has touched a chord in relation to the popular folk wisdom that 'everyone has a double', and that this indicates a special – even magical – kind of affinity. Certainly, people he has photographed are reported to feel there is some kind of ineffable connection between them.

Indeed, it is difficult to believe, when confronted with a striking resemblance between unrelated people, that there can be no connection between them, or no essence of each somehow inhabiting the other, or no mystical filaments running between them. There is a striking example of this in a moving and powerful book by Jackie Stacey, called *Teratologies: a cultural study of cancer*, in which she weaves a very personal autobiographical account into a book that explores how cancer is perceived, experienced and theorised (Stacey, 1997). Stacey has an epiphanal meeting with a look-alike when she is on holiday in Crete, recovering from surgery and chemotherapy:

> I had lost eyebrows, eyelashes and hair, and that does give a person an unusual look. I wore a scarf or a hat in public, but I did look different. Certainly no one else looked like me. That is, until two women walked towards me, one of whom wore a pale blue headscarf wound round in a recognisable turban style. She also had that rather uncannily naked look of someone with no eyebrows or eyelashes. She looked completely familiar and yet totally unfamiliar at the same time. . . . A youngish woman (in her twenties?) who bore a strange resemblance to me had suddenly appeared as my mirror image in a street in a small Greek village. (Stacey, 1997: 18)

Stacey describes being thrilled and excited by this encounter, and disappointed in herself for being so English as to maintain a polite distance and not approach and speak to the woman. But the strange coincidences continued as she discovered that the women were staying in a holiday cottage that was: 'Next-door-but-one: this was too much to bear; I had to go and speak to them. *My whole body buzzed with the excitement of coincidence*' (Stacey, 1997: 19, my emphasis). She recounts the barrage of questions and answers that went between them when they met:

> What kind of cancer have you had? (I never know which tense to use. Nor do I). Well, it's very rare. So is mine. It's called a teratoma. A teratoma? So was mine. You had it removed, and an ovary too? So did I. And chemotherapy? Bleomycin, etoposide and cisplatinum. Me too. I've got these strange scratch marks on my skin as a side-effect. So have I. I'm having AFP tests every week. So am I. My tests are clear so far. So are mine. I've been taking high dose vitamins. So have I. I've tried all the alternative medicines. So have I. I've been seeing a healer. So have I. They offered me a wig, but I refused. So did I. I've read all the cancer books. So have I. But I've never met anyone else . . . Nor have I. (Stacey, 1997: 19)

In this mutual revealing and sharing of intimate and traumatic experiences, Stacey comments that 'caution lost out as the pleasures of recognition drew me in' (Stacey, 1997: 19). This 'stranger than fiction' meeting was the start of an ongoing allegiance which was challenged only when the women were shocked when the resemblances between them that had seemed immutable started to fall away – as one continued to recover while the other suffered continued illness, surgery and treatment until 'now four years later, I almost dare not say that we might both be in the clear. We still have tests. ... And we don't have a shared narrative any longer' (Stacey, 1997: 20).

What a fascinating story! The 'strange' and striking resemblance issuing its own urgent edict to virtually compel the women to speak to each other, and to create or acknowledge an affinity; the mystical workings of chance, coincidence and serendipity that brought them together at this time, in this place, with these sensations and experiences of resemblance, and at this point in both of their lifetimes. There is a strong sense of charisma and enchantment in this meeting and it makes an intriguing and alluring story.

2. Resemblance interactions

Picture this scene if you will. It is a warm and sunny day in July in the north of England, and this is *An Occasion*. There are many such occasions at this time of year in this city. It is graduation season at the University, and observers watch the young graduates eddy around in flocks and flurries of robes and laughter, like crows circling the treetops. They are flanked by small family groups taking pictures and demanding poses and introductions. The members of these groups move with more or less easy assurance, hesitancy, awe, deference and curiosity, in the territory their celebrated young folk have inhabited for the last years, but which is new to them. There is laughter, awkwardness, tension, embarrassment, pride and sometimes there are tears. Every moment of this season throws up arresting resemblances with what one might imagine to be extraordinary spontaneity, were it not for their regularity. Younger and older versions or conglomerations of a face, a laugh, a walk, an animation or a way of being can round the corner at any moment or volley across the square to ambush the observer or the passer-by. Echoes of resemblance materialise in double takes and half glances. A thousand smorgasbords of personal provenance are out and about on parade.

Now we are inside, at the after-graduation 'strawberries and cream' party, and the graduates and families and friends dressed in their finest are milling around animatedly. The room is warm and this is a scene of flushed faces, with bursts of excited laughter punctuating a noisy and genial hubbub, and chinking glasses of prosecco. The atmosphere is celebratory and the formality of the day is beginning to loosen, with a general sense of relief that the ceremonies are over and the graduations are done. In the corner is a professional photographer along with a couple of researchers. The photographer is taking pictures of family groups, and one of the researchers is conducting vox pop style interviews with them about whether they think they resemble each other.[3] The families are happy enough to do this as family resemblance seems a natural topic of conversation today, and in exchange for volunteering to take part in the research they get to keep the photos.

One of the graduates, Jane,[4] is there with her mum and dad. The three look rather strikingly like each other, with similar colouring, facial features, mannerisms and smiles. And there is something else about them and how they are together that speaks of relatedness, so that even from across the room they seem to exude an aura of kinship. The researcher asks if they think there are resemblances between them and Jane doesn't hesitate in replying that yes, she '*always* gets the family resemblance thing'. She laughs and says that *everyone* is *always* saying 'you look just like each other'. Either they say she looks just like her dad, or just like her mum, or she is a 50/50 split of them. She admits she can see it herself, especially in photographs. It isn't easy to say which 50 per cent she gets from each parent, but she reckons her nose, eyes and face shape are from her dad, and then there is *just something about* her mum's face that is similar to hers, but that is harder to pin down.

Jane's mum and dad both agree, but then her mum adds that actually, she thinks Jane looks 'considerably more like her father'. 'Got the same shape eye bags!' interjects Jane, to her father's amusement. Jane's mum is thoughtful though, adding: 'I've been told that we have similarities, but I can't actually work out what they are specifically.' The interviewer asks whether there are other resemblances in the family – does Jane resemble anyone else? 'No', chorus Jane and her dad. Her dad explains that she has a brother and 'you couldn't tell they were related'. Jane resolutely agrees, more serious now, adding that they are completely, *one hundred per cent* different. She couldn't be more emphatic – this is a young woman who does not wish to be seen as resembling her sibling.

Jane's mum, who has been continuing to look thoughtful, is doing nothing to hide a quizzical expression. Does Jane really not think she resembles anyone? Not even on her dad's side of the family? Jane moves quickly to try to nip something in the bud; she wants to settle the matter, 'No, I don't think that I look like anyone in the family', she says, without a smile, 'and *especially* not my brother.' Sensing some tensing of the atmosphere, and that something is bristling privately between the three of them, the researcher looks to Jane's mum for a response. Jane's mum is speaking to Jane, smiling, quizzical and pursuing her line of discourse despite Jane's attempt to draw a line. 'That's interesting', she says, 'because I was under the impression that you thought you looked more like dad's side of the family.' 'No, no, no', say Jane and her dad in unison, and the researcher feels an urgent imperative to change the subject. 'What about temperament and personality, that kind of thing?' she asks, hopefully.

There is what seems like a long pause, in which no-one speaks and the background hubbub is suddenly more audible. Eventually, Jane's mum fills the gap, but only to say that she couldn't answer that question. Her smile has faded now, and everyone looks a bit awkward. '*I can*', says Jane's dad brightly, apparently saving the day. He has said almost nothing up until now, 'I'll answer that. Jane's much more like me, because we do things very quickly, we multi-task, we get everything done, we've got no patience, and we don't do things slowly, we don't wait around, we don't like wasting time, we *hate* wasting time. If we're doing something together, we get it done really efficiently. And we both move at quite a speed.' The three of them seem happy with that, and Jane quickly agrees with her dad. Definitely, she says, her personality comes more from her dad's side. Jane's mum though has something to add. 'That's absolutely right', she says. 'There's no way I can keep up with them in terms of speed, but I'm more extrovert, and Jane's more like me in that way I think.' The interviewer is interested in this, and turns to Jane to see if she agrees. But Jane is unconvinced, and she is pulling a face, 'Okay', she says slowly, in that way that means it is not okay. 'You don't look like you do agree', says her mum. 'Whatever', replies Jane, stony faced, almost petulant. 'Whatever you think.' 'Perhaps you can talk about it later', the interviewer ventures, in a jovial attempt to move things on. 'No?' persists Jane's mum, 'but at a party I, erm . . . ' She catches Jane's glowering look and decides not to pursue the sentence. 'Okay', she concedes. 'Okay', says Jane.

This interchange was one of fifteen similar encounters initiated by the 'Living Resemblances' project team on that graduation day, and all of them enabled us to observe and be involved in group dynamics around family resemblances. There are some common themes that emerged, and that the case of Jane and her parents help to illustrate.

A familiar conversation topic and form

From this encounter with Jane and her parents, as with all the other encounters we had that afternoon, it was obvious that 'family resemblance' was a *familiar topic* in these family and relationship groups. People readily exchanged well-worn stories and jokes about resemblance, often recounting what others had said in the past about resemblances, as Jane and her parents did. It seemed that the frequency and strength of third party observations of resemblance were an important measure of how valid or real they were considered to be. The *form of the encounter* was clearly a familiar one for resemblance talk too: people were used to having these kinds of interactions with each other and, like 'passing the time of day' or discussing the weather with an acquaintance (Morgan, 2009), they were familiar with the idea of a relative stranger asking them about or commenting on their resemblances at an event such as this when intergenerational groups of relatives were assembled together. As we were part of the

interactions, we were able to experience the sensations and animations of them – including the talk, the gestures and the atmospherics.

Resemblances as striking, fleeting and capricious

Encountering people in groups like this meant that, as researchers, we
were thrust into the dynamics of how resemblances were playing out
through our own experience and involvement, albeit for a short time.
Sometimes, we found ourselves being struck by resemblances between
the people we were meeting, so that we were personally encountering something that many people in our study also told us about: that
there is something powerful and almost magical in the sheer capacity
of some resemblances, almost literally it seems, to *strike or hit you* as
a physical and visceral sensation. A resemblance that hits you feels
authentic and irrefutable. In the case of Jane and her parents – even
from across the room – the resemblance between them was striking.

Of course you might say that the circumstances and the situation
of the graduation event were such that onlookers (and especially
researchers like us who were studying family resemblances) might be
expecting to see them. Part of the fun of such occasions is, after all, to
look for them. And yet I do not think it is possible to train yourself into
the shock of recognition that being struck by a resemblance involves,
and in fact such 'training' probably works in the opposite direction
because it invites a more studied and scientific attunement. When
we looked afterwards at the photographs, for example, they revealed
some clear resemblances, and certainly being able to peruse a photograph allows time to trace and ponder over resemblances, and even to
try to pin them down 'scientifically' by measuring and comparing face
shapes, noses, eye colours and so on. But there is something especially
powerful and arresting about apprehending a resemblance in 'real
time', in the moment you are involved in, where the animations and
dynamics of an encounter with all its gestures, glances, voices, movements, sounds, textures, ways of being, demeanours, in/tangibles,
auras and atmospherics can mean that it comes as a full-on sensory
shock of recognition. The physical sense of being struck can be all
the more powerful because you have not had time to pin it down
and it feels the very opposite of studied and scientific, leaving you
intrigued as to where it came from and how you recognised it. It can
be powerful because the resemblances are so strong (being discernible from 'across the room' as with Jane and her parents for example)
as to feel astonishing or uncanny. Or it can be powerful because the
resemblances seem to hover or flicker there for a moment, and then

vanish. We know from our own experience as well as the accounts of people in our study that being hit by a resemblance feeds into inter-actions as the perceiver finds themselves staring or doing a 'double take', or feeling impelled to comment on the strength of the likeness, or to tell and retell the story of it afterwards.

People sometimes talked, as did Jane, about resemblance being dis-tributed amongst relatives. A prominent theme was the idea that people can share *'bits' of resemblance* – same nose as dad, same general look as mum, same intelligence as grandma, same character as aunt, same colouring as brother, same musical talent as both parents, or a 50/50 percentage split for example. People told us that such 'bits' of resem-blance can circulate and crop up haphazardly around a kinship group. Sometimes these were clearly discernible, but often, although these resemblances might be strong, they were confusing to the senses and a focus for conjecture. For example at one point in my interaction with them, it seemed as though Jane was the centre point in a morphing pro-cess where the features of one parent segued into the other, so that an aura of kinship linked the three of them, broadcasting their relatedness. Then later, when talking to them, I could perceive similar mannerisms and physical features playing between them in different moments and gestures. There were other cases too where there seemed an aura or a fluid interplay of features, creating a kind of 'family look'.

Importantly, people said that resemblances can be grown into and out of, and can appear in people in different times (and in different generations) and places, sometimes fleetingly, and sometimes as a life stage. The idea that resemblances were seen as *changing, unpredict-able* and even *capricious*, came across strongly. One way in which the sense of capriciousness of resemblances emerged was in some people's intrigue or engagement with the *absence of resemblance in the blood line*. Some were fascinated or bemused by resemblances in their family that did not closely follow the 'blood line'. Some, like Jane in relation to her brother, were glad to assert them. We were given examples of absent resemblances and alterities between close blood kin, and conversely their presence in distant kin, step kin, in-laws or non-related others. These can be a point of contention, and we can appreciate that different parties may have different interests here in postulating some kind of link; and this leads me to the next point.

Negotiating and 'settling' resemblances

There were lots of *negotiations and debates* amongst the groups we encountered about who resembled whom, how much and in what ways, as well as about whose comments on these matters held sway in the family, and whether comments and pronounce-ments on resemblance had to be accepted, or whether they could be resisted. Sometimes, people had fun comparing their percep-tions of resemblances with each other, to see whether or not they agreed, and sometimes tensions were brought to the fore. Stated resemblances were sometimes challenged, causing consternation, as we saw at one point with Jane and her parents. This suggested to us that resemblances may not necessarily ever be settled in families, and that interactions like these are part of a process of ongoing negotiation. More than negotiation, perhaps we might think of it as a process of *perpetual settling*, since these exchanges seem often to be characterised by a participant wishing to draw a line to assert a fixed truth, yet at the same time it is clear that no such conclusion is reached. In Jane's case, for example, the different participants each attempt to *settle* what the resemblance patterns are at various points in the conversation. But the interchange does not produce resolution, and one senses that each time resemblances come up in conversation in this group, a perpetual process of settling will con-tinue to be staged.

Sometimes, resemblances were clearly sought after, or delighted in, but also they could be rejected, denied ('I don't agree', or 'I can't see it myself'), or bickered over, even in these short interviews. We observed different *alliances and positionings* going on between members of each group (such as the interesting and somewhat counterintuitive agreement between Jane and her dad in the example above to say that she does *not* resemble his 'side' of the family, and also perhaps throwing into question the mum's interpretation of resemblance pat-terns involving Jane more generally). People were sometimes left out or cast onto the margins in these ways, and others drawn in closer. In some cases, it was likely that divorce and separation of parents had made the context in which resemblances were being claimed or tus-sled over more highly charged or poignant.

Some of these negotiations appeared to hinge on who was better at 'seeing' or spotting resemblances; often there was a sense that there were differences in people's apparent capacity to perceive them. This included some banter around gender, with some of the men being portrayed (by themselves and/or others) as less skilled than women in resemblance spotting. It seemed that men were more often 'allowed' to admit in a jokey way to being not very good at resemblance spot-ting, or not particularly interested in it, or to present themselves as 'just going along with' what others said. That was the case even though several men who took this stance did subsequently come forward with a form of resemblance judgement, as Jane's dad did, in a move to 'settle' the matter of a disputed resemblance or to establish clarity in the face of uncertainty. But not being a skilled resemblance spotter did not seem to threaten the men's sense of self. By contrast, for some of the older women (including Jane's mum) the matter seemed a bit more serious, so that not being good at resemblance spotting, or getting it wrong, felt awkward. It was perhaps not something a mother should admit to; nor for others to say about them.

An uneasy combination of the potent and the trivial

Overall, these were fleeting and jocular encounters about a familiar subject that can be seen as insubstantial, and that routinely generates laughter. In that sense the interactions were inconsequential and trivial, yet what was striking was how highly charged some of them became, and how quickly – as we see in the few minutes of interaction with Jane and her parents. It was clear that important things were at stake, nerves were touched, and resemblance was a force to be reckoned with, taking us into people's complex and sometimes difficult personal affinities of closeness and opposition. Talking about resemblances in this context produced, for some, an *uneasy combination of the potent and the trivial*. Joking and awkwardness of this kind, as I have already argued, is a combination that tends to signal that something important is going on.

3. Resemblance stories

Family resemblances make good stories. In another part of our 'Living Resemblances' project we conducted ethnographic interviews (with a different set of participants from the graduation day encounters). Here we mostly interviewed people as individuals, or sometimes as couples, and that tended to produce less in the way of resemblance interactions, but, on the other hand, a great many stories of encounters with family resemblances. The following three sets of resemblance stories are particularly revealing in relation to what emerged about the nature and significance of resemblances in each case. I report the stories using extracts of verbatim dialogue, with some sections highlighted, because these draw attention to important ways in which resemblance stories are told. These cases highlight particularly well the most striking themes to emerge across our study as a whole, and I then go on to draw these together with examples from other interviews, to discuss some of the insights that I think we can draw.

Mike and Faye:[5] a couple in their thirties, with a baby boy
Extract 1: Faye 'in bed with' her brother-in-law

Mike: Well, in terms of my brothers we all look very similar. Especially my older brother. I think you've [to Faye] commented that I look like him.

Faye: Yeah.

Mike: To the point that when I shaved my beard off, you were like – 'no, that's your older brother!'

Faye: **[Laughing] I was sharing a bed with my brother-in-law. 'This is freaky'.**

Mike: And in fact someone erm, I think, **oddly enough I bumped into** one of my brother's friends somewhere and **I didn't know him** and **they thought I was him to that extent** and he's three years older than me . . . But in personality we're extremely different.

Extract 2: You are the father!

Faye: Yes, you **definitely** look at the face [of their baby son] all the time and **think oh**, he looks like granddad today, **oh** now he looks like Uncle Stewart [Mike's younger brother].

Interviewer: Does this change then?

Faye: It does, it does totally, yeah . . . I think his face structure's changing isn't it? **Most people say** he does look very much like me, we can see **bits of** Mike's dad. **When he's asleep** he looks like Mike. And then bits of Stewart in him **from time to time** as well.

Mike: He reminds me in many ways of my younger brother, Stewart when he was a baby. Sometimes I look at him and think mm, you know.

Interviewer: That's interesting.

Mike: **Very interesting yes** [mock suspicious tone]

Faye: **You are the father!** [laughter]

Extract 3: In real life, you can tell

Faye: That's Mike's family [indicating photos], they all look different there but **when people are sitting in a room** they will say 'oh you do look alike'.

Interviewer: That's interesting, so the photo sort of hasn't captured the essence of . . .

Faye: Hasn't at all, no. And they look different there, but **in real life, you can tell**.

Extract 4: Faye's 'icy cold and weird' family line

Interviewer: How do you think that someone as nice as your mum came from someone like her? [referring to grandma Gretel who Faye has said is cold, judgemental, deeply unpleasant]. What's your take on it?

Faye: **I don't know because my mum's a twin** . . . [her twin is] called Stanley and he's like my grandma.

Mike: Uncle Strangely.

Faye: Uncle Strangely we call him cos he's so weird . . . I think it's **genetic abnormality**, if you look **along this side** of the family [gesturing to the family 'tree' she's drawn], you see rifts. People who aren't talking to other people, secrets, silly things . . . if you go **up above a generation** there's just **more weirdness**. Almost like this kind of mental illness that's **broken** out, or social illness, whatever, where they just can't get on with people. Whereas everyone else, all the other grandparents – complete friendliness, warm heartedness, but there's just icy coldness **there**. . . . What my parents say is when I was very little, I looked just like my grandma Gretel, I had behaviour patterns a bit similar to hers and **they worked hard to stamp it out**.

Isabel, divorced, mother, aged fifty-five

Extract 1: Isabel's son and her ex-husband

Isabel: They're quite similar in not being . . . settled down, grown up people. And yet he hasn't lived with his father since he was two years old so there's no nurture about it then, so there's a nature thing there . . . I think **there must be something that's just there** in that because that's such a strong resemblance in a way that I think there must be some gene thing there. Yeah.

Interviewer: Do they look alike?

Isabel: They . . . don't really look alike. Actually they do look a bit alike. They sound alike.

Interviewer: Do they? Their voices?

Isabel: Yeah, their speaking voices. It's their **voices and mannerisms**.

Interviewer: That's interesting isn't it, where that comes from.

Isabel: Particularly, because . . . Well obviously they've had connections with him but **not the close kind of connections that you'd get when you get, you know, such similarities**. So his laugh may be the same and his hand gestures can sometimes be the same; the tone of his voice can be the same. So it's **a nature thing** isn't it?

Extract 2: Isabel and the generations of women in her family

Isabel: Well physically my sister and I are absolutely like peas in a pod; we are peas in a pod. **Now more so. There was a time when we weren't**. She's fair and I have, well I wasn't fair before I got it coloured [Isabel's hair is fair now], but we're very similar, my sister and I are very similar and we've become more similar I think.

Interviewer: In the kind of people you are as well as how you look?

Isabel: Yes . . . Yeah although she's more timid than I am . . . Er no, timid is the wrong word, that's a loaded word isn't it. Reticent I think. [long pause] [Then] . . . I think there's the bossiness which **runs through** our family, the **female line** which I don't think is a particularly admirable trait.

Interviewer: **[Laughing]** It has its uses though?

Isabel: **[Laughing]** But it's got us through a few scrapes probably, this toughness of mind but I don't think it's a particularly attractive trait and erm, impatience. My mother and I, well we all three actually, we all three have that [her mother, herself and her daughter]

Isabel: Yep. Yeah so there's definitely **a female thing which is very strong** in my family and some of it isn't terribly admirable as I say.

Extract 3: Isabel and health resemblances

Isabel: We **carry weight** in the same way, we both, we all struggle with that. I've got a gammy right knee which is exactly what my mother started with before she got arthritis so there are definitely physical **tendencies** that are similar. I'm just trying to do something **not to exacerbate** it but yes arthritis is **bound to hit me** quite **soon** I think. 'Cos I look at her when she started and I think she was just about the same age as me.

Extract 4: Isabel and her grandchildren

Isabel: Emily [granddaughter] is just very like Rachel [daughter], in fact she's exactly the same as Rachel because I was thinking now of course they take photographs of children all the time and families don't they? But we didn't take many photographs when my children were young so I've got few photographs and I couldn't have told you what Rachel looked like as a baby. But from **the moment I saw** Emily I keep calling her Rachel because she is so strongly like her. Not just physically but in **her way she carries on** really [laughs]. She's a **very strong character**. You know how it is when older generations constantly muddle up your name and that's exactly what I'm doing. I can't even remember quite what sort of relationship I have with the different ones, you know I've lost it really! Sometimes, is it my sister or my daughter you know!

Interviewer: [empathetically] Well it's not surprising if everybody *will* look alike is it? You know, what are you meant to do? **[Laughter]**

Isabel: It is interesting, but Emily, it's really **struck me** when I saw Emily, **not as a tiny baby but as she is now**. She's walking now and **moves around**, yeah, she's just like her Yeah, **I shall be calling her Rachel before too long** . . . I'm trying desperately still to call her Emily.

James, late twenties, no children or partner
Extract 1: Being slightly mystified
James: George [maternal uncle] **died before I was born** so I **don't know** him, or I don't really know his **side of the family**. The **weird thing** is I was thinking about resemblances and the thing that **people always say** is that I take after him [Laughter] which is quite bizarre . . . I was at my Nan's, she's got a photo of him in the Navy and it's like '**oh my God that literally looks exactly how I look now!**' So I do think that and I think a kind of manner, a kind of **way of going about things**. I don't know, my **mum always says** 'You're so much like my father'. So . . .
Interviewer: So, how do you kind of deal with that?
James: Well I'm **slightly baffled** really, **slightly mystified**. I mean I can see it with looks but in terms of what that says about me I don't really know.
And later . . .
James: This confusion I have, say with me and my grandfather, **I wonder** so how does that affect my relationship with my mother? You know, it's like I'm reminding her of her father but **I have no idea what that means**.
And later still, in relation to discussion of longevity of many of his kin:
Interviewer: Do you think that kind of bodes well for you?
James: Hopefully, although I do take after [points to George on family tree] **[ironic jocular tone]**
Interviewer: [Laughter] oh yeah so you take after the one who died before you were born! Did he die of natural causes?
James: Well lung cancer, so smoking.
Interviewer: Okay, and do you smoke?
James: I used to . . . **But anyway**.

Extract 2: Skipping a generation
James: the way people talk about how Dorrie was like very sharp, very bright and very sparky, certainly cheeky. That's what Sophie's like. So I **always think** with Sophie and Dorrie, almost that the resemblances may have **skipped a generation**.

Extract 3: Resembling his father
James: It [family] doesn't give me a sense of belonging. I think this is one of the ways that I think **I'm profoundly like my father** in that I kind of feel like I have to create my own separate systems you know and kind of emotional world or something. I don't think my family does give me a sense of belonging. I think more my friendships.

When we look at these cases together, some common themes emerge which also connect with the themes identified interactively in the graduation encounters, but here they help us to see how they play out in resemblance *stories*. We see, for example, all three sets of stories referring to the idea that resemblances can *hit you in an instant*, and the exclamatory sensation of that moment. Faye uses the word 'oh' and an animated mode of speaking to convey her experience of being struck and surprised by shifting resemblances – 'oh, he looks like granddad today, oh now he looks like Uncle Stewart'. Isabel says 'from the moment I saw Emily I keep calling her Rachel . . . it's really struck me'. And James recounts seeing the photo of his late Uncle George and feeling 'oh my God that literally looks exactly how I look now!' This idea of the sudden physical impact of resemblances, or a shock of recognition, and their capacity to shock or make people exclaim, make resemblances feel external, authentic, powerful and ineffable. This was echoed across our interviews as a whole.

Some of the stories about being hit by a resemblance were clearly stories that had been told before. Faye's parents' unwelcome realisation that, as a baby, she resembled her grandma Gretel perhaps falls into that category; or Mike's recounting of Faye's exclamation that he *was* his older brother when he shaved his beard off; or James's comment that his mum 'always' says 'you're so much like my father', as though she is perpetually being hit by the resemblance, and telling James so. Here is an example where another interviewee, Marilyn, told a story about the birth of her daughter:

> Marilyn: But when Jo was born, the very first time they put her in my arms, brought her onto the ward and I looked at her, she was the image of her dad. Now, an hour later I couldn't see it.
> Interviewer: Oh right, Gosh.
> Marilyn: Just that first glance she was the image of him.
> Interviewer: Yeah, what do you think it was that made you think that?
> Marilyn: I don't know. It, I suppose you get used to it, but, yeah, it, it had gone the next time, I looked for it the next time but I couldn't see it.

This rather epiphanal story is about a resemblance that appeared, momentarily, and then was gone. The story evokes wonder, and is intended to, partly because it is about birth and the first (external) touch between mother and daughter, and also because of the magically elusive nature of the resemblance which draws the father of the child into that first embrace too. That the resemblance was there one second, and gone the next, despite Marilyn's effort to find it again, gives it more rather than less potency. Katherine Davies and I have written about this as an epiphanal story of 'the moment of perception'

(Mason and Davies, 2009). This resemblance is a thing of mystery; alive and existing somewhere between the child and the father, with a will or agency of its own. In Marilyn's account, the resemblance manifests itself according to an ineffable agenda, and it will not be bidden into existence. This confirms its authenticity and reality, because although the resemblance was subjectively perceived, it refused to be conjured up to order. Indeed, one could say the point of the story (or one of the points) is precisely to demonstrate that Marilyn did not invent this resemblance or summon it up through wishful thinking or a concern that her partner might feel excluded from the special moment of new birth. Her story chimes with folk understandings of the transient, capricious and mysterious character of resemblance – and indeed with ethereal presences discussed in part 1 – and establishes the power of a story that Marilyn has clearly told before and will tell again.

This experience of being hit by a resemblance in a moment of perception echoes Benjamin's concept of 'profane illumination', which Michael Taussig describes thus:

> Surely the theory of profane illumination is geared precisely to the flashing moment of mimetic connection, no less embodied than it is mindful, no less individual than it is social. . . . The unremitting emphasis of the analysis [here] is not only on shock-like rhythms, but on the unstoppable merging of the object of perception with the body of the perceiver and not just with the mind's eye. (Taussig, 1993: 23–5)

I like the idea of the 'unstoppable merging of the object of perception with the body of the perceiver' not only because it is suggestive of bodily knowing, but also because it hints at a kind of *unknowledgeable* knowing. This might be felt as the opposite of studied knowledge or even knowledge that comes with experience, precisely because you did not know it until it hit you, or seared itself into you.

It became clear in the course of our research that resemblances (and especially the idea that they have a life of their own and can hit you) *make a good story or anecdote*. I do not mean this in the sense that these stories were fabrications or somehow less true than other aspects of people's accounts, but instead that certain key elements of good storytelling were often present. These include: an everyday 'relatable' setting or context, strong characterisation, the dramatic element of surprise in unexpected action or coincidence or paradox that connects the characters, sensations in all senses of the word, an 'aha' moment of realisation and partial resolution through the connections that are then drawn, and yet a pervading sense of ineffability, mystery and enchantment. Indeed, the stories often left one with the conclusion that, in the words of many of our interviewees, *'there must be something there'*.

Many people told such stories of how they or others had been approached in public places or 'in the street' by strangers who had been 'hit by' a resemblance and felt compelled to say so. As we saw above, this happened to Mike who 'bumped into' a friend of his brother's who he had not met before, and who mistook Mike for his brother despite their difference in age and personality. Although such encounters do not necessarily, in themselves and on the face of it, have any deep relationship to family dynamics or negotiations, as perhaps Marilyn's did, they do make good stories and can make people feel they are witnessing or experiencing something rather potent – as indeed with Jackie Stacey's example in her book *Teratologies* of the strangely coincidental meeting with a woman who so closely resembled her – such that the observer feels they are in the presence of something magical and simply *have to* comment on and draw attention to the resemblance. The idea that a resemblance can be seen by strangers or acquaintances in a public 'chance' encounter (where the implication is that there is no personal investment for the narrator or the characters in the story in claiming or spotting a resemblance) adds to people's sense that the resemblance must be real and objective. When woven into a resemblance story, this has the effect of strengthening the narrator's argument. Here is a variation on this theme, from an elderly widowed interviewee called Edith:

> Edith: On Wednesday night I was in the club playing bingo . . . and a lady came in, now she's elderly like myself, and when I went down near her she said 'Hello' and then when I moved away from her and sat back to where I was sitting I looked at her and I thought; 'my word, Kate is going to look like you when she's your age'. Now Kate is her daughter who I know through darts and when I looked at Mavis, which is the mother, and Kate, in my mind . . . the absolute likeness is *there* only of course in an older person . . . That is a real life incidence that's happened this Wednesday night and it just struck me and I was sat there and we weren't doing anything and the person who sits next to me, we usually talk, but she was chatting to somebody else and I was just sat there looking around and it suddenly struck me.

Edith's story is different from Marilyn's in that the revelatory moment being described involves people who are acquaintances, encountered in an everyday public setting, unlike Marilyn's story of people deeply significant to her, at a very special time. Indeed, part of the point of Edith's story is precisely that resemblances can sneak up and strike you in mundane and everyday situations, and her attunement to the sensory register in her relationships with acquaintances connects with Morgan's ideas discussed in the discussion of sensations in part 1 of this book. But the stories are similar in other ways. As Katherine Davies and I argued when discussing these cases, both situate:

> the resemblance and the moment of perception in a social, sensory and physical context, and in a particular time, place and environment. These kinds of animated and contextual stories create a sensory tangibility to the resemblance being described, and imbue it with an evidential quality. . . . As with Marilyn's story, the nature of the resemblance Edith describes is too momentary, mobile or animated to be recorded or 'captured' apart from in the telling. (Mason and Davies, 2009: 598)

That idea that resemblances can *come alive through mobility, animation and interaction* is reflected in Faye's comment above when she was showing us photos of her husband Mike's family. She says 'they all look different there' but 'in real life you can tell'. The static and two-dimensional photographs did not capture the essence of the resemblances, but because photographs are widely assumed to have evidential qualities ('the camera cannot lie' – despite widespread photo editing), Faye may have sensed their potential to spoil the story and thus felt the need to assert the evidential objectivity of 'real life', thus making her argument more convincing.

It is interesting too that in many of these accounts and stories of resemblances coming alive, unlike in Faye's example of Mike's relatives, the two or more people who were said to resemble each other were not physically present at the same time. Edith, for example, said she looked at her elderly acquaintance, Mavis, and her daughter Kate, 'in my mind'. James's mother was constantly 'seeing' the resemblance between him and her deceased father. Indeed, many of the people involved in likenesses in our interviewees' accounts had lived in different eras, with a resemblance being drawn between the living and the dead, or between younger or older versions. This meant, as with Edith, that the perceiver was processing the resemblance in their 'mind's eye' (Mason and Davies, 2009) or, more accurately perhaps, in their sensory imaginations, because the resemblances involved were not always or only visual/visible ones but involved the full range of senses including ethereal, extra-sensory, in/tangible perception too. Importantly, although the moment of perception was an instantaneous one, giving the sense of an impact, its potency was based on the suddenness of an 'in-the-moment' affinity with a set of animated and sensory memories that might have been stored away or even forgotten over a long time. Take for example what Isabel says about her granddaughter's resemblance to her own daughter, Rachel, as a baby – in the absence of ubiquitous family photos Isabel had forgotten 'how Rachel was', but when she saw Emily she perceived the resemblance 'not just physically but in her way she carries on'. Spotting resemblances like this makes ordinary people into witnesses and narrators of conjunctures that are both acutely arresting and brand new, and yet have the resonance and depth of time and maturity. We might think of these as what Barthes, in his essay on photography, 'Camera Lucida', calls a 'punctum': a 'sting, speck, cut, little hole – and also a cast of the dice. A photograph's *punctum* is that accident which pricks me (but also bruises me, is poignant to me)' (Barthes, 2000 [1980]: 27). But what I think adds potency to these moments of perception of resemblance across time, and to pick up on a theme I developed in 'Sensations', is that the punctum is an intriguing mix of resemblance and *discordance* in time.

These epiphanal moments suggest that there is something interesting going on in the play between *time and resemblance*. This was hinted at in the graduation encounters, and emerges as a strong theme in resemblance stories. In all three examples of Mike/Faye, Isabel and James, for example, we see resemblances that can be fleeting and transitory, coming to the fore or receding in different moments, times and eras, or in certain situations, and these temporal features are important elements in the stories. Mike's resemblance to his brother appeared most clearly when he shaved his beard off. Faye and Mike's son dips in and out of resemblances to various others on different days, or when he is asleep and awake. Isabel's son and ex-husband both do and do not look like each other, but especially they sometimes echo each other in their mannerisms and voice, despite not having spent long periods of time in close connection. She and her sister have grown alike where they used to be different. James's sister Sophie seems to have a similar character to a now deceased great aunt he has heard stories about, leading him to feel that resemblances have skipped a generation. I shall return to a discussion of time in the final part of the book.

We get a hint from the cases of Isabel, James, Mike and Faye of a strong theme in the data that people have different 'investments' in perceiving resemblances, linked to the different times, eras and moments in their lives. This is not at all to say that people always calculate in an instrumental way the advantage or disadvantage to themselves or others before noticing or commenting on resemblances; although as I suggested when discussing the graduation stories, it is clear that alliances and positionings go on around resemblance, and that resemblance is part of power dynamics in and between families. There may also be different things at stake for men and women. But the experience of being hit by a resemblance suggests a lack of conscious calculation, although there may be a certain 'readiness to perceive' that perhaps gets more fertile as people grow older. If we take the case of Isabel, for example, we can see here an older woman who has lived through more times and more stages in her own and other people's lives and development than has, say, a much younger man like James. In Isabel's narrative, we see a woman who cannot help but stumble across resemblances more and more: she has more times and experiences to summon up and store away, and more family generations that she can animate and compare in her 'sensory imagination'. And perhaps the shortcomings in her memory that she bemoans only increase her tendency to assemble comparisons across time. James, on the other hand, relies on family stories about his deceased Great Aunt Dorrie's sparkiness to make a connection with his sister and to suggest that a resemblance has 'skipped a generation'.

Added to that, Isabel – with her children and grandchildren – has a strong interest in descendent as well as ascendant and lateral generations in her family. Her positioning and experience as a mother, as indeed also in the case of the younger Faye, ties in with a strong interest in her own children and in how they are turning out. James does not have children, and in general seems to have less personally invested in resemblances both up and down the generations of his family, even though he has been hit by the resemblance to his uncle and does not quite know what to make of it. His focus though is more on what the resemblance between him and his uncle, or his father, might mean for his mother – he cannot quite understand if it means something, or if it means nothing at all. He puzzles over the relationship between family, resemblance and a sense of belonging, explaining that he feels a stronger sense of belonging with his friends than with his family. The ultimate irony in what he says about this though is that he sees the imperative he feels to create his own 'emotional world' outside of his family as making him 'profoundly like my father'. Thus although James's account on the one hand suggests he has a limited or lesser investment in resemblances than others in his family, and indeed in our study, on the other hand what he says is peppered with acknowledgement of their potency for him as well as for others.

So it is not surprising that Isabel has a stronger interest than James in descendent generations, not least because of the perhaps rather prosaic reason that she has more of them. She clearly also feels some *responsibility* for how not only her children but also her grandchildren 'turn out' as people (see also Mason et al., 2007), and there is a slightly guilty collusion in the female line that she describes. Yet the way in which Isabel describes resemblances that live across the generations, eras and moments of her family members, and the different moments in which people seem like others (at *their* different moments), gives the lie to the idea that people do actually 'turn out' as unitary subjects in a sequential, incremental and ultimately-to-be-concluded-during-one's-lifetime process. This connects with Katherine Davies's interesting argument in her study of young people's siblinghood, that the process of 'turning out' – far from representing personal development as an incremental journey to a neat conclusion – is one of perpetual motion, flux, negotiation and unfinishedness (Davies, 2012).

It seems that resemblance stories reveal that neither resemblances, nor the people connected through them, are unitary or settled subjects; people are not singular or fixed packages of characteristics and identities, even at one point in time. And resemblances also are not total, fixed or static either. We have seen in the cases I have discussed, for example, how resemblances are always in flux and playing with time, as well as how people see 'bits' of resemblance between others – and those bits can range and vary across character, spirit, ways of being, physical characteristics, gestures and so on. People can (and frequently do) both be and not be alike. Here is another example, from Clare, a mother talking about her young son.

> He doesn't look like my father but just his whole energy and mannerisms are very, they just remind me so much of my father. And he's only two and he can't speak properly yet. My father is very mercurial and he'll get an idea and he can act on it and you can tell he's thinking about things and you can almost see the cogs going and Jack's very like that.

Clare's focus on 'energy' as something that connects her father and her baby son is a useful way to think about how our other interviewees conceptualised resemblance, and points to something in the nature of resemblance that is absolutely fundamental/elemental, yet is easily (ironically) forgotten: that is their *inherent and irrepressible relationality*. Of course we know on one level that resemblance can only make sense as something arising from comparison between two or more phenomena. But resemblance is more than a mode or process of comparison. Resemblances, as we have seen in the interviewees' accounts, *are alive in the relations between people*. This means they

cannot be reduced to sets of capacities and characteristics that are
assumed to be possessed by and passed between individuals (seen as
unitary subjects). Instead, resemblances *are the connective charge.*
They are the relational energies, flows and forces. They are not simply
points that are put in contact, or even the process of comparing them.
It is these relational energies that spark a sense of recognition which
can carry the force of an impact when it 'hits' you. Consider this
example:

> Janet: In fact it's really strange because I went on holiday to Ireland a
> few years ago and I was with a group of people and this lady came up,
> and it's no word of a lie, this lady came up to me and she said 'I don't
> mean to be rude' she said 'but you don't know somebody called Jim
> Spencer do you?' and I went 'yeah, it's me dad'. She said 'I thought
> it was' she said 'ooh, you aren't half the image of your dad.' And I
> thought, and yet, I mean to look at me, I don't think I am, you know?
> I mean I'm not like, you know, white hair, big tummy, and I'm thinking
> 'What? Do I look like me dad?' [laughter]. But yeah she said she'd just
> seen that, the link, that 'she must be a Spencer that one' you know.

There are familiar themes in here: the epiphanal story, the resemblance
that hits a third party, the appeal to objectivity and to evidence in the
role of the stranger and the way the story is told, and the incredible
('no word of a lie') nature of it. Yet it also clearly shows resemblance as
something that lives between and around people. Janet lists the characteristics and traits her father possesses, but goes on to point out that
she has none of these. Instead, in trying to figure it out, she says that
the stranger saw *'the link'* – a connective charge perhaps, certainly a
relational and somewhat ethereal 'aliveness', that connects them. She
is referring to a relational association and not a set of characteristics
possessed by any one individual, nor in this case even a literal physical
similarity between them. It is as though the stranger had 'perceived'
(in both multi-sensory and extra-sensory ways) a Spencer family aura
or a family 'look' that is so much more than, and cannot be distilled
down to or tracked back to, the sum of its parts.

'She must be a Spencer that one', or he has 'the 'Mackenzie eyes',
or there is 'a female thing which is very strong in my family' – just like
Thomas Hardy's 'family face' – all suggest that such resemblances,
whether or not you can physically see or perceive traces of them in
individual persons, are in themselves emphatically *not* individual. It is
more that they travel in the ether between people, ephemerally occupying or inhabiting their charges, sometimes leaving traces in them,
often exploding into a connective charge between them that has the

power to startle and surprise, and always taking expression in inter-stices and connections.

This sense of resemblances having an *ethereal life somewhere* – often referred to as *'there'* – outside of and between persons, across time and space, ineffable and mysterious – was suggested again and again in our interviews, and in the language and metaphors the people we spoke to deployed. The idea that resemblances can be glimpsed from time to time, or that they surface at will, or crop up/pop up, or indeed that they 'hit you', or that they are irrepressible or inevitable, or that they track along (unpredictable) paths or follow (inexplicable) patterns – all of these indicate that they live somewhere, potently and capriciously, anarchically even, just outside our grasp or our control. Sometimes they can take shape in a discordance or a 'punctum', where sensations in the present are unexpectedly 'pricked' or tickled by others from the past. Yet sometimes resemblances can only be perceived when people are animated and mobile, and viewed 'in the flesh' rather than in a photograph for example. Equally, we had exam-ples where people were struck by a resemblance in a photograph that was somehow not visible in 'real life'. Indeed, as Katherine Davies and I have argued, there is perhaps something mystical about the idea that a photograph can capture a whole other interstitial world of resem-blance that is existing 'out there', but that the 'naked eye' cannot see (Mason, 2008). The suggestion that although not visible to human consciousness, this world can seep or bleed into what Benjamin calls an 'optical unconscious', through photographs, is an interesting vari-ation on the idea of resemblances having an ethereal life *somewhere* (Benjamin, 1999: 512; Mason and Davies, 2009). We can see this ideal of resemblances living somewhere in Faye's suggestion that if you go 'up a generation' 'along this side' of her family it is like a mental ill-ness has 'broken out', or that her parents worked hard 'to stamp out' certain of her apparently inherited childhood behaviours. Or Isabel's that 'there must be something that's just there', perhaps a 'gene thing' or a 'nature thing' between her son and the father he's had so little contact with. Or her suggestion that bossiness 'runs through' the 'female line' and is 'very strong'. Or the arthritis that is 'bound to hit me'. Or James's idea that resemblances across generations are weird and mystifying, and that they can 'skip a generation'. All of these modes of speaking and imagining resemblance, in different ways, see it somehow as a living force, with its own energies, potency, capacities for contagion, gestures, characters and conduits – such as family lines, sides, generations, even genetics and nature. Yet even though people sometimes referred to genes and genetics, or nature (versus nurture), there was no indication that they really meant 'genetics' as defined by scientists. Instead, they used these terms when they were struggling to capture in words and to explain the mysterious potency of a life force that formed such a routine yet magical part of their everyday experience of relatedness. 'Genetics' and 'nature', in that sense, were both shorthand and metaphor for something altogether more experiential, ethereal and sensory than any scientific concepts.

The other undercurrent in all of this of course is to do with the unsettling elements of resemblances as both ineffable forces outside of our control and understanding, yet potentially speaking of highly important things. People often used the terms 'weird', 'strange', 'freaky', 'uncanny', 'spooky', and couched what they were saying in a joke or laughter, indicating uneasiness. This is partly because resemblances are perceived not only in sensory but also in extra-sensory ways as discussed, and hence seem inherently magical. But also, people were variously intrigued, fascinated, scared or bemused by resemblances and what they might mean or signify about personhood (their own and other people's), being alive and mortality. We saw that James struggled to understand what resemblance meant for him and for his relatives in this way, yet he has experienced their potency. And reflecting a common theme of uneasiness, we saw Faye being unsettled by potential implications of incest or infidelity arising from her husband's startling physical likeness to his brother, such that she joked that 'this is freaky', 'I was sharing a bed with my brother-in-law'. We have seen many examples of people who are astonished and intrigued that two relatives who look alike are 'completely different in character', or that a resemblance simply cannot be explained by the parties having spent time together or even having known each other. In all these cases, resemblances seem to disrupt what we think we know about the unitary nature of ourselves as persons, as well as the identifying characteristics that make a person the person that they are. It is hard for people to understand what the essence of the resemblance is, and whether it needs to be taken account of in how we understand who people actually are. But people undoubtedly find resemblances, alterities, and the processes of wondering and speculating about them, utterly beguiling.

Offspring
A person's child or children. An animal's young. The product or result of something.

Progeny
A descendant or the descendants of a person, animal, or plant.
Person
A human being regarded as an individual.
Relation
The way in which two or more people or things are connected. A thing's effect on or relevance to another.
(ODE, 2005)

4. The still-beating heart

In July 2014 in the UK a poignant and moving interview was transmitted on the BBCs 'PM' radio programme. Eddie Mair, an award winning broadcast journalist with an exceptional talent for conducting powerful, resonant and sensitive interviews, spoke to Freda Carter and Scott Rutherford. Freda was the mother of John Carter who had died aged thirty-three, and whose heart had been anonymously donated for transplant. Scott Rutherford was fourteen years old when he received John's heart in a life-saving operation several years before the interview.

The extraordinary story they told was of their revelatory 'chance meeting' at a church service about organ donation, where Scott was speaking about his experience of receiving a donated heart. Freda was there and indeed she had attended other similar services in the past. She saw in the programme that a man called Scott was going to do a reading and, although organ donation is an anonymous process in the UK and recipients rarely meet donors' families, she had known that the recipient of her son's heart was called Scott and was a young teenager at the time. 'When Scott stepped onto the podium, I saw immediately that this was a young man who would have been a teenager six years before. The maths fitted. When he started talking, he said that a John had given him his heart. I nearly collapsed' (Johnston, 2014). Apparently, some of the professionals present at the service, on hearing Freda's story, approached Scott to see if he would be willing to be introduced to her, and he said yes.

Here is an excerpt from the radio interview:

Freda: [Scott is audibly emotional in the background as she talks]
It was just a miracle. I always knew that my son was living on in

somebody. Kidneys and liver and everything are very vital organs. But a heart you can feel beating. You know love comes from your heart. Happiness comes from your heart. And our John's heart was still living on. And he had such a big heart. He was such a lovely boy you know. He was so loving and caring. And I thought well I need to meet this boy that's got my son's heart and when they said I could meet him, well, I was overwhelmed, I was upset, I was hysterical. It was just amazing, you know, I was getting what I wanted. And when I saw him, I thought well if I picked someone out of this whole wide world to have my son's heart, I'd have picked Scott. Because I loved him. I loved him as soon as I saw him. And I went down the back of the church towards the front and he just opened his arms and I went into his arms, and it was such a moment I'll never ever . . . I'll take it to my grave with me because I seemed to bond with him straight away you know. And when I felt John's heart beating, well that was it. You know, he hadn't died in vain. For all we would have loved him to have lived, if he'd lived it wouldn't have been our John because he'd have been poorly and he wouldn't have coped with that because he was such a healthy . . . he was into football he was into sports, he rode his bike, he jogged, and if he couldn't do that he wouldn't want to live. But there was Scott standing in front of me with John's heart, and it comforted me so much. We took John's death very badly but for me meeting Scott and knowing he was living on, I'm so happy about it. And I loved Scott as soon as I saw him you know. But I didn't want to overwhelm him with lots of questions and that, you know, he was only a young boy. I'm a pensioner and he was just a young boy and I didn't want to frighten him or overwhelm him so we just met, and he said he'd had this letter and I said 'please send it to me' and he did and I was so happy.

Scott: I know I had the letter [written] for 5 years and I always found it a bit of a struggle to send off because you're trying to take into con-sideration obviously John's mum and dad's feelings and I'm trying to take, get a hold of mine, and I always found it a very difficult thing to send off to say 'thank you'. But then once we met at that church and then his family came up to me and Freda asked if she could feel his heart beating and I took her hand and I held her hand to my chest and I always remember I said of course you can feel the heart beating, mind you it's a very strong one, and then we all shared this beautiful moment where we all came and had a bit of a cuddle and a cry and we all felt this heartbeat. And then Freda took my hand and she said 'please send your letter' and I knew then that I had to send this letter off, and I felt this instant connection with the family and I knew I had to go to John's family so they could see the change in [between] the past, and in what they had allowed me to do, and how much my life is different. Now I'm very, very thankful to be alive. And John and his family . . . are my true life heroes. These people saved my life, and if it wasn't for these people, and John, then I wouldn't be sat in this radio station doing this interview.

The background to this piece was a push in the UK to tackle the problem of a shortage of donor organs because recently bereaved families were often refusing to allow their deceased relatives' organs to be donated. Appeals for organ donors often centre on *beneficence* (you can help another to live, and give the gift of life), *equity* (wouldn't you want someone to have donated if you or a loved one needed it?) and *fairness* (it is unfair that good organs are unused when people on the waiting lists for them are dying). This was the context in which this story was aired.

But it is interesting here that the story suggests a different kind of affinity and connection than beneficence, equity and fairness: this was a way for a part of John – some would say the central and defining part, his heart – to continue *to live* in a very visceral way, and not only in a spiritual 'afterlife' kind of way. That promise of a further life in a real and pulsing sense, and its value to John's mother, Freda, is very powerful, and quite possibly a more compelling message for relatives of potential organ donors than the comfort in beneficence that may be gained in knowing their loved one's donated organs have helped others to survive. It is that pulsing transfer of life, and the sensory-kinaesthetic relationalities of it, formed by chance – possibly magic or fate – that make this a compelling story.

The *moment of revelation* is presented as a gripping narrative – in the Church, and then rehearsed again on live Radio. The *mystical workings of chance and serendipity* are a crucial part of the story as well – chance that is patterned by the different parties' actions, feelings and decisions. It nearly didn't happen, might never have happened, but that it did is made sense of in terms of a kind of 'meant to be' fate, constituting a magical connection between Scott and John's family, made before even the beating heart is put centre stage, when Freda sees Scott's name in the programme, and does the maths. This speaks alluringly of an ethereal, other-worldly, ineffable connection drawing these people together, making it happen.

These elements come together to create an affinity in the *elemental and magical nature of the bond* between Freda, John and Scott. The way the story is communicated in the media (of course it is impossible to know whether this reflects what different parties feel actually happened) is a celebration of the power of a mother's love and her special insight and intuition. Although other family members are mentioned in passing in different reports of the story – John's father, and John's wife for example – it is Freda who spots the connection with Scott in that moment in the church. Importantly, it is not a professional who works it out for her, and Freda herself doesn't do it in a rational or scientific way – she says 'it was illogical' and 'I was hysterical'. And it is Freda who is enfolded in Scott's arms, and who asks if she can feel the heart beating, and Freda whose hand Scott takes first and puts to his chest. The connection with Scott was immediately potent and was a magical rather than a rational accomplishment. It is interesting that although the transplant was achieved through medical skill and scientific accomplishment, the affinities here seem to be thoroughly magical and enchanted.

We can also see that the moment of connection, when Scott put Freda's hand on his beating heart, derives its potency also from *what has happened before* – the moment depends on a history, both of literal connection made in the physical transplant, and in the ethereal magic that made the connection happen, and especially also in the *'wondering'* that all parties have been engaged in. Freda talks about knowing that her son was living on in other people, and Scott talks about writing the letter to his donor's family but being unable to post it. There is a strong sense of each wondering about the other, and that they have already been 'in touch' before they knew each other or met, through mutual wondering.

Of course the connection also derives potency from the sensory-kinaesthetics involved, and especially from the *importance of touch, feeling and pulsing* – hand holding hand on chest, and of feeling and sensing, almost hearing the beating heart that was physically inside Scott, and for Scott feeling the hand he was holding to his chest over his heart. The sheer viscerality and alive/lived nature of this experience was almost overwhelming for the participants. The last time Freda experienced that heart it was beating inside her son. 'There was Scott standing in front of me with John's heart.' The cultural understanding and also the sensations of the heart are important here – as the organ that is at the emotional and spiritual centre or essence of the person, and the motor of life, but also that can have its own life, can somehow branch off and be independent through transfer and's transplant. In a way, we might say that Scott's life is an *offspring* of John's, or of his heart at least.

It is clear in this case that this connects more than the two men – it is likely to have 'kinship consequences' for their relatives too. If a heart transplant, both literally and symbolically, creates a relationship where a life is *an offspring* of another life, then we might imagine this being factored into people's thinking about what it means to be related. A heart perhaps is not like gametes which are thought to reframe and change 'blood' or 'genetic' ties now and for future generations. But then the potency of the affinities in this case suggests it is something like that. The story's popular fascination and appeal echo or give shape to the idea of some kind of elemental and magical kinship.

5. Nordqvist and Smart's donors as 'enigmatic presences'

Donor conception can raise awkward questions about offspring for those receiving the donations, and their families. These especially concern how those involved think of and live their relatedness in the context of donated gametes, and the more general questions raised about lines of kinship. Social and technological developments in this field have arguably been important in bringing about an intensifying engagement with complex questions about what constitutes con-nections of kinship, and particularly those linking what we think of as parents, their children, their offspring and wider kin. The fact that, for example, it is possible for a woman to gestate and give birth to a child grown from the egg of a donor (who might for example be her cousin, or an anonymous stranger, or her sister, or her friend); or indeed that she and her husband might use the sperm of a donor (who might for example be anonymous, or a relative of her husband, or a friend); or that the woman's wife might have donated the egg (with a similar range of relational possibilities); makes for some com-plex negotiations around who constitutes a parent or an offspring, who is related to whom, and by what system of reckoning. There are further challenges when we try to work out by what order of kin rela-tionship different parties are connected. Consider the first scenario I have cited, where a woman gestates and gives birth to a child grown from her cousin's donated egg; how do we calculate the order of kin relationship between the cousin-donor's father, for example, and his niece-recipient's child? One version would be to see him as the child's great uncle – if the parent–child link is reckoned in *social* terms – because he is the uncle of the woman who is the child's social mother. In this case he would also be the child's great uncle if the parent–child link is reckoned in *biological* terms, because he is the uncle of the woman who has gestated and given birth to the child. But if the link is reckoned in *genetic* terms, then he would be the child's grandfather, because his (presumably genetic) daughter's donation of gametes via her egg would constitute her as the child's genetic mother. As Edwards has pointed out, 'assisted reproductive technologies create kin as well as offspring' (Edwards, 2014: 44). Of course such systems of 'reckoning' draw on and are forged in cultural understandings, habits and practices, as well as socio-legal forms of regulation, ethical frameworks, and people's everyday living of personal life in different contexts. But the complexities and transformations that characterise this field of living make it fertile ground for exploring some affinities of ineffable kinship.

Petra Nordqvist and Carol Smart's 2014 UK study of the experience of donor conception from the point of view of receiving parents and grandparents provides some important insights here (Nordqvist and Smart, 2014). Their study includes the experiences of recipients (and parents of recipients) of gametes from both known and anonymous donors, describing the relationship with *unknown* gamete donors as an 'enigmatic' one, where the donor is always an 'absent presence' or a 'ghost in the room' (Nordqvist and Smart, 2014: 107–9). Recipients create a relationship of sorts with anonymous donors, or at least many of them do, through the curiosity and unease they harbour about them – what did they look like, what was their character like, does the child resemble them, will they grow to be like them, does that particular talent that the child has, uniquely in the family, come from the donor? With identity release programmes such as those in the UK where donor offspring (if they know they are donor conceived) can elect to trace donors when they reach the age of eighteen, some recipients felt this absent presence as a potential future threat to the kin relationships they had worked hard to create: some feared the possibility that someone with a claim to be the 'real' or at least an 'alternative' genetic mother or father might turn up unexpectedly, or be turned up in a search initiated by their donor conceived son or daughter. At the very least this would produce knowledge of connections that could potentially be construed as kinship (with genetic reckoning) and that it might be difficult to know what to do with. There was similar unease amongst some about making any moves to identify donor siblings – namely those siblings created through the use of a common anonymous donor. Nordqvist and Smart argue people had an underlying worry that this might open the door to alternative (genetic) kinship claims or a potentially 'unlimited kinship' that they feared neither they nor their children would be able to contain:

> There is forever an underlying, unresolved tension in the donor rela-
> tion. The donor is not understood as a parent, nor as family, and yet
> the genetic contribution means the donor (and his or her relatives) can
> *potentially* claim to be connected. . . . There is a constant potential for
> the donor to fall into the kin category despite being positioned and con-
> ceptualised as non-kin. (Nordqvist and Smart, 2014: 123–4)

Some therefore tried actively not to 'know' about, or not to dwell
on these matters, or they avoided certain topics of conversation
(Nordqvist and Smart, 2014: 110–13). But the threat of unwanted
or unlimited kinship that might potentially be a potent connection
could lurk unpredictably in the shadows for families where the donor
had been anonymous, however much recipients and their relatives
asserted the predominance of social over biological ties.

In others, where the gamete donor was *known* (including family
members and friends), families worked to try to negotiate a kinship
that simultaneously recognised the donation of gametes but contained its kinship potential and potency, for example by defining it as
a special gift rather than a kin tie, or by minimising or attempting to
neutralise the significance of genetic material. This could be problematic however, as it needs all parties who are potentially involved or
might feel they have a kinship claim to go along with this version of
what constitutes a tie or indeed an affinity. There is a kind of reciprocal
and multi-directional relationality in kinship that makes it difficult for
personal visions of what it means to be asserted.

In cases such as this, Nordqvist and Smart argue that as well as seeking to emphasise the importance of *social and relational aspects of
parenting* and upbringing whilst containing or minimising the genetic
ones, some also consider that the *biological* processes involved in
gestation and giving birth – often perceived through the substance
of blood rather than genes – confer a strong kinship affinity in themselves; they are ways in which the essence of a person or of kinship
(the gestational mother and their family) might be seen to pass physically or biologically into another (the child). Some people in Nordqvist
and Smart's study felt that non-genetic pregnancy, gestation, birth
and physical nurturing could 'leave traces' in children that became
manifest and there for all to see, including in family resemblances
(which earlier facets showed to be a potent force) (Nordqvist and
Smart, 2014: 127). Nordqvist and Smart argue that this gestational
transfer involves separating the meaning of the categories 'genes'
and 'blood', and thinking instead of the idea of 'blood food', thus
'activat[ing] a line of kinship between mother and baby based in the

body' (Nordqvist and Smart, 2014: 127). This is important because it is a potential challenge to the perceived determinacy of genetic kinship, but it is one that is made in *biological and physical more than social* terms. It also clearly establishes that the concepts 'genetic' and 'biological' are not synonymous, which enables parents in these circumstances to downplay the significance of genetic links yet still emphasise the biological ones. This idea of gestationally conferred biological kinship is a theme that is echoed in anthropological research (Edwards, 2014; Konrad, 2005; Sahlins, 2013), some of which argues that it is not only the physical processes of gestation and giving birth that appear as significant in connecting people by kinship, and leaving kinship 'traces', but also the sharing of certain foods, including breast milk and foods from ancestral lands and labour (Edwards, 2014; Sahlins, 2013). Edwards (citing Weismantel, 1995) comments that:

> a child can be made 'one's own' by eating the same food over time. . . . The point to make is that feeding a child over time *is not a symbolic or ritual act* that transforms the non-related child into one's own, *but a material bond* created through shared food making up the same flesh. (Edwards, 2014: 48, my emphasis)

At the same time, Nordqvist and Smart point out that the lack of physical traces in the form of family resemblances can be a painful reminder that the child is somehow not one of the family, or of which parent in a couple did and did not contribute genetic material. One sperm donor recipient (a genetic birth mother) in their study reported a kind of guilty pleasure that she must keep secret from her partner when she notices resemblances between herself and the child. As indicated, resemblances that do not seem to fit into the family can also establish the haunting and unwelcome (for parents) presence of a donor. We know also that donors who 'wonder' about offspring created through their donations, as well as donor conceived people who consider or do seek out their donors or their 'donor siblings', are equally fascinated by questions of family resemblance (Freeman et al., 2014).

Perhaps unsurprisingly then, given the apparent kinship potency of family resemblances, Nordqvist and Smart found in their recipient families that people would sometimes be keen to 'map family resemblance across non-genetic relations', taking pleasure in remarking upon (and sometimes in the process interactively creating) a resemblance between a child and a non-genetically related relative. Such practices of 'kinning' have also been observed in studies of transnational adoption where resemblances (for example between Asian babies and European adoptive parents) although not immediately self-evident, are nevertheless routinely remarked upon and created in kinship groups with the effect of establishing both kinship and national identity and belonging (Howell, 2006). We now also know that processes of 'matching' in fertility clinics and informal arrangements are frequently designed to increase the chances that any consequent child will resemble both parents (where there are two), often by seeking to ensure that donor characteristics like hair, skin and eye colouring mirror those of the non-genetic parent. In heterosexual couples, the logic is that something from both parents then goes into 'the mix' to be determined by the usual lottery and chance, in the same way that they would in non-assisted reproduction, enabling them to 'pass' as a traditional genetically connected family (see, for example, Haimes, 1992; Hudson and Culley, 2014). In lesbian families, where passing as traditional is not usually possible in the same way, there is nevertheless evidence that, in selecting donor characteristics, couples 'aspire to create what can be understood as a phenotypical resemblance between . . . the non-birth mother and the child' so that, although there would not be a genetic connection, there would be something that was almost as good, expressed in physical or biological resemblance (Nordqvist, 2010: 1135).

6. Konrad's 'nameless relations' and 'transilience'

In the mid-1990s Monica Konrad conducted an ethnography of privately run assisted conception units in England, involving fieldwork with female ex-donors and ex-recipients (Konrad, 2005). Her study took place in the context of a national regulatory regime where all assisted conception conducted in clinics was anonymous, and before identity release was made mandatory for donors in the UK in 2005. The UK law prohibited payment for donation but allowed expenses. What is especially interesting about this study for considering affinities is that Konrad pursues an analysis of *kinship* and gender, that explores donors' positioning in what she sees as ambiguous (but nonetheless *kin*) relationships between 'procreative strangers'.

Interestingly, the women Konrad spoke to downplayed the potential for donor eggs to create kinship-genetic connections with offspring. This may be a gendered phenomenon, as other studies have suggested that male gamete donors seem less willing to downplay such

connections (Almeling, 2014). Konrad's female donors used 'deper-
sonalised formulations', for example stressing that 'the egg has no
particularly privileged status as a reproductive capacity of the body',
thus implying that 'the connection between donors and recipients is
not [carried in] the biological substance of the egg itself' (Konrad,
2005: 69–70). Konrad argues that the women are not proprietorial
over these 'body parts', but at the same time when reading Konrad we
can see that the donations do have intriguing relational consequences.

Their donations were made in the context of what Konrad calls
'clinical euphemisms' operating in the donor conception programmes,
which suggested that the women were 'donating chances' and
'making gifts of life', underplaying any suggestion that donation created any kind of relatedness (Konrad, 2005: 68). We can see that
some of Nordqvist and Smart's recipients were wishing to appeal to
this logic in minimising the role of genetics. One can imagine that
the possibilities are differently gendered here, partly because of the
different ways in which donations of ova and sperm are secured.
But it has also been noted in other research that despite attempts
in donor conception processes to neutralise gamete donations from
men *and* women into 'genetic material' without kinship or relational
potential or consequences, male sperm continue to have a greater
'gendered social power' than female eggs. Richards, for example,
argues that sperm are viewed as having 'greater determinative power'
as a 'genetic connector' than ova (Richards, 2014), whereas in law it
tends to be gestation and not genetic connection that confers mother-
hood (McCandless and Sheldon, 2014).

In some senses, this way of thinking seemed to fit with the women's
unwillingness to claim ownership of their eggs. However, at the same
time, and not entirely at odds with that idea of a 'gift of life', the
women recognised that their donations could 'effect a change' that
could transform the lives of others, and Konrad argues that the metaphor of 'initiation' is important here: 'Several women seem to want to
think of themselves as some kind of generative point of new inception
and growth' (Konrad, 2005: 72). So there is potentially a potent line
of connection here.

This had the twin consequences of, on the one hand, increasing
the ova donors' sense of self-esteem and moral worth, sometimes to
the extent that the women felt they had earned a kind of celebrity
status; and on the other hand, of fostering a sense of kinship between
them and their (unknown) recipients. This was a rather female kind
of kinship, and seemed to be grounded both in empathy for another
woman's (or couple's) plight of childlessness, and also in being the

'generative point' in the female physical process of creating and growing a baby in which donor and recipient were both engaged. For some
of Konrad's donors there was that sense of being in it together and
contributing to a joint purpose, but also something more ethereal in
the connections that resulted: 'there's got to be something between
us' (said one donor), 'it's the most peculiar thing to try to explain'
(Konrad, 2005: 73). Konrad thus argues that the practice of donating eggs thus involves 'extensional agency' on the part of the donor
(Konrad, 2005: 73), who is effectively extending parts of her-self, in
a non-proprietorial way, into another set of relations. One could perhaps argue the toss about whether ova donors do have any feeling
– however small – of proprietorial interest in the offspring generated
through their donations as at least some men appear to do (Almeling,
2014). However, the suggestion that ova donors feel a kinship connection *with the woman recipient* is different from evidence about
male sperm donors and their recipients who, if anything, are more
likely to be viewed as having a procreative or even sexual connection
(Almeling, 2014; Edwards, 2014).

For Konrad, the kinds of relations that are established, especially
under conditions of anonymous donation, form what she calls 'transilience', and this is a fascinating concept involving what she calls
'non-relations'. She argues that transilience is:

> a non-possessive modelling of personhood in which non-relations, rather
> surprisingly, are shown to be integral to social agents, as well as central
> to a subject's sense of her or his own core ambivalence. . . . When
> anonymised ova donors and anonymised ova recipients talk about their
> non-traceability, they are recording *how the non-link already makes
> them – and their children – into real, embodied non-relations.* (p. 243,
> my emphasis)

Her discussion of transilience is innovative and important, because in
it she is insisting that the non-relations between anonymous donors,
recipients and offspring are in fact *relations*. That these things are
not just *nothing*, nor are they simply transitory events or exchanges
without legacy, is clear from Konrad's research and that of others,
including Nordqvist and Smart. People who have been involved in
donor conception expend a lot of mental energy in *thinking and
wondering* about others to whom they are connected through the
process (for example donors, recipients, offspring, wider kin). Often
these will be others whom they do not know, have never met and (in
the case of potential offspring from donor gametes) whose very existence itself is not certain. Through 'transilience' Konrad argues that

these processes of thinking and wondering, and feeling connected through 'non-relations' and 'anonymous sociality', constitute kin relations in themselves; they are lines of kinship, and potentially potent connections:

> within anonymous sociality, *active not-knowing* sets up 'unfinished' relations whose unconcealing makes persons 'transilient'. Such transilience can be accessed from the moment the reproductive gift makes its first appearance. Namely, the fact that multiple sets of recipients may receive eggs from the same genetic donor, the fact that successful conceptions lead to the spatial dispersal of half-siblings across discrete families, to say nothing of how the donor herself imagines her particular acts as relations of transilience. But transilience can also be approached as the process of *projective kinship*. When donor-conceived children reach maturity and want to know more, or suspect they should know more about their genetic origins, their enquiries set in train the relations that make their persons 'transilient'. Transilience here is activated by known 'half-knowns' or by what is simply imagined and not yet known. Its cultural space is the occupancy *between concealment and revelation* – nobody and nothing can be transilient when it is directly encountered. (Konrad, 2005: 180–1, my emphasis)

Transilience, then, involves wondering, imagining, thinking about unknown others out there who you (or others related to you) might be related to, but in ways which are hard to pin down. It is active relationality in itself; it *is* the links and connections, forces and flows. In that sense, transilience is part of an imagining of kinship that does not require us to conceptualise relations as being between persons who are unitary individuals contained in discrete bodies. Instead it involves flows and circulations in time and space, extending or projecting kinship.

For Konrad, an egg donor is an 'ambiguous progenetrix' (p. 102) who 'extend themselves from out of the procreative power of their bodies' (p. 119). In coming to that conclusion, she is proposing what I think is a radical rethink of the idea of kinship as a set of bio-genetic relations between persons (who have unitary bodies mapped onto their persons). Instead, she makes an argument that requires us to reconceptualise both the idea of *time*, and of the *unitary body-person*. She says the 'body parts' involved in ova donation:

> do not belong to specific named persons, but become apparent as the multiply detached parts of persons' extensions/extendible selves. Parts are not owned as persons' past productions, but circulate as 'other' time

and in 'other' social space, both as the collective extensions of 'someone' and, relatedly, as a type of common substance. (Konrad, 2005:
125)

How these circulate as 'other times' and 'other space' is an open
question, but we can see the ways in which transilience might spread
potent ripples of affinity. The increasing evidence about the significance of 'donor siblings' for example (offspring created from the
same donor gametes) can be interpreted in the frame of transilience.
Konrad comments from her own study:

> We do not yet know how children will react to the news their mother
> once gave away her eggs to help someone else have a child before they
> themselves had been conceived and born. The knowledge is instantly
> 'relational' since it exposes the existence 'somewhere' of a genetic half-
> sibling. It is relational and specifically transilient in nature, because it sets
> up irrelational kinship. (Konrad, 2005: 118)

Progenitor
Person or thing from which a person, animal, or plant is descended or
originates; an ancestor or parent: *his children were the progenitors of
many of Scotland's noble families.*
Progenetrix
No entries
(ODE, 2005)

7. Super-donors and dubious progeniture

On 19 January 2015 a BBC Radio 4 series, 'Out of the Ordinary',
focused on the stories and apparent motivations of what have become
known as 'super-donors' – men who by their own accounts have
'sired' multiple offspring through donor insemination. Although they
advertise quite openly on the internet and social media, these men
operate outside the UK regulatory system, which sets a maximum of
ten families that can be created through any one man's sperm. And
although it is illegal to require payment for donated sperm, many of
them charge around £50 per donation when using AI (artificial insemination). A sperm recipient interviewed on the programme explained

that many will, however, donate for free if the recipient will accept NI (natural insemination – a euphemism for penetrative sex).

There is a growing debate and research interest in the potentially exploitative nature of such relationships between donor and recipient, where women who long to have their own biologically related children, but who cannot afford the clinic fees for regulated assisted reproduction, may be coerced or some say 'groomed' into oppressive, dangerous and violent sexual encounters, and/or financial extortion (McQuoid, 2015). Where such circumstances exist they make another euphemism of the term 'donor'. This is partly because such conception encounters, and the lead up to them, are characterised by an agenda of coercive male gratification rather than any form of gift relation. But also, they can be euphemistic in cases where 'donation' is not simply freely made in a single encounter, but where a more ongoing or permanent set of relations ensue either because the first donation attempt fails and subsequent conception encounters take place, and/ or where the donor does not simply wish to donate and then claim no proprietorial interest in any offspring.

There have as yet been only a few studies into the motivations of sperm donors, mostly focused on men whose donations are legally regulated and made through clinics. The relative absence of research is probably partly because the socio-cultural framing of assisted reproductive technologies has tended to be on providing substances (in this case sperm) for use in 'treatment' for fertility problems, or to enable conception. These locate the need for and interest in creating a baby (and hence in progeniture) unequivocally with the recipient(s) and not the donor. As a consequence, the sperm donor is divested, in the discourse at least, of the idea of progenitive agency – it is either not thought relevant or appropriate (indeed it may feel too much of a risk to the parental rights of the recipients) to consider them in that frame. Mohr notes this absence of research and argues that 'sperm donors have been disregarded as people in their own right' (Mohr, 2014: 163). Consequently, debate around motivations for sperm donation has tended to focus on the relative merits of altruism versus economic reward in the donation (of a substance), rather than the nature of a donor's interest, or otherwise, in progeniture. Overall we should not therefore be too surprised that surveys of donor motivation do not suggest a personal interest in progeniture as a common motive, or indeed a motive at all (for example, Bay et al., 2013; Thorn et al., 2008). In surveys based on structured precoded questions, this may not even be offered as an option for respondents to select from.

But more qualitative work, as well as journalistic reports into illegal super-donors such as those featured in the Radio 4 programme, reveal motivations that are more to do with the idea of progeniture itself. Donors in the radio interviews talked proudly of high productivity rates of sperm, and high success rates in conceptions, one claiming 'I am getting success every 10 days'. They talked of a competitive order, with rankings of donors based on their success rates available on the internet. One said: 'I'm good at it. I'm very proud. If there was a Guinness book of records I'd probably be in it.' Another was proud to sometimes donate five times a day with a high 'success' rate, and that his first 'success' was to a woman who was on the pill, presumably he felt indicating the potency of his sperm.

In terms of motivations, the programme identified a clear genetic – progenetic – interest amongst the super-donors. One said, 'I like helping people', but when further pressed said, 'I do things to opti-mise how many genes I do have', and explained that he actively seeks to create donor siblings – advertising this on his website – because his understanding is that people with siblings are more likely to go on and have their own children (thus perpetuating his genes) than only-children. So there would ultimately be more of his genetic off-spring and descendants in the world. Another donor, who claimed to have twenty-seven children born from his donated sperm, and nine ongoing pregnancies, said that his motivation was: 'Simply to pass on my genes. I want lots of mini-mees all over the world because you know, I like to consider myself, fairly intelligent, quite a successful human being.' The man who claimed to have twenty-seven children likened his donating activities to 'stamp collecting', explaining that he insisted on having contact with the recipients, and required updates on the progress of any pregnancy, and then on any offspring, three to four times a year 'forever'. Some recipients, 'spermjackers' as he disapprovingly referred to them, had to his mind reneged on the deal and broken contact after they had received his donation. He used the information gained from those who kept in contact to keep detailed spreadsheets, charting the development and key milestones for all of his 'offspring'. The men interviewed were cagey about whether their own partners knew about or condoned their donations. One said that his wife would 'go crazy' if she knew, and that she would see it as him cheating on her.

The men interviewed very clearly considered themselves as pro-genitors of offspring with whom they would have an inalienable and powerful genetic link, and although they expected the recipient-mothers to keep in touch so that they could track 'their' offspring, there was no sense of wanting to create a wider feeling of kinship.

There was clearly no suggestion or assumption that these 'super-donor' men were simply providers of a facilitating bodily substance to assist someone else's kinship, or even that they were making a 'gift of life' in the way that Konrad's ova donors imagined themselves. Heredity and genetic connection were the foremost matters of concern for them.

8. 'The Seed' by The Roots, featuring Cody Chesnutt

Here is a piece of music that you should listen to. It is an infectious belter of a song by the North American band The Roots featuring Cody Chesnutt. The song was from their album 'Phrenology', released on 26 November 2002 (Geffen Records and MCA Records). Wikipedia describes it variously as 'a hybrid mix of distorted rock, hip-hop and psychedelic soul', 'featuring a little bit of funk' with a 'catchy hook that stays with listeners for days'. I think that is a pretty accurate description (Wikipedia, 'The Seed', consulted 5 March 2015). The lyric is morally ambiguous, with a suggestion of non-consensual sex and forced pregnancy, focused around the metaphor of 'the seed' and its supposed role in heredity.

The song lyric is generally agreed amongst commentators to have a dual meaning. Partly it is about a charged and forcibly procreative sexual relationship, relying on what Richards in another context has described as the dominant '"gardening" metaphor of man the sower of seeds and women the fertile ground that nurtures them' (Richards, 2014: 35). Arguably though, the metaphor in the song is more aggressive and dominant than gardening is usually thought to be, with the repeated line in the chorus, 'I'll push my seed somewhere deep in her chest'. And partly it is thought to be metaphorical of the desire to subvert some of the safe and staid musical conventions of the time, planting the seeds of a more authentic genre drawing on hip-hop, and forcing a gestation and birth of that genre, as for example in the line 'If Mary dropped my baby girl tonight I would name her Rock'n'Roll'. It uses forceful and aggressive phallic and sexual imagery and metaphor to make these points, and celebrates the idea of male genetic potency and determinacy in heredity. The progenitor is the man and his seed creates the offspring which will keep his legend alive; Mary does not seem to have much to do with it other than being a vessel.

The song's potency is not simply in its assertion of such messages, but is also in the visceral sensations of the music itself – ironically these aspects are often disregarded in analyses of the socialities of music and fandom. It is infectiously likeable and alluring in part because it is sexy, cool and deeply appealing musically. It is a song that moves the listener with its rhythm and pace, whether or not they can discern the words and their meaning. I for one had the ambivalent experience of finding the sound, vibe and movement of the song appealing before I had discerned the nature of the lyric. The lyric and its sentiments, once discovered, sit very uncomfortably with me. But of course it is difficult post hoc to unlike a piece of music you like, on principle and on reflection. The song is highly sensory-kinaesthetic and it motors along in a way that creates bodily empathy, involvement, and makes the listener/audience want to move with the rhythm and sing along. It bundles these together almost irresistibly and unnoticeably with the suggestion of thrill and potency in the possibility of being the pro-genitor of offspring who will keep the faith and go forth in one's own image – peopling the world.

Layering the Argument: Affinities of Ineffable Kinship

The facets in this section have focused on questions of resemblance, 'offspring', progeniture and heredity, and throughout we have seen glimpses of a kinship that is haunting, ineffable, mysterious, sometimes magical and often potent. The facets, in a sense, constitute an invitation to tune into ineffable kinship as both a way of seeing, and something of an ether in which affinities can flourish. Here I want to consider what that kind of attunement can enable us to apprehend, by exploring what characterises affinities that are created through these kinds of ineffable kinship, and consider why they seem so potent. I shall just pick out a few of the important insights from the facets, to layer into my argument about affinities.

Metaphors of genetics and heritability

If we are receptive to the idea of ineffable kinship, we quickly notice the *power of analogy and metaphor* in this domain. It is interesting to note these types of linguistic devices are used by scholars and scientists, musicians and artists, just as much as they are used by 'ordinary' people. The facets were peppered with metaphors and I have discussed some of their significance already. In a way, we are so used to living with both scientific and everyday metaphors of connection, descent, heritability and progeniture that we barely notice them or how they play into our ways of conceptualising these things – in fact, arguably the terms 'genetics', 'kinship' and indeed offspring are just as metaphorical as are those we more readily recognise as being so, such as, for example, 'in the blood', 'taking after', 'being the dead spit' and 'peas in a pod'. And yet these do of course help to create or echo certain versions of the nature, direction, irrefutability and ineffability of the connections involved, and this has been a concern for some scholars and scientists, especially where those different versions are in contention.

Nordqvist and Smart are interested in idioms and metaphors that people use to talk about kin relationships, and argue that there has been a shift from 'blood' to 'genes' over the last fifty years in popular discourse (and earlier in scientific discourse). *Genes and genetics* are powerful contemporary metaphors, and Nordqvist and Smart point out that these terms are routinely in everyday usage and indeed this was the case in some of the facets, where the argument 'it must be genetic' was used, sometimes in jest, sometimes in pleasure, sometimes in anxiety, to talk about an ineffable resemblance or potent connection.

In one way, we could argue that the whole point of donor conception or collaborative reproduction is to create a biologically borne/born or genetically related child, and the concern to manipulate family resemblances (for example between the child and a non-genetic parent) through 'matching' underlines this. As Konrad points out,

> The uptake of biomedical technology can be seen as both responsive to and reconfirming of genetic inheritance ideology. To ensure the making of 'good' matches, the normative space of the assisted conception clinic ultimately succumbs to, and encourages, the biogenetic bias and pretensions of many prospective parents as would-be recipients. (Konrad, 2005: 142)

And yet as we saw in the facets, the appeal to genetics amongst people involved in assisted conception is perhaps not so simple.

However, the apparent geneticisation of society, and the proliferation of certain accompanying metaphors, has been of concern to some 'natural' scientists because of their tendencies to obfuscate rather than illuminate. For example, the life scientist Steven Rose has produced a fascinating and robust critique of the role of metaphor and analogy in the development and popularisation of 'ultra-Darwinism' and the particular version of theoretical genetics where heritability is understood through a total genetics paradigm. He documents what he sees as the pernicious process whereby 'information-theory' in particular, developing at the same time as genetic science, became the 'metaphor within which genetic theory was . . . formulated' (Rose, 2005: 120). He charts a series of metaphorical leaps whereby genes –

in a dangerous and irresponsible shorthand – were first misread and misrepresented as being '*for*' traits and characteristics (for example, the idea of a gene for eye colour and then, more dangerously, for conditions like schizophrenia), an idea that gained popular credence. He shows how subsequently genes, apparently benignly, were cast as lengths of DNA which could be turned into *codes* for protein synthesis in a 'one way *flow of information*' where DNA 'had become the master-molecule' (Rose, 2005: 120, my emphasis). Rose's point is that these metaphors have shaped and skewed the scientific process, as well as dominating popular messages fed to ordinary people with a misleadingly irrefutable message about the determinacy of genetics, and about how they should understand heritability, transmission and indeed biological science. Here is what he says about the popular geneticist Richard Dawkins's role in this theorisation and popularisation by metaphor, for example:

> Consider, for example, the euphoria of this account in *The Blind Watchmaker* in which he [Dawkins] considers a willow tree in seed outside his window:
>   'It is raining DNA . . . It is raining instructions out there; it's raining tree-growing, fluff-spreading algorithms. That is not a metaphor, it is the plain truth. It couldn't be any plainer if it were raining floppy discs.'
>   This is fine writing, great fun to read, so much so that it has found its way into anthologies of scientific prose. But it is misleading in almost every respect. You might ignore the trivial fact, irritating to a biochemist like myself but airily dismissed in the paragraph containing this extract by the grand theorist, that the seeds contain a great deal more than DNA: there are proteins and polysaccharides and a multitude of other small molecules without which the DNA would be inert. But you cannot ignore the blunt statement that 'this is not a metaphor', for this is precisely and at best what it is. It certainly isn't 'the plain truth'. Nor is it a statement of homology or analogy. It is a manifesto. (Rose, 2005: 121, citing Dawkins, 1986)

Rose's anger about the misuse of metaphor and the dominance of a simplistic theoretical genetics it helped to forge and to usher in is almost palpable. His more recent work with the sociologist Hilary Rose has sought to document how the many failures in the bio-genetic promise of a panacea for various ills of disease and heredity are due to the cumulative factoring in of simplistic dogma from the start and 'the gene sequencers' failure to recognise the sheer complexity of humans as biosocial creatures' (Rose and Rose, 2012: 2). For Steven Rose that complexity had to involve recognising humans as organisms living in environments (there are some parallels with Ingold's anthropological view of processes of 'being alive' here [Ingold, 2011], and his more recent work on organisms as 'ensembles of relations' and humans as 'biosocial becomings' [Ingold, 2013: 8–9]). Rose and Rose want us to understand both the complexities of biology, and the interaction of the (also complex) social and the biological, before we begin to make arrogant and far reaching knowledge claims about human development and life. Their book *Genes, Cells and Brains* show the not dissimilar processes that have led us from what they call 'Genes'R'us to Neurons'R'us in two decades' (Rose and Rose, 2012: 2–3).

Of course there has been some softening of genetic determinist dogma more recently, not least in widespread scepticism in light of its manifest failures to become that promised panacea, but also with, for example, the advance of the field of the science of 'epigenetics', or what is sometimes known in more popular discourse as 'the influence of the environment on our genes', which complicates understandings of heredity so that, as Rose and Rose put it:

> Genes are no longer thought of as acting independently but rather in constant interaction both with each other and with the multiple levels of the environment in which they are embedded. (Rose and Rose, 2012: 73)

If we are in search of scientific sensitivity and complexity, this is clearly better, but metaphors still abound that belie those complexities, and that also (from my untutored perspective as a non-scientist at least) leave something of the supposed pre-eminence of genetics as 'raining instructions', for example, unchallenged (see also Ingold, 2013). Consider this excerpt from Nessa Carey's popular text *The Epigenetics Revolution*:

> When scientists talk about epigenetics they are referring to all the cases where the *genetic code* alone isn't enough to describe what's happening – there must be something else going on as well. . . . There has to be a *mechanism* that brings out this *mismatch* between the *genetic script* and the *final outcome*. These epigenetic effects must be caused by some sort of physical change, some alterations in the vast array of molecules that make up the cells of every living organism. . . . In this model, epigenetics can be defined as the set of *modifications* to our genetic material that change the way genes are *switched on or off*, but which don't alter the genes themselves. . . . We are finally starting to unravel the *missing link* between *nature and nurture*; how our environment *talks to us* and alters

us, sometimes forever. (Carey, 2012: 6–7, my emphasis of some of the key metaphors)

The idea here that the environment, or 'nurture', or even the social, alters us by switching genes on or off, or modifying 'the script', seems to see the 'environment' in something of a bit part where ultimately, although seen as influential, it is only really considered relevant for what it does to genes, which are still the key players, the motors in the process. Disappointingly, I have not seen a great deal of evidence in research developments so far of any very sophisticated understanding of what 'the social' or 'the environment' might be, nor how we might be embedded in 'it' (see part 3 of this book) and, importantly, according to Rose and Rose:

> Despite the lip service paid to 'the environment' by those modelling genetic effects, their formulae have a manifestly false built-in assumption that the effects of genes and the environment are almost entirely additive and can be teased apart by appropriate statistical methods. (Rose and Rose, 2012: 212)

But where does this take us in thinking about affinities, and the role of genetic metaphors of connection and heredity? Nordqvist and Smart argue that the ubiquity of genetic discourse, softened or otherwise (and they argue it *has* softened from the idea of 'immutable blueprint' to a script), does not mean that people have all signed up to a genetic determinism in their everyday lives, and in fact in their study they identify a 'profound paradox . . . that genes both matter a great deal and yet do not really matter at all' (Nordqvist and Smart, 2014: 145). Interestingly, they describe observing, in how their study participants talked, a commonplace 'slippage between very different explanatory metaphors' such as on the one hand the scientific-information informed and minimising metaphor that gametes are a just 'pinhead miniscule bit of data', and then the 'homely, almost horticultural' metaphor that a gestational mother is the source of life because she 'grows' her babies. In places they suggest that parents and grandparents in their study were quite instrumental in their use of metaphors and kinship reasoning, so that they 'were very adept in combining the apparently unblendable into accounts which sustained their connection with the children they were raising who were not fully their genetic kin' (Nordqvist and Smart, 2014: 162). And yet this was not entirely an instrumental process, as in other places they stress the haunting absence and threatening presence of donors, with their lurking potential to be repositioned as kin. Interestingly, they suggest that where genetic links are seen as weaker, 'kinship thinking' of the kind that stresses non-genetic links and metaphors gets stronger. Konrad too talks of the importance of metaphors of growth, nurture and feeding (sometimes through the metaphor of blood) that are used as a way of conveying the potency of affinity that is bestowed in gestation of donor ova (Konrad, 2005: 153). Nordqvist and Smart use the rather lovely metaphor that people 'dip into a reservoir of ideas, many of which have competing epistemologies . . . to explain different aspects of the work of creating kinship' (Nordqvist and Smart, 2014: 158). This ties in with the important anthropological work on 'the new kinship', especially that of Janet Carsten, that sees kinship as 'one of the most important areas for (most people's) creative energy' (Carsten, 2004: 9).

Poetics and the 'frisson' of ineffability

I think we can take from all this the idea that people are not simply genetic dupes, and that metaphor, and indeed mixing metaphors, might be an important way in which people can be creative about how they live kinship. The fact that people can comfortably hold onto interpretations and metaphors that appear to be contradictory suggests that they are not driven to use metaphor as a way of showing they have signed up to a dominant truth or a single framework. Indeed, I think we can see from this that 'ordinary' people are rather good at something that scientists who operate within a single paradigm are famously bad at: namely, traversing and experiencing everyday life connections between, for example, what we might think of as the genetic, the biological, the social, the cultural, the spiritual and so on, and understanding that there are no walls between these. People are routinely used to living such traversings in personal life, and would probably make better transdisciplinary researchers than most scientists do for that reason. People know that 'the genetic' is never just or only 'the genetic' – it is also always social, and always magical, and always ineffable for example, and these things segue and blur into and out of one another. People know that this is what life is. Added to that, I think scientists are probably more convinced of (or invested in) the singular and ultimate truth value of their metaphors than the rest of us are about ours (or theirs), or at least they are more fretful about their exactitude. Take this excerpt from Rose for example:

> In attempting to interpret and change the world, we often operate by
> analogy – by likening the process or object we are studying to another
> whose mechanism we understand more fully. Analogies, however, are
> hazardous tools. Often they are merely metaphor, and the likeness we
> imagine is *poetic rather than exact*. (Rose, 2005: 303, my emphasis)

I completely agree with his analysis of the dangers of power and
dominance of certain metaphors. But actually I think Rose was on
to something else here that he did not intend to be, and that he did
not quite see, but which is just as important, in his implied dismissal
of *mere* metaphor, and of *poetics* rather than exactitude. We saw the
significance of poetics in, for example, Hardy's 'family face'. I want
to go on to suggest that it is the very poetics, lyricism and creativity
involved in metaphor, and the fact that metaphor is sometimes used
to make light of something that may be troubling or arresting – and
yes also the inexactitude and slipperiness – that convey and express
the potencies of affinity. In fact, I would go so far as to say that there
is something about the very nature of metaphor – that it involves
a tension between 'mimesis and alterity', or a resemblance/alterity
between a thing and an Other thing that it literally is not – that
makes it particularly suited to expressing and channelling potent and
intriguing *discordances* of affinity (see 'Sensations'). Taussig's ideas
on 'mimesis and alterity' are fascinating here, and although developed in a different context and with different aims, I think they have
a resonance with what I am saying about metaphor, discordances,
poetics and affinities here. Consider this excerpt from his argument:

> Pulling you this way and that, mimesis plays *this trick of dancing between
> the very same and the very different*. An *impossible but necessary, indeed
> an everyday affair*, mimesis registers both sameness and difference, of
> being like and of being Other. Creating stability from this instability
> is no small task, yet all identity formation is engaged in this *habitually
> bracing activity* in which the issue is not so much staying the same,
> but maintaining sameness through alterity. (Taussig, 1993: 129, my
> emphasis)

I like Taussig's idea of an *impossible but everyday trick of dancing
between the same and the Other*, and the suggestion that this is a *habitu-
ally bracing activity*. I think we do just get on with discordances and
impossibilities in our everyday lives, and that doing so gives a *frisson*
of something; it is bracing. When applied to metaphor the bracing activity can be a highly lyrical and poetic one too. There is an
everyday poetics in the use of metaphors, and this is most certainly

connected to what is called 'affect' these days, although most discussions of affect neglect it (for an exception see Sopory, 2005; see also Cameron, 2011, for an interesting discussion of metaphor and empathy).

We have seen in the facets that metaphors come into play when something of their everyday experience of resemblance, or of offspring, bothers or excites people – a frisson – or where it is mysterious or ineffable. I strongly think that people use the terms 'genes' and 'genetics' to indicate an everyday *ineffability of kinship* that may be fearful or troubling, joyful or fascinating, or sometimes magical or mysterious; but in the facets it is clear they rarely if ever use it to say anything literal about genes. It is not simply that they misuse or misunderstand the term either. There is plenty of evidence to support the idea that people do not literally mean genes when they talk about genetics, both in the facets and in existing work. Indeed, Martin Richard's useful chapter on the concept of genetic connection neatly points out that the term 'genetic identity' does not make literal sense, although it is commonly used to suggest, for example, that a donor conceived person may have a right to know their genetic identity. But if that can mean anything literally, it would be providing donor offspring with the genome sequence of their donors, yet he suggests that 'I do not think that DNA alphabet soup is what donor offspring are perceived to lack'. 'Genetic information', he points out, 'itself does not individuate people. It is not a kind of molecular essence of personhood' (Richards, 2014: 37). 'Genetic identity' does not make literal sense, and Richards argues that donor conceived people who want to know their 'genetic identity' actually probably want to know about the circumstances of their conception and the people involved. I might go further and suggest, following my arguments in the 'Sensations' section, that this might even involve knowing something of the sensory-kinaesthetic characters of them, and knowing whether there is any family resemblance. And it might involve some receptivity to ideas of ethereality and magic too in how these things might be channelled or capriciously living inside and beyond the persons they can surface in.

If we think of metaphors as lyrical and poetic, we should also see how they can be funny, and clever, and appealing, and scary, often because of the very mimesis and alterity they hold together in tension, and the analogies they imply. Metaphors of heritability and connection in the facets were sometimes playful, sometimes fearful, in what they evoked about affinities. Where scientists with a manifesto and on a mission may use them in an attempt to persuade, or bemoan the lack of exactitude in the analogy, in everyday life metaphors are often used in jest (by saying that something too complicated or trivial to be 'explained by' genetics is genetic), or in passion (the desire to populate a world with mini-mees), or in fear (of a lurking inevitability of a donor who may have 'genetic' credentials for example), or in self-deprecation (recognition that you have 'inherited' a negative trait), or in criticism (of a female line in the family with none-too-attractive characteristics), or in sheer poetics (where metaphor enables a lyrical evocation). This is reminiscent of Tipper's important arguments about irony (discussed in the 'Sensations' section), and her gentle criticism that scholars of animal–human relations can be 'too earnest' and fail to see the joke and, ironically, also that the joke is important (see also Brown, 1977, on irony). In saying this I do not wish to suggest that metaphors are unimportant – far from it – but I think we are wise not to get too exercised when thinking about affinities at least, over how well their *content* matches whatever we think the scientific or empirical reality to be, because more often it is *discordance and the frisson – a tantalising and thrilling tension of mimesis and alterity –* rather than exactitude in the match which is the point of them and which gives them their charge.

Metaphors and mixed metaphors then are ways in which people live with and express the intriguing discordance of affinities in a lyrical or poetic register – ways which can be charged with pleasure or fear – and where life scientists and social scientists looking for a more rationalistic or categorical version of reality will remain puzzled or irritated by an apparent dissonance that they itch to resolve. For that reason, among others, I think we should not dwell too extensively on the *substantive meaning of 'genetic'* in people's reasoning. And when we move beyond this, we can see many other metaphors and ideas at play which help us to better understand the potency of ineffable kinship affinities.

Wondering about what is circulating and relating

We saw the potential significance of 'wondering' in the discussion of sensations in part 1 of the book. This is also striking to the reader of Nordqvist and Smart, and Konrad, in the importance of curiosity and *wondering* in the lives of people whose families have knowingly been touched by anonymous donor conception. Nordqvist and Smart talk about 'curious questions' and Konrad identifies 'cascade(s) of "I wonder" questions' (Konrad, 2005: 171). Wondering comes across strongly as an act of affinity, and as a way in which people animate and create meaningful kinship, even if they do not ever meet or know those donors, or offspring, or donor siblings, or donor grandchildren/parents, who they are wondering about. Just as important is what Nordqvist and Smart identify as the act of 'trying not to think about it' (that is, donor gametes and what that might mean) amongst some of the recipient parents in their study. I do not think this implies that people who have received anonymous donor gametes fall into two camps, however – as in those who wonder, and those who do not. On the contrary, in fact I think the activity of wondering is highly likely to incorporate periods of 'trying not to think about it'. To put it another way, trying not to wonder, is simply an extension of wondering. Both are part of the same process, using the same energies, drawing on the same assumptions about why this might matter, and engaging the same relational thinking. Of course trying not to wonder does nothing to defuse the potency of any of this.

Konrad's concept of transilience also involves wondering as an activity that connects people who are unknown to each other through anonymous sociality. It involves a shift in perception from the idea of kinship as *people or persons who are related* in a fixed, either/or sense, to an emphasis on kinship as *processes of connecting and relating.* Konrad explains for example that, 'A notion of persons as "transilient" draws upon elements of *extension, imagination, regeneration, dispersal and diffusion, circulation and multidirectional flows*' (Konrad, 2005: 49, my emphasis). Ideas (and metaphors) like flows and circulation, along with multi-direction and diffusion, emerge, as we have seen from Konrad's own research, but also have many echoes in the facets in this section on the forces and flows of resemblance, and in the experience of creating offspring or being part of 'an offspringing' that may or may not involve 'gametes'.

The sense that ineffable kinship affinities *are alive in an ethereal circulation of transfers, forces, flows and energies* comes across repeatedly and strongly in the facets, as we have seen – in metaphor and otherwise; for example we see them in the sense that activities of wondering and transilience constitute, in themselves, ineffable kinship affinities; we see them in some of the prominent themes, motifs and metaphors from the facets such as the idea that there *must be something there*, or a timeless *family aura*, or 'family face', or in *coincidence, serendipity and fatefulness*, for example in *chance encounters* or glimpses 'in the street', 'across the room', or through a surprise find of a photograph. These are instances of the *everyday magic of live connective forces and flows going on 'out there', 'somewhere', and outside of linear or familiarly encountered experiences of time.* And we see them too in the familiar yet magical knowledge and experience of being *'hit by'* a resemblance (implicit in the very idea of a striking resemblance), or a connection, or an aura, or an energy, or a spirit or feeling of kinship – which can be experienced as a 'punctum', or a piercing conjecture about kinship or mystery, or the manifestation of an 'optical unconscious'. And even though resemblances can be matters of debate and therefore, by implication, of interpretation, there is also something that feels outside of subjective interpretation about the experience of being hit by one. Being hit by a resemblance can provoke a 'double take', evocatively described by Stacey thus:

> The momentary delay holds two contradictory perceptions in tension: what I have just seen is unremarkable; what I have just seen demands a second look. Taken aback, I am literally taken back. A backtrack prompted by a perceptual disturbance, the double take feels like the mind catching up with the body, which has already reacted. The head has turned to see again, as the sense of the significance of the unforeseen belatedly enters our consciousness. The double take is both physical and psychic, conscious and unconscious, visceral and imaginative. (Stacey, 2010: 257)

Such encounters, clearly, are full of sensation and extra-sensory potency. Just like when a resemblance hits us, I think we feel – physically, psychically, viscerally and imaginatively – the force of something almost elemental, or outside the normalcy of the social somehow. These moments, or these experiences, are heavy with something – a *frisson; a tantalising or exciting breach in our ways of understanding* perhaps, and especially maybe sociological ways of understanding that do not usually bring together all these dimensions. At the very least, such moments constitute an unsettling of conventional binary divides in our modes of explanation, and enable us to glimpse the possibilities of connections, or parallel goings on – ethereal or otherwise – that we can hardly imagine.

What I want to suggest is that these themes are seams in the sensation of living that are both ordinary and extraordinary – the extraordinariness of the claim that there is 'something there', for example, rests on a knowledge of the way of the world that is both familiar and slightly outside our grasp. It unsettles the distinction between what is tangible and intangible, what is sensory and extra-sensory, and of course what is of the body, the mind and perception. It also suggests that the 'unstoppable merging of the object of perception with the body of the receiver' needs to incorporate another, more

ethereal layer. Such ephemeral flashes of recognition, are glimpses
– I want to suggest – of a way of the world that is both familiar and
slightly outside our grasp; a world that we know and do not know all
at the same time, and that is always there, and we are always part of.

Once again, the theme of *in/tangibility* is clearly crucial here. These
experiences and encounters traverse the supposed tangible/intangible
divide with ease and alacrity. They do this partly because they disrupt our supposed tangible experiences of linear time in the here and
now, with piercing disjunctures, conjectures, edicts and glimpses of
an ineffable kinship that lives outside of time, yet also pops up and
inhabits the present, the past and the future. By way of explanation,
let us consider resemblances and in/tangibility.

One of the fascinations of resemblance is that it often seems to
defy any temporal or other rules of regularity including genetic
ones, but also ideas of social conditioning and social construction.
Resemblances can appear or hit you in a flash, in a gesture, or a
look, or a sound, or an expression, only to disappear when you do
the double take or try to hold everything still. Or they can appear in
the style of Benjamin's 'optical unconscious', in an image that is held
still by the shutter on a camera producing – or capturing – a resemblance not visible to the naked eye because what we are looking at
is always busily moving and living. Resemblances may appear in bits
and pieces, not in whole likenesses, and not all in the same time or
era, and these kinds of vagaries seem to fascinate people.

What kind of thing, therefore, is resemblance? What kind of in/
tangibility do resemblances speak of? What do they make us know?
I think these questions highlight what Gordon refers to as 'the
always unsettled relationship between what we see and what we
know' (Gordon, 1996: 194). Resemblances are sometimes only
partially or ephemerally seen like fleeting ghostly presences and
coincidences. Sometimes they leap up and hit you with their visible
or almost palpable force. Sometimes they recur. But much about
resemblance is not quite seen, or is not seen at all, but it is known
in ways that are sometimes more tactile and bodily, sometimes more
ethereal or spiritual or extra-sensory, and sometimes more sensory-
kinaesthetic. Resemblances draw together the visual, the audible,
the olfactory, the tactile, the imagined, the ethereal, magic, nature,
bio-genetics and the socio-cultural into a visceral everyday knowledge that is both articulated and unarticulated. And they trouble
the distinctions between those things, especially perhaps the socio-
cultural, the natural and the bio-genetic. Resemblances that pop
up haphazardly across generations, in some people and not others,

apparently defy laws of science and genetics, as well as social conditioning or social construction. Most importantly for my current argument, resemblances exist at the interface of and 'trouble' the distinction between the tangible and the intangible, the sensory and the extra-sensory.

I began this section by saying there is more to kinship than the affinities I would discuss here, and of course that is true. But the facets and the discussion I hope do something different than simply extending our knowledge of forms and types of kinship, by drawing attention to something we (sociologists, social scientists) forget about sometimes; which is that *people find it fascinating to consider and to wonder about what is circulating and relating* when affinities of ineffable kinship come into being, and to be open to a range of possibilities about that, and to even enjoy the discordances and uncertainties of it all. I do not mean here that social scientists should do more wondering about this so that they can pin it down, define and categorise it all. I mean people find these things fascinating to wonder about, and the ways in which they wonder – not just cerebrally but through full blown sensations and experiences – is telling of what the energies, forces and flows are, as well of course as being integral to them.

We social scientists too readily think of *categories of kin*, or different kinds of *kinship practices*, or *types of relationship*, for example, instead. But actually I think in the process of living, people show themselves to be fascinated by and fully involved in forces, flows and circulations that suggest something kindred; some kind of ineffable and elemental connective energy that does not settle into a social scientific mindset about systems of kinship. People are tantalised by these live wires of ineffable connection in all their mystery, force, anarchy and capriciousness. People know we are not all 'unitary' persons who are somehow fixed in static and individuated relation to each other by a thing or framework called kinship (or a family tree); they are enchanted, puzzled and sometimes full of wonder about this experiential knowledge that will not be contained or settle into reductive theories or factually accurate metaphors, at the same time as they know this to be just normal personal life in the living. People are perfectly ready to accept and engage in (to borrow from Taussig) 'the impossible but everyday trick of dancing between' (Taussig, 1993: 129) the tangible and the intangible, the rational and the magical, the 'of us' and the 'elementally outside of us', the parochial and the boundless. The idea that affinities arise in energies and forces that are in themselves of interest, and that do more than simply connect fixed points (such as unitary persons), will be developed further in the next part of the book, where I move on to consider how we might layer an understanding of ecologies and socio-atmospherics into the argument.

PART THREE

Ecologies and Socio-Atmospherics

Why Ecologies and Socio-Atmospherics?

In this part of the book I want to continue to develop the argument that affinities are connective charges, forces and flows, rather than static relationships between fixed entities. Here I want to focus on some of the ways in which affinities might arise in and through some form of ecological connection, for example with places, things, environments or surroundings. I want to consider how an ecological and atmospheric attunement can provide further insight into the potencies of affinity. As with the previous two sections, this is not a separate or contained endeavour: I want to layer an ecological sensibility into my arguments about affinities as sensations and ineffable kinship.

The *Oxford Dictionary of English* (2005) says ecology is the study of 'the relations of organisms to one another and to their physical surroundings', and it is these kinds of relations and potential affinities that I want to tune into in this section. That idea of looking at relations not only between organisms but with and between 'surroundings' is a useful one because it attunes us to 'living in the world' as an ecological activity and process. This helps to bring into focus things, places, technologies, surroundings, atmospheres and environments, and the affinities that implicate and involve these. We can see, however, that the idea inherent in the ODE definition of organisms existing in relation to physical surroundings already assumes a certain ontology that, in fact, we may wish to question insofar as it implies that organisms are fixed entities or that surroundings are physical or material solidities. We need a more radical and open sense of ecology, and in seeking this I again take inspiration from Tim Ingold's ecological anthropology; he conceptualises living beings as simultaneously biophysical organisms and socio-cultural beings, whose elements, layers and lines are in multiple relation with the 'continuum of organic life' and those energies, forces and atmospheres that we encounter as places and spaces, structures and things (Ingold, 2011, 2013, 2015). In accord with Ingold, I do *not* wish to ascribe an inanimate 'object-ness' or flat materiality either to non-human lives or to things, forces and energies in the world. Nor do I wish to see these merely (or conceptually) as the 'contexts' for or backdrop to human life.

Thinking about ecologies and what these might be has taken me on a route through a range of literatures in ecological anthropology, environmental ecology, cultural geography, multispecies ethnography, human–animal studies, posthumanism, material culture, as well as into literature on walking, weather, and more. The different studies I have encountered en route, and the movements, revelations and lines of argument they represent, are fascinating and illuminating. For example, there are important studies, some of which I will consider, that ask telling questions about 'things' and relationships, including analyses of what people wear, own, use, keep, dwell with and in, give or throw away, lose, pass on to others as gifts or inheritance. Some of these studies shift our thinking about 'things' in really exciting ways by inviting us to imagine or notice that things have *lives* which insist we move beyond a literal reading of their materiality and their apparent 'thingness' and into the relational forces and energies that animate and entwine them. For sure, we can see that material, sensory, physical and animate textures and properties of things work in ways that enliven, symbolise, materialise and sometimes problematise the everyday realities of relationships. To go further and say that things – even apparently inanimate ones – have *lives* is more radical and exciting because it forces us to confront energies other than human agency. I am especially interested in that idea, and with how it feeds into a way of thinking ecologically about affinities that is at the same time intellectually controversial and totally in tune with everyday life and experience.

An ecological and atmospheric attunement also demands that we pay attention to the meld or the goings on not only of things and human lives, but of other lives and livings. That involves challenging both the arrogant and naïve primacy of human life and perspective that is so firmly rooted in different versions of culture and 'the establishment' around our world, and hence also the idea of 'nature' or 'the environment' as *backdrop*, or *setting*, or *landscape* or *context*. Once we do that we feel the solid ground of the taken-for-granted slipping away from beneath our feet, forcing us to question conventional analytical and categorical separations. I mean especially those separations between human and non-human (much better conceptualised as 'more-than-human' [Whatmore, 2006]) lives – and organisms, and things, and technologies, and nature, and 'the environment', and 'the climate', and elements and forces (of weather, 'nature' and otherwise), and time and space in the sway of life itself. Radical thinkers, researchers and activists who want us to decentre human agency and perspective, and think in terms of 'multispecies lives', or 'the mesh', or 'entanglement', or 'assemblages', or 'happenings', or 'ensembles of relations', are right in my view to unsettle the comfortable (for some) old intellectual certainties that were so at odds with what 'living in the world' is actually like.

We will move in this part of the book through facets selected and written with the aim of suggesting and illuminating a more radical and open sense of ecology. The facets touch on animate places, things, technologies and journeys, as well as weather, before returning to the overall argument about affinities, and layering in some of the insights drawn from an ecological and atmospheric attunement. A crucial theme that emerges throughout is that we need an attunement to what I am calling *'socio-atmospherics'* if we are to understand both the scope and nature of ecologies and their relationship with affinities. In light of the facets and the insights that come from them, I shall ultimately go on to argue that we need more than a technically thorough or holistic ecological attunement. Instead we need a version that can capture the 'socio-atmospherics', the dynamics of ecological connection, and the poetics of living in the world.

Facets of Ecologies and Socio-Atmospherics

1. Animate places and things in literature

Nan Shepherd's 'living mountain'

This wonderful little book was written by Nan Shepherd during the last part of the Second World War, but not published until 1977 (Shepherd, 2011; Macfarlane, 2011). It is a celebration of an iconic range of Scottish mountains called the Cairngorms, which form what is also known as the Cairn Gorm plateau. Shepherd's affinity with what she calls 'the living mountain' comes across strongly on every page. The mountain for her is not simply a vast tall thing made of rock, stone and earth, which we can look up at, climb, and look down from. It is all of the life and elements – including water, frost and air, as well as the more obvious plants and animals – that constitute it. It is not simply a surface, but has an inside, and it includes the surrounding atmosphere. Her writing is shot through with a passionately ecological sensibility, and that includes her consistent use of the singular form 'living mountain' to describe her experience of vibrant connection between peaks, plateau, recesses, corries, rivers, life of all kinds, weather, her own senses and perception:

> there is more in the lust for a mountain top than a perfect physiological adjustment. What more there is lies within the mountain. *Something moves between me and it.* Place and a mind may interpenetrate till the nature of both is altered. I cannot tell what this movement is except by recounting it. (Shepherd, 2011: 8, my emphasis)

The shape of the slim book constitutes this 'recounting', as it refuses to be organised in geographically defined sections for example (as many other 'walking' books would do). Instead it follows what for Shepherd is the magic and ineffable nature of the elements, the mountain, and that *something that moves between her and it* in chapters like 'water', 'sleep', 'being', 'life'. Robert Macfarlane, in the introduction to the book, captures something of Shepherd's ecological-philosophical sensibility well when he says: 'the book's form acts out its central proposition, which is that the world will not fall into divisible realms, as an apple may be sliced, but is instead an unmappable mesh of inter-relations' (Macfarlane, 2011: xxiv–xxv).

Consider, for example, this extract from Shepherd's chapter on sleep whilst taking note at how unusual it is that a 'nature' book should contain such a chapter at all:

> No one knows the mountain completely who has not slept on it. As one slips over into sleep, the mind grows limpid; the body melts; perception alone remains. One neither thinks, nor desires, nor remembers, but *dwells in pure intimacy with the tangible world*. These moments of quiescent perceptiveness before sleep are among the most rewarding of the day. I am emptied of preoccupation, there is nothing between me and the earth and sky. . . . To come up out of the blank of sleep and open one's eyes on scaur and gully, *wondering,* because one has forgotten where one was, is to recapture some pristine amazement not often savoured. . . . I do not ascribe sentience to the mountain; yet at no other moment am I sunk quite so deep into its life. I have let go my self. The experience is *peculiarly precious because it is impossible to coerce*. (Shepherd, 2011: 90–1, my emphasis)

Jon McGregor's city that 'sings'

Jon McGregor's novel *If Nobody Speaks of Remarkable Things* is what one might call an assault on the senses. He begins, defiantly almost, in a sensory register, conjuring immediately an atmospheric feel of a city and its rhythms. Any reader will recognise at least some of this and 'feel' the city he is creating. The novel begins:

> If you listen, you can hear it.
> The city, it sings. (McGregor, 2002: 1)

McGregor has said his novel is about the anonymity of city life and the damage that transience does. It is set during a swelteringly hot summer in a northern English city, and involves snatches of the lives of

residents of one street of terraced houses, and the uneven reverbera-
tions of a piercing event, that is nonetheless small in the life of the
city and from the perspectives of national media. Most of the characters are unnamed and referred to by their house number or other
visible or descriptive characteristics only ('the man with the carefully
trimmed moustache', 'the boy with the white shirt', 'the tall girl with
the glitter round her eyes', 'the girl with the short blond hair and the
square glasses', 'the man with the ruined hands'). This was a move
that irritated some reviewers, but was clearly intended to immerse the
reader in the sensations of city street living, where people don't know
their neighbours' names but do know certain things about them, and
do see/hear/encounter them – noticing what they do in the street
and what can be seen and heard through windows and walls (there
are links here with Morgan's ideas about 'acquaintances', discussed
earlier; Morgan, 2009). What the novel conjures for me is a strong
atmosphere of city life, in a neighbourhood, with lives lived outdoors
one hot summer. Actually what emerges is not complete anonymity
and certainly not disconnection, but rather a connectivity characterised by sensory awareness, situatedness, and partial observational
knowledge of each other's lives. McGregor creates a multi-sensory
experience of the living city – a northern English city in a rare heat-
wave. Whether or not you have been part of a set of atmospherics like
this, you are likely to find it evocative and resonant.

The beginning sections move quickly into an evocation of this city
at night time, or more particularly in the hours between one day and
the next, including a rare moment of nocturnal silence. Again, the
reader can *feel* this city, and knows the time of day/night, the atmospherics, the vibe.

> So listen.
> Listen, and there is more to hear.
> The rattle of a dustbin lid knocked to the floor.
> The scrawl and scratch of two hackle-raised cats.
> The sudden thundercrash of bottles emptied into crates.
> The slam-slam of car doors, the changing of gears, the hobbled clip-clop
> of a slow walk home.
> The rippled roll of shutters pulled down on late-night cafes, a crackled
> voice crying street names for taxis, a loud scream that lingers and cracks
> into laughter, a bang that might just be an old car backfiring, a callbox
> calling out for an answer, a treeful of birds tricked into morning, a whis-
> tle and a shout and a broken glass, a blare of soft music and a blam of
> hard beats, a barking and yelling and singing and crying and it all swells
> up all the rumbles and crashes and bangings and slams, all the noise and

the rush and the non-stop wonder of the song of the city you can hear
if you listen the song
and it stops
in some rare and sacred dead time, sandwiched between the late sleep-
ers and the early risers, there is a miracle of silence.
Everything has stopped. (McGregor, 2002: 2–3)

Haruki Murakami's 'pulsing' city

McGregor's city is a living, animate, mass of connections and atmospheres, and I think there are parallels here with Murakami's depiction
of night-time Tokyo in *After Dark* as animalistic, organic, breathing:

Eyes mark the shape of the city.
Through the eyes of a high-flying night bird, we take in the scene from
midair. In our broad sweep, the city looks like a single gigantic creature
– or more like a single collective entity created by many intertwining
organisms. Countless arteries stretch to the ends of its elusive body,
circulating a continuous supply of fresh blood cells, sending out new
data and collecting the old, sending out new consumables and collecting
the old, sending out new contradictions and collecting the old. To the
rhythm of its pulsing, all parts of the body flicker and flare up and squirm.
Midnight is approaching, and while the peak of activity has passed, the
basal metabolism that maintains life continues undiminished, producing
the basso continuo of the city's moan, a monotonous sound that neither
rises nor falls but is pregnant with foreboding. (Murakami, 2008: 3)

Both McGregor and Murakami portray city and neighbourhood as
vital, creaturely, both familiar and strange, potentially dangerous and
alluring. They both invite the reader to imagine cities as viewed from
above – Murakami 'through the eyes of a high-flying night bird',
and McGregor implicitly lifting the roofs off the differently numbered
houses to observe the inhabitants, or viewing them in the street from
an upstairs window. Then the authors periodically zoom in, then back
out, always tuning all senses to the atmospherics of living in these
worlds, and their rhythms, atmospheres, weather, chances and near
misses, anonymity and fleeting encounters – so that you feel their
weightiness without ever being certain which will turn out to be the
most potent. Both, it seems to me, hint at the vital precariousness and
the almost random potency of city relationships.

Barbara Kingsolver's Africa as an 'attendance in my soul'

Kingsolver's *Poisonwood Bible* is a story of the wife and four daughters of an obsessive Baptist missionary, and their experiences in the 1960s in what was then the Congo. It evokes powerfully and viscerally the way relationships, environments – in this case the African jungle and the capricious extremes of its climate, its flora and fauna – and socio-cultural-political contexts, are woven together. The extremes of the contrast between the family's background in Georgia, USA and the conditions, and relationalities they find themselves entangled within in Africa, help to emphasise interweavings that are, I want to argue, always there, but rarely observed in analyses of everyday life. The books speaks in the alternate voices of the female characters, and here is an excerpt from the mother and the missionary's wife, Orleanna:

> Once every few years, even now, I catch the scent of Africa. It makes me want to keen, sing, clap up thunder, lie down at the foot of a tree and let the worms take whatever of me they can still use. I find it impossible to bear. Ripe fruits, acrid sweat, urine, flowers, dark spices, and other things I've never even seen – I can't say what goes into the composition, or why it rises up to confront me as I round some corner hastily, unsuspecting. It has found me here on this island, in our little town, in a back alley where sleek boys smoke in a stairwell amidst the day's uncollected refuse. A few years back, it found me on the Gulf Coast of Mississippi, where I'd returned from a family funeral: Africa rose up to seize me as I walked on a pier past a huddle of turtle-headed old fisherman, their bait buckets set around them like a banquet. Once I merely walked out of the library in Atlanta and there it was, that scent knocking me down, for no reason I can understand. The sensation rises up from inside me and I know you're still here, holding sway. You've played some trick on the dividing of my cells so my body can never be free of the small parts of Africa it consumed. Africa, where one of my children remains in the dank red earth. It's the scent of accusation. It seems I only know myself, anymore, by your attendance in my soul. (Kingsolver, 1998: 99)

Kingsolver tells a story of lives permanently changed and inflected by visceral experiences bound up, in this case, in the sensory memory of a place, Africa, which is more than a place; it is a place-time-relationality-ecology-worlding-sensation, and in this it has parallels with Murakami's pulsing city, McGregor's city that sings and Shepherd's living mountain. I am following Heidegger here in using the term 'worlding' to suggest the generative and ongoing sense of 'being in the world' rather than the more static idea of a world composed of things which are fixed material states (Heidegger, 1971). What Kingsolver's character Orleanna feels, remembers and experiences about Africa as an 'attendance in her soul', is her encountering of, her doings with, her movement and her 'worlding' through *that* time, *those* relationalities, *those* engagements with the earth, the plants, the weather, *those* particular losses that she and her daughters endured, and so on. Like Shepherd's sense of something that 'moves between' her and her mountain, and of sliding into pure perception through sleep, Orleanna's memories of these experiences and atmospherics come unbidden – they assault her at unexpected moments, connecting with something that feels like it has infiltrated and is alive deep in her soul.

2. Atmospheric memories of animate places and things

The atmospherics of a teenager's city

When she remembers it, she remembers – or perhaps she conjures – particular atmospherics. Underage drinking – 'the vodka and lime days' – in the city pubs. Never any need for ID back then, especially for girls, but oh the excitement of transgression. The Spa Tavern, loud, smoky, crowded old city pub, 70s music on the jukebox – a group of four of them linked and giggling their way up the alley, city smells, cheap perfume (Avon's 'Occur'!), hairspray, pub smoke, grubby darkness, probably rats down there in the dark. The night they saw an arsonist round the back of the Echo building, his guilty glance towards them, like a hunted animal, as he kindled the fire in a back alley near the dustbins. Warm nights, and then cold ones, wet ones, and the cheap, thin and tight fake sheepskin-lined zip-up jacket she wore that never kept her warm enough. The click of her shoes on the cracked pavements – peep-toe high heels, vertiginous platforms, twisted ankles, sore and irrevocably mutated heels and toes. Pencil split skirts, trevira dresses, backless tops, hotpants, clothes she had made herself (thrown together in an evening) – clothes that always took some arranging, getting the straps right, the side slit right, hiding the unfinished seams. Clubs their parents didn't allow them to go to, so they went anyway with careless lies. What parents didn't know wouldn't hurt them. Northern Soul, in this Southern English City. Having to be where the right music was – hearing it throbbing through the night air – the right dancing, the right people. Running up the back of town past the Arundel Towers for the last bus home – sometimes there was time for a greasy cheeseburger at Larry's stall – watching him fry dubious beefburgers, onions and mushrooms through the hatch in his van, in winter leaning her face and hands in to catch some of the warmth. Scoffing those delicious burgers whilst running for the bus, soaking up the vodkas and lagers and lime, greasy faces, onions dropping down their fronts, laughing, hiccoughing, gasping for breath in the cold air, ducking the rain.

The smell of the number 47 bus, the journey like passing through a decompression chamber gradually turning them from inhabitants of one world into those of another, and the creepy mile-long walk home alone from the bus stop through quiet, scary tree-lined suburban streets, with middle aged people sleeping oblivious to her danger and fear, snoring in the darkness behind their closed doors and windows, so different from the safe vibe of the buzzing city centre seven miles away, wishing her shoes didn't 'click click clop clop' so much. Her ears still buzzing from the music, limbs alive from dancing and running, rerunning the excitement of the evening's encounters. All this sound and vibe in her, jarring with the sober quiet of her sleeping-parent home, as she fumbles and rattles her key in the door, greeting the smiling sleepy dog and trying to stop his tail from thump thumping against the door or his claws from scratching too noisily on the floor, and trying to creep silently up the stairs whilst actually bumping and stumbling like a stage drunk.

Her parents thought the city too dangerous, but for her it always felt safer and peopled. The quiet strange dark of suburbia seemed more dangerous. And anyway she was always with her friends – the ones who also sought the thrills and risks of the city, away from their suburban homes. The ones who didn't only want to hang out with other middle class white kids. The night the city football team won the FA Cup and everyone was hugging, singing, cheering, being carried on each other's shoulders, even those of them who had no interest in football. She remembers the feeling of sitting on the shoulders of an older boy, the warm feel of his shirt and football scarf in her hands – grasped for stability – all laughing and singing in a potent moment of physical closeness where acquaintanceship became special and important in shared celebration. He died a couple of years later of a brain tumour – a shock discovery for her many years later, remembering that moment, vital with celebration, and feeling a special association although she barely knew him.

These are night-time images, scenes, atmospheres, of lights and dark, and sounds and smells, associations, routes and ways through a 1970s port city, before the all-night culture had become the norm. Concrete, modernist architecture, no concessions to 'nature' except in the parks and then finally when the high street was pedestrianised, the circular concrete-pebble dashed planters that became their sitting and hanging out places, or more often their strutting past places (she rarely sat still for long), on bored Saturday afternoons. Many of her memories are of routes and ways, going somewhere, journeying, weaving and clopping through the city. She hasn't been back for many years now, although she has visited once or twice in the interim since those times, and she might have taken a peek on Google Street view in a quiet solitary moment. Somehow she expects the ways and their landmarks are still there – that she could walk that alley to the Spa Tavern, and run the back route to the bus station past Arundel Towers and Larry's Burgers – even though she knows it has changed almost beyond recognition in its city makeover, in turning itself into a shopping centre, a city of the twenty-first century, through different shades of local authority management, different phases of urban development and regeneration, the creation of swanky office and apartment blocks, retail centres, and urban green spaces, and of course different demographies, migrations and emigrations of inhabitants, different accents and fashions and sounds and smells and sights on the streets. She recalls, in fact, a taxi ride circling the city sometime just a few years ago, peering through the window and trying to map onto these shiny new glass buildings and lights and major roads, the old concrete and brick structures, and the ways and routes they made through that other place/time that used to be here and still is here, as a layer underneath or beyond somehow, just like it is a layer in her. Suddenly seeing a familiar building from those times, in a sea of the unfamiliar, but not being able to make it work as an anchor without shutting her eyes and going to that place/time and those atmospherics.

Anat Hecht's 'tangible memories' of home

Hecht's essay on tangible memories focuses on a single case study of a woman in her late sixties called Nan, and the way in which the homes of Nan's past have come to be reflected in – even actively curated in – her current home, and in various memorialisation practices that she engages in (Hecht, 2001). Nan had an 'uprooted childhood', having at the age of seven been wrenched, along with her younger brother, from the cramped convivial hardship and poverty of her working class childhood home in the tenement buildings of the 'Wee World' of Abbeyhill in Edinburgh, Scotland, to be sent to the Scottish countryside as a war evacuee. After that, her mother died, her father went into the army, and she and her brother ended up in a Children's Home, never returning to the 'Wee World' where she had been the happiest. When Hecht met and worked with her, Nan lived with her husband in south-east England, where she had lived all her adult life, in a house that was an 'Aladdin's Cave of reminiscence' and which was 'jam-packed with books, photographs, past-time ornaments and several, rather unusual, collections' (Hecht, 2001: 124). Hecht calls this Nan's 'private museum of symbolic roots' (Hecht, 2001: 124) and as the essay proceeds, it becomes clear that Nan is quite some collector – of things and stuff, memorabilia and mementoes – with the conscious aim of creating, preserving, curating, passing on and disseminating memories of former times and eras and specifically places, people and relationships. A lot of the things she collects and curates (some to be displayed in her home, some in association with local museums) are things of the time or place, rather than the things that actually belonged to her or were passed down her own family; all of those things and homes were lost – when her childhood was uprooted, and subsequently when the 'Wee World' was demolished. Things clearly play a very active role in constituting Nan's autobiography, which she narrates to Hecht through the homes, places, times, characters and relationships she has lived in and with; these fall into clear eras combining the historical times, with childhood 'stages', changing material and spatial resources and fashions, and personal-relational events. Significantly the stories are full of sensations. The things that Nan furnishes her home and life with symbolise these associations and meanings, and Hecht emphasises their tangible ability to evoke potent albeit less tangible feelings, memories, reminiscences and nostalgia.

The play on in/tangibilities in Hecht's concept of *tangible memory*, and the shifting, fluid and atmospheric relationship between them, is very interesting. This is especially so in her emphasis on what she calls Nan's 'sensory journey' (Hecht, 2001: 130), where sound, sight, touch, tastes and smells, animate her story. In relation to sound, Nan sings childhood songs, and her 1940s and 50s 'Wee World' Edinburgh accent grows stronger as she delves further into the past. With touch – Hecht cites the very materiality of Nan's things and the way in which she has tended them and self-consciously built them as a tangible, touchable collection, designed to evoke. Descriptions of tastes and smells pepper Nan's stories of being an evacuee – receiving lovingly wrapped parcels from her mother, with an apple each for her and her brother, yielding a wonderful scent when opened.

Perhaps the most powerful and remarkable aspects of this sensory journey though are the elements that Hecht discusses under the theme of 'sight', although I do not think sight as a single sense does justice to the multi-sensory in/tangible nature of what is described. Nan is 'forever searching for, as well as creating, visual representations of her geographical roots' (Hecht, 2001: 131). Not only does she look for historical photos, maps and illustrations of the places she has lived, but she has made her own detailed aerial view sketch maps of the layout of 'Wee World' Abbeyhill area as it was when she was a child living there, as well as the internal layout of her home at that time. These are wonderfully illustrated and highly intricate. And there is another series of sketches of internal views of key rooms, in her various homes, which are fascinating not only for their period precision and detail, but also for their use of light and shadow, including one drawing which has the sun streaming in through the kitchen window in her first adult home (reproduced in Hecht, 2001: 132–5). What is so interesting here is that she is able to conjure a world, a family and relationships, a home, a neighbourhood, things, qualities of light and shade, atmospherics – all now lost or past – that she can journey through and narrate, complete with sensory animation, illustration and maps. As Hecht suggests:

> The fusion of emotions and senses that accompany and support Nan's story enables her to recapture and convey the sense and essence of her experience, making her memories more tangible for both her audience and herself. (Hecht, 2001: 130)

Karin Widerberg's atmospheric memories of 'the homes of others'

Widerberg uses memory work techniques to explore what she calls 'the doings of gender, class and ethnicity' in her childhood memories of being in the homes of her friends in Sweden. She explains that:

> I was struck by how it all came back to me, things I thought I had long forgotten. And how . . . I could recall details of furnishings and even smells. By knocking on the door or ringing the bell, I positioned myself on the doorstep ready to be let in. (Widerberg, 2010: 1181–2)

Widerberg's method is to think and remember herself into the homes and atmospheres by writing 'experience stories'. She starts at the front door, and writes her stories in the third person, which she argues enables her to take the stance of an observer and to inspect the detail of her interactions and experiences. She argues that the perspective of a child (albeit through the extra lens of adulthood) is particularly enlightening because:

> Children come and go in the homes of neighbours, friends and rela-
> tives. There they will encounter grown-ups positioning them as children
> and not as grown-ups. As such, a child can be ignored, enjoyed or be
> a disturbance. For adults, a child is valued differently to how adults are
> valued. But children are, of course, also valued differently due to their
> gender, class and ethnicity. The power to define this situation rests with
> the adults and the child visiting the home is at their mercy. So as not to
> put a foot wrong and be thrown out, the child has to discover 'the house
> rules' accordingly. (Widerberg, 2010: 1184)

Such childhood experiences are therefore likely to be etched almost
tangibly into memory. Indeed, Widerberg's stories are full of sensory,
material and atmospheric memories, which tell us in very animated
ways about relationships, and the 'doings of gender and class', rather
than just the sterile or abstract categories of these things. Here is an
extract from her story of the home of a friend, Iréne, whose family
lived over the road in Widerberg's own middle class suburb and who
were clearly aspiring to the same secure middle class status, but who
were mocked for putting on airs and trying to be posh:

> The kitchen bench is made of marble with only one sink. In the corner is
> a gas stove. A small table with three chairs is situated along the empty
> wall, from which a door leads into the hall where Iréne [friend] sleeps
> in a bed that can be unfolded from the wall. A drape separates the hall
> from the living room were Folke [friend's father] lies sleeping on a couch
> beneath which there is a bed to be pulled out for Mrs Löfberg to sleep in.
> The living room also functions as the parents' bedroom and is furnished
> with heavy furniture comprising three big armchairs, a round table and a
> huge desk in the corner. . . . In the bathroom they [Iréne and Karin] have
> fake brown dog poo and both of them start to giggle when K takes it
> out and puts it on the floor of the hall. They hear Folke turn over, on the
> other side of the drape, which makes them giggle even more. . . . Mrs
> Löfberg comes out and tries to hush them. She is not angry with them,
> however, and goes to Folke instead, and they can hear her talking to him
> in a low voice. The drape is drawn back and Iréne and K are allowed to
> enter the living room. The room smells stale and of farts. Folke is red in
> the face, but looks content, lying big and fat in his trousers and shirt and
> braces with a paper next to him. (Widerberg, 2010: 1185–6)

Widerberg knows that she was influenced when she visited her friend's
home by the views of others, especially her mother, and the knowledge that this family were ridiculed for their attempts to emulate the
ways of middle class people. She says that she was accompanied in
her visits by these perspectives. She also acknowledges that her sub-

sequent life experience, including becoming a feminist and a sociology professor, is part of how she filters and remembers her past. Both of those ideas would not be unfamiliar to those who wish to study oral histories, but I think what is interesting is that she also makes a convincing case for the idea that her memory work method enables her somehow to *encounter* – not just remember – her friends' homes in an animated and what I would think of as an ecological way, full of their sensory, material and atmospheric presence.

What does all this say about what goes into experience of place and memories of places? What does it imply about what place is, and what affinities with place are? What it shows is, I think, that we need to focus on the *encountering* of ecologies if we are to start to understand the potencies of connection with places. There is more going on in ecologies than 'just' the emergent qualities of a physical or even temporal place, or of atmospheres; and at the same time encountering involves more than the corporeal or bodily reception of these things. Encountering ecologies involves a place-time-relationality-ecology-worlding that is full of sensations but also of the extra-sensory and the atmospheric. There is an emanation, a circulation in all of this and the atmospherics are a *socio*-atmospherics, because they entwine 'the social' and 'the cultural' (whatever we might understand those to be) into the ecological.

3. Animate technologies, vehicles and journeys

Phone feelings

Almost everyone has a mobile phone these days. Although there are still inequalities in access to mobile phones by age, gender, and level of personal, household or national income, such devices have nonetheless become almost ubiquitous. Not only that, but people take them almost everywhere, leading to 'first world' concerns about hygiene and harmful radiation (Leedham, 2013). We tend to expect people who we encounter to be carrying a phone somewhere about their person. We look at and touch our phones a lot, and we stroke them and tap them, possibly we love them.

Like other people, I usually have my phone with me, or very close by, but I do not think I love it and, actually, there is a lot that annoys me about it. The predictive text sometimes really grates on me, so at odds is it with what I might want to say. I resent the near constant pressure from Facebook, Twitter or email hosts, to commandeer my phone as an aperture for their repeated, wheedling and inveigling inanity and marketing assaults. I resent the grinding drudge of email, at any and all times of day and night, when I have only left my phone switched on because I've set the alarm. I feel invaded by surveillance when any app I open wants to know my location, and I am not so naïve as to believe, in this post Snowden era, that 'they' do not still know my whereabouts even when I've declined the option to 'allow' my location. The look and feel of the phone in my hand is OK, but does not move me or particularly interest me. Yet I keep it warm in my pocket, and indeed prefer to wear clothes with pockets to accommodate it. I touch and stroke it, I gaze into it, I speak and sometimes laugh or curse (in)to it, I wipe and clean it, I have mundane, trivial, affirming, affectionate, curt, businesslike, and sometimes intensively significant encounters through it. I nurture it. There can be no question but that this phone is an intimate of mine, and in fact I think I spend more time in its company than anyone or anything else's.

Of course my phone puts me in touch with those who I want to be in touch with, or who want to be in touch with me, and that is crucial, but it would be wrong for me to assume that is all there is to it. Certainly it offers a way of having minor, quick-fire or regular interactions which have a certain unique quality, avoiding the stilted formality of 'special occasion' talk, and allowing the saying of things that are not always possible to say when physically together with others. It is interesting that the interactions, despite their quick-fire brevity, can ironically be more potent, more emotional, more funny, more incisive, more cruel, more eloquent. In text exchanges, there is something powerful and arresting about the look of the text on screen – the almost animate nature of the words and symbols. I have saved some texts that have a special significance. And of course phones are fundamentally about and enabling of time and the times, and they are also about places and spaces. They enable modes of location in 'real' time and space of ourselves and others, and they create and mediate our sense of and our engagement with place, cartography, proximity, distance, other lives, things and the temporal rhythms of living, on a routine and everyday basis.

Jane Vincent has written interestingly about phone love (Vincent, 2006: 39–44). In a study of people's relationships with their phones in the UK and Germany, she found striking evidence that people were highly emotionally attached to their phones. People depended on their phones – sometimes in ways they themselves felt excessive – for reassurance about and 'constant connectivity' with loved ones (Vincent, 2006: 41). They saw their phone as a way of feeling permanently 'tethered' (not necessarily positively) to intimates, and unwelcome unknown callers too. We know of course that phones and social media can be conduits for stalking after all. But also phones could give rise to quite potent emotions, such as panic when someone is separated from their phone, or fear that it might be lost, or the thrill of receiving an intimate text in public (Vincent, 2006: 40). In explaining how phones facilitate relationships and connections, Vincent talks of what she calls the 'buddy space', created between people when using phones, as a crucial part of their attachment to their phones. Interestingly though, this is not simply a 'live' space that is established only when a call or a text is in progress. It is more to do both with the relational 'affordances' of the phone, and the fact that this is not just *some generic phone*, but it is *my phone*. Vincent explains:

> Each time the use of the mobile is initiated it invokes the absent presence of the other buddies who can be accessed via the device, whether or not they are actively engaged in mutual communications at that time . . . the device 'holds' the memories, the sentiments that are associated with the text messages and numbers stored on the phone, the appointments, the ringtones chosen and the pictures. . . . However . . . people's attachment to their mobile phone is not the result of a solitary pre-occupation with the device but rather it is relationships with others that provide the stimuli for people's attachment to their mobile phone. (Vincent, 2006: 41–2)

In identifying these very personal relational affordances, Vincent's argument is more complex than the familiar one that people love the connections the phone enables, and not the phone as an object. She shows that the phone itself, its sensations and materialities, and the relationships and the characters in the buddy space are all implicated in each other. She argues, for example, that,

> We interact with a mobile phone in a way that we do not with other computational devices – we fondle it, we clutch it in times of crisis ready to turn to it and dial for help or solace, and we know that our loved ones are doing the same, probably at the same time. (Vincent, 2006: 42)

Vincent explores the senses of touch, hearing and sight, and shows that they are intrinsic in people's relationship with the phone itself, for example holding and fondling, personalising ring tones, looking at messages and images. She argues that the strength of emotional attachment to phones 'is in part due to the senses being pierced by all that the device engenders' (Vincent, 2006: 44). 'All that the device engenders' is a way of saying the device's affordances, but also I think it can imply more than that. If we are to understand phone love we have to have a sense of what a phone *is*, and I think Vincent's study opens up our thinking about that, beyond the unhelpful polarisation of either a material object or a set of relations. Vincent does not go on to theorise what is involved, but I like her attention to personal phone love in a field where other theorisations are more concerned with societal, human and existential transformations, or the relationships between the abstract concepts of the social and the technical, that are associated with digital communications (for example, Fortunati, 2002; Kinsley, 2014; Madianou and Miller, 2012; Scott, 2015).

The threaded worlds of train travel

There is a longstanding connection between walking and philosophical thinking and writing. The new generation of walking writers like Robert Macfarlane, and their predecessors like Nan Shepherd, as well as academics, writers and philosophers including Woolf (1985), Ingold and Vergunst (2008) and Tallis (2013), all associate walking (especially country and hill walking, but also suburban and metropolitan strolling in the case of Woolf and Tallis) with philosophical thought. For all these writers, immersion in the environment at a walker's pace, and taking time, is a key part of their philosophical and ecological thinking, helping them reflect on the meaning of being human. Walking brings them to the place they need to be, literally, metaphorically and metaphysically, to write about life as an ecological set of connections.

For me, travelling on a train can do something similar, although I do not claim the same quality of philosophical thought. Unlike the connection between walking, thinking and writing (where I have to think while walking and then spill my thoughts quickly and retrospectively into text when I get home or to the office), train journeys are times when I find myself actually writing, not just thinking about it. Often I will be physically scribbling, usually by hand, sometimes on my laptop, whilst on the train to and from work or going to a meeting. Sometimes in these circumstances I have experienced an urgent flow in the writing that can sometimes elude me in the more comfortable and conducive surroundings of my study at home or work.

What is it about the place, the train, or the journeying, or the atmosphere, that makes this happen? Would I say I have an affinity with train travel? This would not be predictable from the facts: I am no train enthusiast, and my train journey to work for example is short (just thirty-five minutes) and fairly squashed and uncomfortable. So this is not about time for reflection, nor is it to do with having lots of space around me, or peace and tranquillity. The train is never quiet. There is a hubbub of noise from other passengers. Laughter and conversation, tinny sounds and pulses escaping from earphones, coughing, sneezing, nose blowing, and there are announcements about which station we are just arriving at or have just left, or apologies for our delay. The train itself makes noises – loud rattling, vibrating, banging, sliding, whooshing, electrical buzzing noises, the loud din of the diesel engine, accelerating and decelerating, the bumping heft of the train on the rails. The seats are quite cramped and I never choose a table seat, preferring the more hermetic privacy of the 'airline' style window seat where I can create my own tiny cramped space, albeit with my knees pressed against the back of the seat in front. The train is usually uncomfortably hot, especially in winter when the heating is in overdrive, and there is not enough space for anyone to take their coat off. But unpredictably it can be too cold. When it is wet outside the train and its passengers generate an internal fug that doesn't smell too good (especially where the carriage contains a phantom farter), and is a combination of bodily and train outputs that steams up the windows and feels full of germs. We all sit in damp coats and shoes. I wish we could open the windows, but I know other people would say it is too cold, too draughty. And yet despite or perhaps because of all this, there is something about the constellation that train travel produces for me, of surroundings, places, journeying, and a certain sensory sensibility, that enables me to think and write. Here is an account written in the real time of a journey:

> I am writing by hand and I am scribbling, fast, and drawing lines and connections on my notebook.
>
> There is an amiable anonymous hubbub in the train which is full of sounds, smells, looks, feel. I am too hot, I am squashed in, it is difficult to balance my notebook on my lap, the sun is coming up behind trees and buildings and is flashing a staccato of bright/dark through the grimy window into my eyes and onto the page. It doesn't annoy me though – actually I'm pleased the sun is out, and I don't mind feeling too hot when it is sunny. I am in my own world and space, here amongst the anonymous amiability of fellow travellers, all heading in the same direction although off to different places and things, all moving together forwards for now I am conscious of all this as I write. It is in me; I am in it. I am part of an atmosphere.
>
> We are travelling, moving. I am in thrall to the movement, the going, the journeying. I am not moving my limbs or body very much, but we

are moving, quite fast for this little old train. What engages me is that we are covering ground, moving through territory, scenes and places which we are momentarily part of. We are a place journeying through places.

I am repeatedly looking up, looking out of the window, looking back down, and writing, always also fully conscious of the atmospheric 'we' of the train. In the moments of thought between actually writing, when I am composing, or reflecting, or just waiting, I look up and out of the window. I *stare* out of the window. This must look like an unseeing kind of stare, a thinking-about-something-else and not registering what is there kind of stare. Except I do see. This is both an absent and a penetrating stare, and I do register what is there as well as what is here; I am *taking in my surroundings*. I am *really* looking, and yet sort of not looking. And when I look I am connected with hundreds of separate tableaux, each a look long, framed by my window, drawn into the 'we' of the train as it hurtles along.

Shapes, colours
Textures
Movements, flashing and whizzing
Light, streaming, shafts
Reflection, the inside – 'the we' – superimposed on the outside
Clouds, sky, vapour trails, glittering little planes
Shadows, flickering, crazily switching from light to dark
as we rattle through
Fields, mud, grass, hedges, marshes
Fences, railings, razor wire
Gates, trees
Vegetation, urban and rural
Sheep, horses, a donkey, birds
Someone loudly arranging a meeting on their phone
Water, rivers, canal, lakes, ponds, puddles
Chimneys, poles, rubble
Houses, suburban and city, windows, gardens, back alleys
Worlds I imagine are there
Cars, a jeep, bikes, lorries, trains
Roads, more roads
traffic lights, roundabouts, junctions
pavements, level crossing, lone figures
station, platform
knots of people
clothes, bags, headscarves, paper cups of coffee
artless graffiti
industrial buildings, office blocks
church, mosque
rubbish, bridges

people get on, crowded train, hubbub changes
hum of Asian Yorkshire voices, accents
Grey stone, red brick, concrete
a dog with its walker in an urban field stops to look at the train
I am envious of that simplicity
Neat housing estates, messy estates, allotments
a jogger
Walls no longer joined to anything, just standing there
Leaning and crumbling
Geese, more horses, canal locks, a mule
A sharp laugh
Agri-buildings, rubbish tip
Moss, lichen, whitebloom, detritus
Insides of railway bridges, dark, dangerous, murky
Thrumming hubbub, warmth
Industrial pallets, planks, storage yards, things I don't know what they
are
Guttural coughing
Leaves, big puddles, floods on roads, sodden fields
Radio masts, railway sidings, urban wilds
Crackling and muffled announcement, no-one can make it out
Cables in giant reels
Silage bags
Petrol station, pylons, overhead cables
Trams, buses, no smoke (how different from the past)
CCTV, brake lights, perfume
Glass towers, distant high rise flats, destination approaching
Corrugated roofs, advertising hoardings, torn billboards
I know where I am, I've been looking
Car parks, waste land, empty playground, things boarded up
Workmen in orange

I am *looking*. I am looking so much I can't record it quickly enough. The
world is flashing by and the world is passing through what is flashing
by. The world is being threaded through the world, at speed. Through
places I am not *of* – I don't belong to these places – except I am and I
do, because I am on the train, participating in this threaded tableau of
world passing through world. I look out of the window with an absent
penetrating stare that connects the hundreds of tableaux, through the
frame of my window and its reflection, with the atmospheric 'we' of this
train, and the flow of my ideas on the page.

Mimi Sheller's 'automotive emotions' and 'feeling the car'

Mimi Sheller's study of what she aptly calls 'feeling the car' in her
article 'Automotive Emotions' is a beautifully drawn insight into the

nature and potencies of people's feelings about cars, and especially about driving. As she says in the opening paragraph, 'Cars are above all machines that move people, but they do so in many senses of the word. . . . Movement and being moved together produce the feelings of being in the car, for the car and with the car' (Sheller, 2004: 221–2). She argues strongly that people's relationship with cars is never a purely pragmatic or rational-actor one, and that to understand the complexity and intensity of it we need to focus on 'the lived experience of dwelling with cars in all of its complexity, ambiguity and contradiction' (Sheller, 2004: 222). She explores aesthetic, kinaesthetic, emotional and sensory responses to and interactions with cars and driving.

It is widely held that cars are linked to identity – the stereotype goes that they are extensions of fantasy identity – and that choosing and driving certain types of car can help to cultivate or promote a certain image. Kent has argued that private car use creates 'ontological security' (Kent, 2016). Culturally speaking, cars are fetishised, romanticised and sexualised, and known to be the object of fantasies about power, personhood and sometimes (so the jokes would have it) male sexual anatomy. In that sense, we do identity work in our relationships with cars, and the corporate interests of car advertising, and key strands in popular culture, reinforce certain sets of associations. But what is interesting about Sheller's approach is that she moves beyond this somewhat limited view that we use cars to try to express ourselves as individuals, or that we feel emotions about cars, 'to show how emotion itself arises out of particular material relations and sensations, and at the same time organizes material relations and sensation into wider aesthetic and kinaesthetic cultures' (Sheller, 2004: 223).

She develops a sensory-kinaesthetic analysis of what it feels like to be in a car:

> Motion and emotion, we could say, are kinaesthetically intertwined and produced together through a conjunction of bodies, technologies and cultural practices (that are always historically and geographically located). . . . Human bodies physically respond to the thrum of an engine, the gentle glide through a gearbox, or the whoosh of effortless acceleration, and in some cases the driver becomes 'one' with the car. (Sheller, 2004: 227–8)

Sheller considers how the way people feel the car in these kinaesthetic and sensory ways is connected to gendered and classed practices and inequalities, as well as historic and national car cultures. So, for example, cars can give a feeling of liberation and can allow a wide range of forms of sociability to those who have the privilege of driving them. She points out that this can be especially significant for young people and for women who can achieve more self-determining forms of sociability and agency with than without a car. Cars can give a feeling of protection, especially of family and loved ones, with the use of child car seats, and safety features, and can enable people practically to care for others and drive them around. Again, what I think is good is that this is more than saying that cars are useful, because of how she ties her argument in with the kinaesthetic of feeling the car:

> The 'family car' is closely integrated into daily or weekly routines and comes to support feelings associated with taking care of loved ones, as well as the sense of liberation afforded to women. . . . When cars become not only devices for escaping families, but also members of families, repositories for treasured offspring and devices for demonstrating love, practising care and performing gender, they bring into being non-conscious forms of cognition and embodied dispositions which link human and machine in a deeply emotive bond. (Sheller, 2004: 231–3)

She follows Thrift in her use of 'non-cognitive thought . . . as a set of embodied dispositions ("instincts" if you like) which have been biologically wired in or culturally sedimented (the exact difference between the two being a fascinating question in itself)' (Thrift, 2001: 36). Thrift in fact develops those ideas further to focus on the role of automobile software and ergonomics in producing 'new forms of "humanization"' in the 'cognitive fit between people and things' (Thrift, 2004: 50), to argue that the sophistication in how such scientific knowledges are now applied to urban environments – for example 'intelligent vehicles' driving on 'intelligent streets' (Thrift, 2004: 50) – produces:

> a studied extension of the spatial practices of the human which consists of the production of quite new material surfaces which are *akin to life*, not objects, and thereby new means of *bodying forth*: new forms of material intelligence producing a new, more fluid transubstantiation. (Thrift, 2004: 49, my emphasis)

This sense of 'hybridization' in 'humanization', and driving as a kind of 'bodying forth', raise important and difficult ecological questions about hitherto sureties in the boundaries between humans, things and environments. I like the sense of 'bodying forth' – like 'worlding' – and think it is suggestive of the kinds of places we might look for the filaments of affinity.

Citing studies by Bull, Gilroy and Pearce, Sheller draws attention to soundscapes. In-car music, for example, 'can heighten the emotional climate within the car interior, or it can be projected into the "dead public space" of the surrounding streetscape' (Gilroy, 2001: 97; Bull, 2001; Pearce, 2000). There are cross-cultural differences in music in cars, and musical contexts, and also there is the importance of music – for example on motorways – in reviving personal memories and feelings.

Lynne Pearce's 'autopia' of driving and thinking

Lynne Pearce's chapter 'What We're Thinking When We're Driving' is based on analysis of her own accounts of eight 'driving events' when she was driving alone (or with her dog) between Scotland and northern England, for various different reasons and durations. It is an introspective piece, designed to 'dive deep into the states of consciousness that attend each driving-event' rather than, or so she says, paying much attention to the environments that she encountered on her journeys (Pearce, 2013: 103).

And yet her accounts are actually full of a sense of place, movement, environment, things, technologies and atmospherics. She refers often to what she sees, encounters and passes through, sometimes fast, sometimes slow: for example, particular and named places, landscapes, mountains, lochs, islands, roads, as well as aspects of scenery, environment, weather and colour like hedgerows, 'waving bracken', 'weeping birch', 'moorland greyness', flowers, grasses 'long and waving', water, rain, fog, sunshine, 'snow-filled, northern gullies', cool temperatures, car headlights, road signs, speed restrictions, shops, garages, 'civilisation', 'desolation' (Pearce, 2013: 93–7). And then there are aspects of the car itself, its internal environment, as well as her control of it and kinaesthetic engagement in the act of driving, and how these things make her feel. She cites involvement in music or its absence, anxiety when a troublesome oil warning light comes on, the challenges and excitement of driving in different conditions:

Once again, water is throwing itself off the mountains in big waterfalls and I am gripping the steering wheel tightly as I accelerate past lorries, blinded by spray, and am minded not to brake for fear of skidding. (Pearce, 2013: 96)

Once I'm through the village and heading up the other side of the loch . . . the traffic behind me starts to pick up . . . I speed up accordingly and quite enjoy it: accelerating out of the bends, holding firm to the road. (Pearce, 2013: 94)

Overall, her accounts are very atmospheric, but what she is most interested to examine are the different moods, affects and modes of thought that she engages in while she is driving. She identifies what for her were four powerful and recurring 'horizons of consciousness' on her journeys – nostalgia, disappointment, anxiety and anticipation. She describes how these were sometimes prompted by what she was perceiving in the moment of driving, or sometimes were more oblivious to her surroundings albeit shaped by them in some way, but were also inflected with memories (sometimes highly sensory ones) of the past and anticipation of possible futures. Importantly, she highlights these elements in different combinations, and shows how they are brought on by the experience of these particular drives. For example, she says 'the past lurks around every corner' and 'I am wired for signs of change' (Pearce, 2013: 98) when on a drive where she is unexpectedly diverted due to a road closure through an area where she had dwelled some twenty years before, and which she has conjured in her imagination often since. She is essentially ready for, receptive to, and bombarded by, nostalgia, as she drives through the visual and atmospheric cues and memories.

She hints at the agentic possibilities that are thrown up by certain drives:

it is . . . sometimes, possible to commandeer the fast-changing perceptual present of the drive as a welcome distraction. . . . By giving myself up to the comforting familiarity of a drive made – along the same route, past the same landmarks – in happier times, I am able to temporarily evade a more deeply distressing scenario. (Pearce, 2013: 99)

She finds she has displaced an impending mood of 'devastating disappointment' with the 'preferable melancholy of nostalgia' as a consequence of the kinaesthetic, environmental and mnemonic combination this driving event has produced for her. And on another drive, in a surge of relief following some anxieties about the oil light in her car and a period in a hire car, she falls into a daydream about making changes to her job and working environment, and she does this at the same time as clocking, engaging with and seeing the world outside the car.

This alert intuition of my immediate, if transitory, surroundings sits comfortably alongside my daydream. I see and dream simultaneously.

> Freshly conscious of these things as serial visual prompts flash by, all things seem possible once more. (Pearce, 2013: 101)

What I really like about this small meditative piece by Pearce is the way she pulls things together in her appreciation of driving *these* driving events, to explicate what she calls the

> temporal binary of our driving-consciousness: thoughts drawn to the past and thoughts projected towards the future, with both compulsions mediated and/or prompted by the perceptual present. . . . These trajectories also feature a utopian (anticipation/nostalgia) and dystopian (anxiety, disappointment) dyad. (Pearce, 2013: 97–8)

She is drawn to a phenomenological approach in understanding these driving events, but ultimately pulls away from it, because she cannot entirely follow Husserl and Merleau-Ponty in their emphasis on 'the primacy of perception in the act of consciousness'. Instead, she wants to argue against any insistence on a presentist kind of perceptive primacy, because she sees her 'driving events' as 'a duration rather than a singular moment of intuition' bringing together 'elements of primary perception, retention, recollection and phantasy in a complex yet meaningful way' (Pearce, 2013: 102). I think they also illuminate the centrality of memory, and of provenance, in ecologies and socio-atmospherics.

4. Weathery weather in social science and literature

Most social scientists, except those who are particularly interested in the changing climate, tend to ignore weather completely, or see it as a variable which can affect other variables (Buscha, 2016; see also Doward, 2015), or as significant only because it tells us about something else, like rules of etiquette and sociability in weather conversations for example (Fox, 2014). But how can we forget weather or see it as not relevant? In my own lifetime's observations of and participation in weather, as well as in my own research project on 'Living the Weather',[6] I have observed that weather is central and crucial in people's experiences of living, and that weather conversations are evidence of people's close attentiveness to and experience of the everyday minutiae and nuances of weather – its feel, and its foibles.

Seen thus, weather conversations, amongst other things, demonstrate that people are always engaged in the process of living the weather, and are usually poised and ready to talk about that engagement. Weather is powerful and affecting, and it is always there in some shape or form, so I think if we are interested in ecologies and socio-atmospherics we should be interested in weather, for its own sake. We should not simply either ignore it or think it only tells us about something else that is thought to be more important.

And let's not forget that weather is very *weathery* in ways that differentiate it from the usual more abstract foci of social science enquiry. We do live *in* weather, as Ingold has pointed out (Ingold, 2011), which, when you come to think about it, somewhat messes up the idea that we can somehow chart and plot 'living' and 'weather' as separate activities or 'effects' that can be thought to have, or not to have, an influence on each other. My point, really, is that it is only if we take an impoverished or one-dimensional view of what weather is – a view that negates our involvement in it, or its very weatheriness – that we can then say that we are not talking about it when we are, or we can say it does not affect our moods when of course it does – because it 'affects' everything (although of course 'affects' is the wrong word). Weather is not a variable, or an effect, or a symbolic device, or a metaphor: it is the very medium of living, the atmosphere of life. As the nature writer Richard Mabey puts it, weather is 'this constant thrum in our lives' (Mabey, 2013: 17).

Creative writers and poets have taken more notice of the weatheriness of weather than have social scientists. Of course it is not difficult to find heavy handed, overblown and trite references to weather in literature. This is arguably epitomised in Edward Bulwer-Lytton's much parodied and ridiculed opening line to his 1830 novel *Paul Clifford*, 'It was a dark and stormy night; the rain fell in torrents' (Bulwer-Lytton, 2010 [1830]: 1). And yet weather can and does appear in more fascinating and subtle ways in literature and I would go even further to say I think we can learn a great deal from literary and creative writers about the nature of weather and its fundamental role in the weave of life.

Alexandra Harris has written about the connections between English literature, art and weather in her impressively researched and alluringly written *Weatherland*. Inspired by Virginia Woolf's *Orlando*, her book evokes a thousand years of weathery 'time-travel' through English culture, and shows that weather is experienced intimately and personally, and yet there are trends and fashions in our cultural engagement with it. She argues:

> as cultural preoccupations change, we find affinities with different kinds of weather. We find conditions to suit us, or from which we need to defend ourselves. *Weather gathers association* and, in a constant exchange of subject and object, our associations shape our experience of weather. (Harris, 2015: 14, my emphasis)

I love that idea that 'weather gathers association' and I think Harris – through her own observations on and analysis of literature – has got hold of something important here. 'English literature begins in the cold', she argues (Harris, 2015: 26), as she documents the frozen frostiness that characterises Anglo Saxon art and literature. But then things change, and, 'turning the pages from the Anglo Saxon elegies to the lyrics of the thirteenth and fourteenth centuries, the air beings to feel milder. Doors are thrown open; the poet is outside and it is spring. He [*sic*] sees the blossom and he hears the birds' (Harris, 2015: 51). As she time-travels forward she discovers 'it is hard to find a description of a rainy night in the early 1700s, but by the end of the eighteenth century the Romantics will take a storm, or even just a shower, as fit subject for their most probing meditations' (Harris, 2015: 15).

Harris writes particularly powerfully about rain in literature and art – unsurprisingly perhaps, given the preponderance of rain in the English climate. She argues that 'for centuries English literature has courted the rain' (Harris, 2014), and explores the connections between rain on the pages, and rainy times as the contexts for the production of great literary works. She talks about Dickens's *Bleak House*, for example:

> the novel Dickens began in the dark November of 1851 and finished the following year, during three months of near-continuous rain. The heavy drops fall ('drip drip, drip, upon the broad flagged pavement') when we first meet Lady Dedlock looking out blankly over a leaden landscape. 'The waters are out in Lincolnshire', and it rains for the first twelve chapters before pausing and raining again. . . . Even when rain stops, it is remembered in the rampant growth of the summer garden at Chesney Wold, mockingly profuse, with peaches basking by the hundred above heaps of marrows. (Harris, 2015: 294)

In Harris's time-travelling analysis, literature grows out of weather, just like Dickens's peaches and marrows; weather is in the weave both of literature and the socio-cultural world – as the watermark in the pages perhaps. And weather is deeply ingrained in and is part of the atmospherics – or what I want to call the socio-atmospherics – of the times.

It is interesting, once one is attuned to it, to notice and be mindful of weather not only in the classics and 'high' literature, but in contemporary novels. The sensibilities of perception of creative writers who have something to say about the world and the experience of living are often, it seems to me, much more acutely attuned to the constitutive nature of weather in everyday lives than are those of many social scientists. Take, for example, this excerpt from a recent novel by the English writer Rachel Cusk:

> He didn't mind the heat, he said – in fact he was enjoying it. He felt like years of damp were drying out. His only regret was that it had taken him till the age of forty-one to get here, because it seemed like a really fascinating place. It was a shame the wife and kids couldn't see it too, but he was determined not to ruin it by feeling guilty. The wife had had a weekend with her girlfriends in Paris just now, leaving him to take care of the kids alone; there was no reason he shouldn't feel he'd earned it. And to be perfectly honest, the kids slowed you down; first thing this morning he'd walked up to the Acropolis, before the heat got too intense, and he couldn't have done that with them in tow, could he? And even if he had, he'd have spent the whole time worrying about sunburn and dehydration, and though he might have seen the Parthenon sitting like a gold and white crumbling crown on the hilltop with the fierce pagan blue of the sky behind, he wouldn't have felt it, as he was able to feel it this morning, airing the shaded crevices of his being. Walking up there, for some reason he'd remembered how, in the bedroom of his childhood, the sheets always smelled of mould. If you opened a cupboard in his parents' house, as often as not there'd be water running down the back of it. When he left Tralee for Dublin, he found that all his books were stuck to the shelves when he tried to take them down. (Cusk, 2014: 32–3)

Here I would argue that weather is not 'just' a device or a backdrop, and neither is it 'only' atmosphere. It certainly absolutely *is* atmosphere (and in the process it hints at why atmosphere is so important and elemental), and it *is* also characters, places, times, events, memories, feelings, emotions and sensations, gender, age, power. Although it is, in a sense, oblique, this does not mean it is merely symbolic or metaphorical. Weather is itself, and it is in the weave of everything else.

5. Writing weather stories

Because weather is so regularly reified as an external meteorological thing, and because we have so many words to describe it – sunny, rainy, windy, scorching, drizzly and so on (although it was not always thus – see Harris, 2015), it can be difficult to articulate the ways it infiltrates us, its sensations and atmospherics, and how we are a part of it or live it. I think this is so even though we intimately know the sensations of weather, and how we interact with and are part of it; it is just that these sensations, which are foremost in our encounters with weather, remain implicit in our talk, as it is easier to use weather labels and shorthands than to pinpoint the connective energies between us and weather. In an attempt to encourage people to articulate these everyday connective energies and sensations, and as part of my 'Living the Weather' project, I ran workshops in which I invited participants to write a short 'experience story', similar to Widerberg's autobiographical experience stories about the homes of others (Widerberg, 2010). I asked the participants to write autobiographically about an encounter with weather, but without using obvious weather words like 'sun' or 'rain'. The stories were written quickly and relatively spontaneously, and they are full of the sensory-kinaesthetics of the experience of weather. Here is a selection:

*

Cold, always cold. Cold to the bone. Something I had never before experienced, even in minus 40 degrees C! Cold that I was not able to escape from; cold outside, cold inside, cold in bed, cold while watching TV. Always cold. The all-pervading damp made it worse. The curtains (thick, heavy, English curtains, a futile attempt to make up for the lack of double, triple or quadruple glazing) felt like how I imagine touching mould would feel: matt, leaving what felt like a residue on my fingers. My clothes were always wet.

*

The revolving door is revolving faster than usual. Leaves in the lobby, hair in our faces, the shine wet jeans have to them, the clattering sound on the top of the roof making us all stop and one by one stand up and move to the windows. Emily's umbrella still pitched, drying next to my chair like a satellite dish. Seasonal clothing, people wearing walking boots (not just the people who always wear walking boots), scowling their faces, holding the front edge of their hoods, leaning forward like the stick figures in Lowry paintings.

*

Will this be the night when Daisy [the puppy] will willingly go outside or are we going to have a battle? The alarm goes off at 2 o'clock and I listen out for the tell-tale signs – what can I hear outside? Silence? Objects swaying and rolling around in the yard? Noise against the windows and roof tiles? I go downstairs and wake her up and head for the door, grabbing my coat for all eventualities. I open the door, we head out. Oh, it's going to be a battle tonight. She cowers against the door, shivers, trembles, climbs onto my feet, scrambles to get back inside. I give up.

*

My skin was wet. My hair was wet. Everything and everyone in those bloody mountains was wet. As I remember it, seven days ago. Big drops were hitting in my face and hands. Small drops, like little spies, were infiltrating my waterproof boots, rucksack and jacket.

*

These stories are surprisingly atmospheric and full of sensation, given their brevity and that they were written without planning or forethought. They show how the writers felt and experienced weather as multi-sensory and kinaesthetic energies and forces (sometimes malevolent – raindrops as 'little spies'), to be battled and engaged with. In the stories, weather penetrates and permeates indoors as well as outdoors – offices and homes for example, as well as clothing, bodies and the spirits of living things. We see in these stories that weather can mark, animate and transcend experiential boundaries between inside and outside and that weather is in the weave of people's sense of belonging and in relationships. The stories show that weather is in emotion, affect, hopes, fears, longings, imaginings, characters, interactions and the everyday – and I think also they show that these things are part of what weather is. Unsurprisingly, therefore, weather can make a good story, and is part of how people experience and can convey the socio-atmospherics of 'the times' or of eras in their lives. It can feel searing and poignant, and in memory it is highly evocative.

6. Socio-atmospherics and the time of the floods

On 26 December 2015, and during the period when I was conducting fieldwork for my 'Living the Weather' study, parts of West
Yorkshire suffered their worst floods in living memory. This was part
of major flooding that swept across the north of England, and into
Scotland, Wales and Ireland. After around six weeks of seemingly
endless rain in the Calder Valley, the last straw was heavy rainfall in
a twenty-four hour period from Christmas Day into Boxing Day. This
released torrents of new rainwater which was unable to be absorbed
by the already sodden and waterlogged farmers' fields and hillsides
or the patches of woodland, or was diverted from previously absor-
bent grousemoors via multiple irrigation channels and drains that
had previously been dug in the blanket bog to enable grouse shoot-
ing. The waters sped across the surfaces of tarmac roads, pavements
and housing estates, crashing down into the populous valleys and
already swollen rivers below. Hebden Bridge, a small and lively town
at the bottom of the hills, and marking the confluence between rivers,
canal and other waterways, suffered badly, with flood waters rising to
shoulder and head height, flooding the many small independent cafes
and shops that characterise this bohemian place, as well as homes and
businesses.

Hebden Bridge had flooded before, most recently three years previously, and some of the residents, as well as small businesses, shops
and cafes, had not long got back onto their feet with extensive drying
out and refits taking up to eighteen months, when the latest flood
descended. But this one was different: a much wider area affected
(and thus many more people, animals, buildings, roads and infrastructure, lives and livelihoods), a much greater depth of water (and
that term is a euphemism for a muddy, sludgy, viscous, grainy, lumpy,
smelly, sewage-ridden form of semi-liquid and debris), greater structural damage with some buildings partially demolished and many trees
uprooted, and for many the prospect of trying to rebuild afterwards
with no insurance compensation, because they had been uninsurable
since the previous flood.

These floods arguably represented an epiphanal moment in many
of the lives affected by them (and those who saw them reported in
the media), shifting perceptions of what constitutes normal weather
and conditions of life as well as places and local atmospherics. The
combination of recurrence and intensification over recent years, and
the sheer geographical scale and coverage of the floods, gave people

a very visceral and granular appreciation of what they were starting to perceive as the everyday realities of climate change, as well
as a stronger sense of some of the local, national and global politics
involved. The floods brought to the fore debates and disagreements
around the policies and failures of a national government who had not
fully funded the promised flood defence schemes or invested in climate change measures like renewable energy; local authorities whose
budgets had been decimated in times of austerity now struggling with
the massive and urgent demands and complaints of communities and
infrastructures in total upheaval; recriminations for farmers, landown-
ers and developers whose land management practices did not seem
to have flood alleviation as their priority (or even on the to-do list); as
well as the manifest evidence of differential impact on and resilience
of the rich and poor in the face of the floods.

Certainly, the floods challenged and created different affinities with
weather. But that underplays the complexities somewhat. Most significantly, the floods and their aftermath have come to define the 'times'
in the area, by creating (actually more like curating) a distinctive conglomeration of 'socio-atmospherics', involving many dimensions of
affinity.

Shock: the power and magnitude of water

On the morning of the floods many people in Hebden Bridge went
down to the edge of the waters and stood in shocked silence, bearing
witness in a kind of collective agitation on this Boxing Day holiday
morning. Water that should have been two or three metres below
bridges was crashing over the tops of them, and car and building
alarms were sounding in a mad frenzy as the town's electrics became
soaked. The town centre was a series of deep lakes, creating wide
expanses that were impassable and looked so much wider than the
familiar network of criss-crossing streets and pavements that were
submerged beneath them. Terraces of houses and shops became
islands and cliffs in this new watery landscape, their ground floor
storeys all but completely vanished. Some car rooftops were just visible above the water, slamming home to onlookers the realisation that
many more cars must be submerged entirely. The night before, as the
waters rose, people had been safely inside, eating, drinking and celebrating Christmas with relatives and friends, when the flood siren (an
old WW2 air-raid siren) went off. Not everyone heard it, and many
who did thought the flood would be smaller and more manageable
than it was. But many shopkeepers, cafe owners and residents were

already struggling with what to save and how to save it – moving things upstairs, or to higher shelves for those whose places were single storey. As it turned out, the higher shelves were not high enough. The siren, which is triggered by the river gauge, went off again in the early morning, a foreboding and confirmatory tone.

And now in the morning people stood and looked and watched and took photos on their phones, and were shocked and numb and shaking with a combination of physical dread, horror, disbelief and guilty exhilaration for the real-life drama they were living. 'How could it come so high?' Those who were trapped inside, with no communications (the phone lines were down), or power to give light or heating (electricity would not be restored for several days), had to wait in raw desperation and despair for whatever was going to come next, and to start working out what they were going to do.

Bearing witness and being in touch

For people who were there or who came to see the worst affected places that Boxing Day morning, the places and scenes hit them like a sledgehammer, assaulting all of their senses, and staying with them. There was a collective sense of bearing witness that came from physical co-presence with others at such an astounding scene, in the face of so much to look at and perceive with all one's senses. There was oddness, unfamiliarity and shock in the noises, sights, smells, feel, and the in/tangibilities of the atmosphere. There was a profound reverence in having been there and having seen it, being excited, scared and in danger together. Bearing witness involved a full-on and intensely multidimensional set of sensory experiences. These experiences would become the stuff of visceral memory and nightmare, and much storytelling in the weeks and months to come, as people recounted their experiences again and again to each other and to non-witnesses, struggling and failing to make words, metaphors, sounds, gestures and superlatives that were up to the job.

Very quickly, knowledge of the flooding became widespread in the locality and beyond. Social media, and in particular a local Facebook group which was established after the previous floods, became a way of spreading real-time news and images, with a greater speed and precision than the national or local news media could hope to muster. Some hungover teenagers, asleep until late morning, learned about the disaster in their town on their phone screens from the familiar comfort of their beds. The news media faced the difficulty of getting journalists into the area in the early days, given that most roads including major connecting routes all along the valley were impass-able. But by using social media, people who were directly caught up and involved in the events, and those who had borne witness, could share images and videos, as well as comments, requests for help, and offers of assistance, with a much wider group. Many people reported that social media were a 'lifeline' during these times. Even people who were Facebook-deniers and had never used social media before signed themselves up, and many became 'social media junkies', watching images and videos of the shocking height and scale of the floods, and checking for updates, again and again, until they were exhausted and wrung out. But people wanted to see, feel and experience it for themselves. Social media helped to connect and provide a channel for a strongly sensory-kinaesthetic involvement to a wide group of people who felt themselves to be affected by the floods. People who lived in the area but had not necessarily 'been there' to witness the flood waters on the day, watched video footage again and again – on their own or with friends and relatives – in shock and disbelief, often with tears running down their faces. The sensory intensity and power of those videos cannot be underestimated – the brown powerful water, the mud and sewage sludge, the noise of the rivers, the eerie sound of the sirens as a backdrop to the pounding rain, the before and after shots that gave shocking testimony to the height of the waters. There were thousands of photos and videos, dramatic and depressing, cir-culating almost wherever one looked. Certain images took on iconic status, especially those that showed the shocking height of the water in familiar places such as shop fronts and streets where the viewer might have done their Christmas shopping just a few days before-hand. Images and film were played again and again, discussions were had, and many requests for assistance or information and offers of help were exchanged.

But being a social media junkie for these people would be wrongly described as a shallow, thrill seeking or voyeuristic gawping at others' misfortune. For sure there is an oddly chilling and despairing thrill in the visual and aural impact of flood footage in one's own area, and of trying to discern familiar landmarks in the watery chaos. But for most of the people involved this was nothing to do with titillation and everything to do with *bearing witness* and achieving or accord-ing *recognition* – just as those who stood in silent shock in front of the floods on Boxing Day morning had done. People using social media were subjecting themselves, often repeatedly, to being physi-cally shocked and emotionally rocked through multiple sensations, in a way that produces not only a visceral and palpable reaction, but also a recognition of and a potent connection with the calamitous nature of what has occurred.

An atmosphere of 'getting on with it'

The atmosphere of incredulity, horror and fascination that was palpable on the streets that first morning, uniting those who were there, gave way later that day and on into the next to massive activity in the town as the water levels receded and the clean-up operation started to get underway. Gradually the vibe changed as people knuckled down, lots of people together, subdued, shocked and busy, working alongside each other. Soon there was what seemed like a whole populace at work, dealing with it, getting on and sorting things out first with quiet, shocked pragmatism, and subsequently with grimly cheerful determination. This was punctuated with occasional jokes and laughter. One woman had a hose and was cheerfully washing out the floors of shops, joking that 'what we need here is MORE water!!' Yet just down the road the scene was awful, with so many houses affected, and heaps of possessions, some topped with Christmas trees and toys, starting to rot in the rain and mud outside each one. It was utter devastation, with misery all around. And everywhere there was nervous distrust of the weather, and what would come next.

The rain eased off for a while, and the sun even came out, and the muddy and debris-ridden streets filled with residents, shopkeepers and cafe owners discovering the worst at their premises, along with many many helpers from the surrounding area and further afield, a scattering of journalists and some 'flood tourists' who had come to take a look. But almost everyone had wellies on and a broom to sweep with. The whole place began to feel alive with activity and determination and yet the devastation and misery were still there, lurking. One of the participants in my 'Living the Weather' project wrote this:

> The sun shone this morning. The weather warm, yellow and benign. As though it had done nothing wrong. The town looking at itself, assessing the damage. Everything covered in thick mud, and people emptying the contents of their shops, their flats, their lives, out into the streets in huge sodden piles. All ruined. The town turned out in force to help with shovels, brooms, buckets, everyone working together to tackle the mess. And the sun shone, as if to make things better. But today's sunshine felt a bit like the flowers and chocolates brought by an abusive husband in the morning to his wife who is bruised and broken from the night before. Almost a mockery.

Sometimes the early clean-up stages lacked efficiency, but things were gradually getting done, and after a day the Town Hall in Hebden Bridge opened up and became an organisational hub-cum-food-and-supplies-bank with the most tremendous buzz and atmosphere. It was bright and warm and packed with people. Free hot tasty food (mostly vegetarian, reflecting the alternative politics of many residents) and drinks were being given to all volunteers and those 'affected by the floods' (the name that was preferred over 'flood victims'). Teams of volunteers who turned up at the Town Hall were deployed to assist in clearing flood-ruined possessions in multiple locations around the town, after the insurance loss adjusters had been (they had to see all the ruined stuff before it could be disposed of). Others were sent out to knock on doors and check for elderly and vulnerable people who might still be stranded without food or power, or to deliver the seemingly endless supplies of hot food that were being donated. The usually white, mono-cultural town of Hebden Bridge was alive with volunteers of a range of ethnicities, including Muslim and Sikh groups, and even Syrian refugees. Many locals in this politically liberal community noted and were angry that some elements of the media underplayed or ignored the significant role of Muslim groups in the relief effort, presuming that reporting such acts of kindness would not fit with the tenor of the national tabloid press's more usual incendiary and Islamophobic content.

Legacies of the floods

Although everyone knew or could see that the 'valley bottoms' were flooded, the waters also carved routes (many new and unexpected) down the hillsides and into the swollen tributaries, scattering debris and causing anxiety and sometimes frenzied preventative activity, and then landslips, flood and structural damage to properties, land, roads, walls, cars and so on, on the way. With an unpredictable and capricious malevolence the waters created anomalies where some suffered badly, while others next door, or down the hill, were not flooded. Nobody in the area though, was unaffected, whether or not the waters had entered their homes.

Obviously there was a great deal of physical ruination caused by the floods. But what was perhaps less obvious although profoundly striking in the event was the way it made people think and feel differently about the emotional and physical geography of the whole area as well as about specific places. On the day of the flood it was suddenly impossible to get from one side of the valley to the other, or to move even short and routine distances. When the waters were there it was impossible and unsafe to try to move around, and many people did take enormous risks, wading and then finding themselves chest high in fast moving water. People found risk difficult to calculate, simultaneously perceiving as a spectacle and yet not comprehending as a risk the ferocity of the rivers which one of my participants commented 'had never tried to kill you before'. Some people got perilously close to the torrents so that they could take pictures on their phones. Some people found they had temporarily lost members of their group in a terrifying few minutes when they had become separated. Some people drove cars into water only to become stranded and in need of rescue, not realising how deep it was, or that even fairly shallow water can pick up a car, float it and sink it further up the road in deeper waters. And as the waters receded, they left in their wake many ways, routes, paths and roads which were blocked by landslips, debris and fallen trees, or were broken entirely. Some people reported with astonishment that familiar parts of the landscape, places and things had just 'gone'. That terminology is very telling; it evokes a vanishing, a thing never to be recovered. It is a bleakly powerful way to convey the shock of permanent loss.

But as well as physically impeding people's movement around the place in the short term, the floods re-sculpted people's mental image and assumptions about their usual ways and routes, and their 'ontological security' in the familiarity of their places more permanently. They found themselves feeling differently about the place, and some were surprised how this feeling seemed to emanate from their very 'core', and that it was manifest even when they were not going outside or trying to get anywhere. Some felt trapped and in need of planning new routes, or simply that they had to think more carefully about how to get from A to B, and to allow more time for their journey. Indeed, damage to roads, bridges, tracks and paths was extensive and many have remained closed. Many prior routes and ways that formed people's everyday geographical, mobile and temporal thinking about the place have gone, some permanently. Where roads are open, travellers are now subject to long traffic delays as vehicles are filtered through inefficient traffic lights in single file past repair works or, more likely, untended piles of rubble and broken road because each broken highway is awaiting its turn for attention in a very long queue for severely restricted public funding in times of austerity.

Many people have felt the visceral impact of loss of physical aspects of the place that were gone or where the changes wrought are so major that it seems it can never feel the same again. Some have been anxious and worried about changes they have yet to discover – damage done that was lying in wait to pounce when they are going about some innocuous activity in their daily lives. And indeed, this routine going about everyday life for almost everyone in the area has continued to be punctuated poignantly and unexpectedly by these dull and draining surprises, which are experienced as a weight (emotionally, physically, literally – as people feel the heft in their bodies and their mood), and an inexorable, always lurking loss. Like a bereavement, people are pulled up short at unexpected moments by the recognition that the dependability and familiarity of their places are suddenly gone and lost, or by the sight of shops still boarded up and sand bags in doorways. Or it hits them as they wake up in the mornings and they realise that this is how it is now: the dull misery of life going on in the face of losses that cannot be repaired, or even articulated sometimes. In some ways, this is like the weeks and months and years that follow the busy focus of a funeral of someone close. Around the time of a funeral pain is raw and acute but is also shared with others in emotionally charged activity, and in dealing with things. But afterwards is a bleaker landscape where the unwelcome losses and changes that have been wrought must now be lived with.

The emotional landscape was bleakest for those who had felt the direct impact of the floods on their homes and businesses, but there was another group who were touched by the floods. These people's premises had not been flooded, and they often felt awkward and uncomfortable with the fact that they felt so profoundly affected. There was a pervasive and insidious feeling of 'survivor guilt' – many people have continued to use that precise phrase – and that, as a survivor, one did not have the *right* to feel affected, or to feel loss, or misery, because one's suffering was so much less than the depth of losses that others had experienced. Almost everyone I encountered during these times who had not been directly flooded and even some who had, described themselves as 'lucky' – feeling themselves to be much more fortunate than others. Indeed, their remarks, and their 'flood stories', were usually prefaced by and then punctuated and concluded with that remark.

Another of the changes wrought by the floods, and possible legacies, has to do with sociabilities. Different associations, sometimes short lived but nonetheless potent, came into being in an explosive cacophony around the places and times of the floods. For example, there were those moments of bearing shared witness in physical and multi-sensory co-presence. Or there were those lines of connection, and sensory confrontations, created and followed on social media.

Or there were people – strangers, neighbours – thrown together in dealing with situations (sometimes emergencies) where they were engaging over and with stinking water, rain, wind, mud, shit, makeshift tools, cleaning products, ruined homes and personal possessions, freezing cold, pitch darkness (no electricity). But also then dealing with things in the light, warmth and steamy shelter of the Town Hall, donating, preparing and consuming food, feeling the warmth of human company, of people going through the same as you. Some people took in animals who had lost their homes, feeling a sharp closeness with an animal in need, and sometimes leading to emotional reunions between animal and owners and new contacts and associations between the humans involved. Sometimes, strangers were in danger together, or feeling the raw power of emotions of misery, relief, gratitude and beneficence in the company of others.

Some neighbours shared impromptu Boxing Day meals because relatives had been unable to get through the floods and there was a lot of surplus food and drink. Others argued with neighbours or strangers about local culpabilities, lack of cooperation, or accused others of building flood defences to look after themselves without caring about the consequences of diverted water for others. Many who were displaced from their ruined homes had to move to live in all kinds of temporary accommodation and new contexts – sometimes with friends, family, strangers, acquaintances, or in hotel rooms and other forms of temporary accommodation. People from the area had sometimes difficult conversations and encounters with 'outsiders' of various kinds, who had either seemed to come to gloat, or more often who 'didn't get it' and who could not understand the potent impact of the floods on every sphere of life for people whether they had been personally flooded or not. In these cases the floods became a carking presence; an irritation in what were hitherto more straightforward relationships.

The time of the floods had sometimes complex and ambivalent effects on people's sense of belonging to a place, its people and environment. Some of those who felt the sense of loss and bereavement had discovered, alongside it, a surprising sense of belonging they had not appreciated beforehand – a visceral feeling that this was *their* town, and the losses were *their* losses. Some of those from outlying areas, or relative newcomers to the area, who had volunteered to help by providing and cooking food, or cleaning up debris, found it gave them a sense of self-worth and usefulness, and a strong connection to the place and its people that they might have wished for before, but that had not perhaps been given the circumstances to flourish. These things could provide not only a strong feeling but also a legitimate claim to belonging. But Hebden Bridge, a town that usually commands much loyalty and affection, strained its relationship with its residents in the time of the floods as well. People found their sense of belonging to place was challenged as that place turned into such an extreme flood zone, known nationally and internationally for this photogenic disaster. Some felt betrayed, and most felt vulnerable to what would likely be worse flooding in the future. Some business owners, who had been flooded before, gave up and decided not to try to reopen. Others refitted their shops and reopened, with an uneasy combination of triumph, trepidation and resignation.

Whereas before, the hilltops and moors, with high winds and rain and colder temperatures, had been seen as the extreme and challenging environments to live in, and the valleys the more sheltered and milder alternative, the severity of these floods produced a sense of inversion, with the valley bottoms now feeling more dangerous, violent and at the mercy of the elements. And everyone – everyone – talked about the weather like never before. There was a nervousness around, with people anxiously checking the weather forecasts, the skies, and the river gauges, when it looked like rain. One man told me there was a new vocabulary on the streets, with words like 'hydrograph, grip-blocking, land management and, increasingly, climate change'. He went on to describe what he saw as a not-so-amicable divorce between people and the weather:

At times like these our relationship with the weather is bound to change; no longer, at worst, a thing to grumble about if it causes mild inconvenience, but a threatening presence as we experience its more devastating effects and anticipate those yet to come. We tend to forget easily enough if past events become even relatively distant but perhaps one of the realities of climate change will be to change perceptions of our weather climate – a necessary change in all probability but one where the long term, comfortable relationship with a largely benign companion sours and changes for good. The divorce can then go either way: a permanent dislike and mistrust or, more constructively, a new respect and acceptance of the changed reality. When the weather is changeable – miserable even – but free of inconvenience it's a lifestyle choice but when it brings suffering and danger it becomes a more solid and threatening presence. It assumes a persona and not one we like that much.

Some have started to wonder – if not to say so out loud for fear of seeming disloyal – about whether the rebuilding and reopening demonstrates a plucky Yorkshire spirit or whether it is short sighted;

whether valley towns like these are lost causes in an inexorable tide of climate change; whether defences and preventative schemes can solve the problem, or whether 'the problem' is the new normal, meaning that more radical solutions will be needed and must be faced.

These ecologies and socio-atmospherics of flooding in Hebden Bridge defined a time – or is it a place? – with its own character – the time of the floods. If we try to explore what constitutes this, we come up with a burgeoning and enigmatic effervescence which is impossible to break down and analyse. It certainly included the involvements, entanglements and sensations of the particularities of weather and weatheriness, the elements, landscapes, things, places, journeys, technologies, politics, socialities, human and non-human lives, stories, narratives and memories. But if we simply try to list all the components in the mix, we miss the haunting and potent feel of it all; we miss the socio-atmospherics.

7. Weather poetics

One part of my 'Living the Weather' project involved recruiting 'weather correspondents' – local people who wrote and talked to me about how they were living the weather during the course of a year. The accounts people gave were either through conversational interviews, or journals, blogs, emails, texts or experience stories written from time to time. The written accounts were often immediate, in-the-moment, unpolished, real-time observations, although some were more reflective pieces; but in these and the spoken accounts it was immediately noticeable that there was an 'everyday philosophising' and a kind of poetics going on. The insightful, lyrical and poetic nature of the accounts was striking, even though most participants were not trying to create poetry or beautiful pieces of creative writing. It was as though the very thing they were seeking to convey – living the weather – was lyrical and poetic in nature, and so that was how it forced itself to be expressed even in everyday conversation. These participants felt potent and charismatic connections with weather, and these were *poetic and lyrical in essence and character*. People were not simply 'being poetic' about the weather. I wanted to find a way of conveying this, so I created some poetry.[7] To do this I used my participants' words, in their original sequence, but I shaped and edited them to uncover and highlight the poetry that was inherent in them.

This required an artistic sensibility, rather than the more usual social scientific techniques of analysis. Here are some of the poems.

*

Seasonal wrongs
It was far too warm,
All the way through
really weirdly warm.
We've got hawthorn in leaf in the hedgerow,
a few days before Christmas
and the grass is actually growing,
actually starting.

Daffodils coming up
always makes me feel nice,
like light at the end of the tunnel.
But it's not been winter yet.
This is not good.
Winter may yet come
and damage all the things that are starting.
Hedgehogs are coming out
and what then when it snows and it freezes?

The trees come into leaf too early,
ash burnt by frost
creates dead wood.
Warm wet winters, fungal diseases
trees get manky.
Makes me nervous,
feels wrong.
Everyone is edgy
what is this all about?

Nature doesn't like it.
She likes it when things go right.
I'd like it to be
how an eight year old draws the seasons
that's what I want.

*

Valediction
There was more light today.
The feelings and emotions brightened the day,
clarified the autumn air,
seemed to bring more illuminance
more lux
more light into me.

It is not the same.
Different and specific emotions
filter, amplify and shift the sky
make the light loud and full.

An autumn day
just the summer side of the equinox tipping point.
We had a journey,
and goodbyes to do today.

The transitions of the season,
the transforming trees,
the warm shifting light,
all provided the setting for a day of change.

Each familiar view today;
the autumn coming to the valley,
weighted with valediction,
stored and fixed for the time away.
The times apart.

The soon-to-come partings
gave a significance to each long view,
as we crossed the high Pennine plateau,
each turn opening a new chance,
a fresh opportunity.

I felt each angle and plane of the sunny landscape
was weighted and potent.

*

Absorbing the sound
When the flood siren went off
I was meditating.
Such an odd experience, sitting there.
That apocalyptic noise
of war and terror
and registering it in a peaceful way.
Feeling every hair
on the back of my neck
and up the back of my head
just prickle up.
And then that sick feeling
'Oh, those people'.
It was quite an experience
just to sit there
and absorb this sound and what it meant.

*

Weather connecting
Weather and the environment
are the same.
The valleys shape the wind
The wind shapes the ecosystem.

People try to ignore it
But we're part of it as well.
The way our world works
is designed to ignore it.

Wearing jeans in the middle of summer,
same jeans in the depths of winter
Irrespective of the weather
or of whether they're appropriate.

People in the country
feel more connected
than people in the city.
People around here
wear big, heavy boots to the pub.
In the city, everybody's still wearing their Converse
all year round
as usual.

Here, in the country,
it hits you.
it's unavoidable.

Layering the Argument:
Ecologies and Socio-Atmospherics

The facets in this part of the book have illustrated aspects of ecologies and socio-atmospherics, by exploring affinities that can arise as sparks and charges in animate places, things, technologies, journeys, weather and, across all of these, in the socio-atmospherics of living. They show that our ecological and atmospheric attunement needs to be open in its ideas of what places, things and environments or surroundings are – in particular we need to understand their subtleties, poetics, atmospherics, liveliness and entanglements with other elements – if we are to grasp the character and potency of affinities that involve them. The affinities explored in the facets all owe their potency in some way to these ways of experiencing and knowing, and indeed to their enigmatic and sometimes charismatic sensations, rather than to more conventional assumptions about places as material territories, things and technologies as inert objects, weather as external and free floating, and people and living as divisible from these.

Here I want to layer these considerations into my overall argument by considering more closely what ecologies and socio-atmospherics are, and what they can reveal – as well as what insights an attunement to them can provide – of the nature and potency of affinities. I shall draw on some strands of contemporary theorising about ecological connections to help me do this, and I shall go on to argue that we need to move beyond the nonetheless worthy aspiration for better technical, or more thorough, or more democratic interpretations of ecologies, because these will still fail to apprehend the spark and charge, the frisson, of affinities. Instead I shall put forward an argument for an ecological and atmospheric attunement that foregrounds the socio-atmospherics, connectivities and poetics of living in the world.

Ecologies as convivialities, assemblages, happenings and animated space

The facets have shown that places, things, technologies, journeys and weather are animated, lively, multidimensional; they are more than 'themselves' as conventionally defined. There is a range of contemporary theory that might help us to conceptualise this and I am now going to consider some important strands.

One of the most influential approaches has argued that we should see the entanglements of *places, spaces, things and lives (human and non-human) as convivialities, happenings and assemblages*. This approach is influenced by developments in cultural and ecological geography, 'affect theory' and 'actor network theory', and is also echoed in polemics like David Abram's *The Spell of the Sensuous*, discussed in part 1 (Abram, 1997). Whatmore, a leading voice in the field, identifies a new enthusiasm amongst some cultural geographers for exploring what she calls 'the vital nexus between the bio (life) and the geo (earth)' (Whatmore, 2006: 600), involving a 'redirection of materialist concerns through the bodily' (Whatmore, 2006: 602). She argues that this constitutes a welcome 'return to the livingness of the world [which] shifts the register of materiality from the indifferent stuff of a world "out there", articulated through notions of "land", "nature" or "environment", to the intimate fabric of corporeality that includes and redistributes the "in here" of human being' (Whatmore, 2006: 602). When she says 'bodily', however, she does not just mean human bodily. She borrows the term 'livingness' from the writer Jeanette Winterson (Winterson, 1997: 85), and uses it to articulate the connections she sees between 'more-than-human bodies and a lively earth' (Whatmore, 2006: 603). Her focus on the more-than-human is crucial, and is defining of a theoretical (and political) turn away from the assumption that 'culture' and 'socio-material change' are solely human achievements and experiences, and to a view that a 'rich array of the senses, dispositions, capabilities and potentialities of all manner of social objects and forces [are] assembled through, and involved in, the co-fabrication of socio-material worlds' (Whatmore, 2006: 604). This approach has some analytical purchase especially onto the kinds of animations of place that some of the facets touched upon.

Hinchliffe et al. (including Whatmore) have studied 'wild life' in the city from this perspective – for example the lives of urban water voles – and they talk of 'the ferment of urban wild things' (Hinchliffe et al., 2005: 656). They argue that water voles should be understood as their complex and dynamic *activities of inhabitation and collaboration* as part of the mixed-up-ness and conviviality of urban wilds. They are articulating a 'recombinant ecology' involving 'biological communities assembled through the dense comings and goings of urban life, rather than the discrete and undisturbed relations between particular species and habitats that are the staple of conservation biology' (Hinchliffe and Whatmore, 2006: 123). Again, this focus on dynamics, ferment and inhabitation (rather than static and divisible entities that are somehow cast as in relation) suggests a useful orientation to the question of ecologies.

In particular, the picture we get from these approaches, and others with a socio-technical perspective on the urban, is one of cities as wild places and happenings, teeming with all kinds of human and more-than-human lives, bodies, topologies, materialities, energies (including water, electricity), technologies, things and so on (see also Guy and Karvonen, 2011). These may jostle or collaborate in dynamic, entangled, parallel, confrontational or non-apprehended ways, and this is what the city, or the urban, *is*. It is assemblage and happening, full of hybrids and convivialities. This unsettles the image of a city as a built material environment and set of infrastructures, designed and engineered by humans, with nature and wildlife in its green parts, or somewhere else entirely – in the country, and with social relations somehow laid on top of this. It also unsettles the idea of human existence as separate from, or ultimately in charge of, this teeming conviviality, with things and materialities as its context or at its disposal. Their point is that 'cities are inhabited with and against the grain of expert design' and that this 'involves ecologies becoming urban, and cities becoming ecological' (Hinchcliffe and Whatmore, 2006: 127–8).

I think this is a really exciting ecological approach to understanding the liveliness of the world. I really like the way these dual lenses of cultural geography and ecological politics lead them to an enlivened and multidimensional ontology of place and ecology – which has some echoes for me of Heidegger's 'worlding' (Heidegger, 1971) and Thrift's 'bodying forth' (Thrift, 2004), and stands in opposition to a static sense of inhabited place. This is a kind of ecological liveliness and mixed-up-ness in places, things and technologies that comes through strongly in the facets in this section – whether that be in animate places, or the dynamics and legacies of a flood, or worlds being threaded through worlds on the train or in the car, or the meld of things, places, dynamics, times and lives that constitute a sense of home, or that are at the heart of our love affair with our mobile phones. So I think this kind of liveliness and entanglement is very important for my arguments about ecologies as these are the very textures, energies and dynamics in which such affinities take shape.

However, despite their emphasis on happenings, and on multi-species relations, or co-minglings of humans and technologies (see Kinsley, 2014), and porosities and associations, ultimately these cultural geographers have specific interests and agendas which do not all chime with my own, and specifically which mean they do not take their analyses forward in ways that necessarily assist in understanding affinities. They are interested in cities, and the urban for example, and some are attempting to make interventions in urban and environmental politics and analysis with their concepts of 'living cities' and 'conviviality' (Hinchliffe and Whatmore, 2006); crucially, these are more-than-human concepts, and manifestos for research, activism and change. This means the arguments are brought back to cultural geography, or architecture and urban planning, where starting and end points for analysis are spaces, places and environmental politics more than they are affinities. They are not seeking to understand that charge of potent and charismatic connection that constitutes an affinity. Significantly, their approach does not automatically or easily lead to an understanding of the association that sears, or the charge or 'punctum' of an affinity. Conviviality describes a scene, or sometimes an atmosphere, or a mode of being together, but does not necessarily illuminate or explain a potent or piercing connection.

I think this is partly because these approaches tend to be – intentionally – somewhat characterless; there is not room for characters in a world of assemblages. And I do find assemblage (not a term used by all I should add), ironically, an oddly lifeless term that somewhat undermines the fascination and flashes of connection that I am trying to express with affinities. In a more-than-human and very worthy democratic concern to decentre human agency and design, what can happen is an underplaying of a sense of directional energy and force, or of traction and creative connections, and sparks of ignition. Ingold criticises what he calls the 'additive logic' of the concept of assemblage where it is used to describe a grouping, because 'what is missing from the additive logic is the tension and friction that make it possible for persons and things to cling' (Ingold, 2015: 7). Whilst I want to take on board much of what is offered by these cultural geographical approaches, I am nonetheless interested in those particular clingings, and tensions, and sparks, and their potencies.

Actually, I think the same goes for the concept of 'bodies' and 'embodiment' which is used quite extensively in these approaches – often for good reasons, but with consequences that lead us away from rather than closer to an understanding of the potencies that are affinities. Whatmore argues that an important contribution of recent cultural geography is to resituate subjectivity as outside of the supposed interiority of human identity, by bringing the idea of 'livingness' to the fore 'as a modality of connection between bodies (including human bodies) and (geo-physical) worlds' (Whatmore, 2006: 603). 'These shared embodiments of people and things', argue Hinchliffe and Whatmore, 'heighten awareness, or form a "biopolitical domain"' (Hinchliffe and Whatmore, 2006: 133). The focus on the livingness and in-betweenness of *more-than-human* bodies is very welcome, as is the expulsion of identity from its assumed home inside human heads or at the end of a process of social construction. And keeping 'bodies' in view helps to secure our attention to the fleshiness and tactility of affinities. Yet I still find the anchoring of discussion in the concept of 'bodies' to be quite limiting – especially when paired only with geo-physical worlds – not least because it leads us away from the idea that living is imbued with characters, or indeed that forces and energies that are more ethereal and in/tangible, weathery and atmospheric, are part of the mix. Hinchliffe and Whatmore argue that 'intercorporeality exceeds the consciousness of "I think" and the "said" of language' (Hinchcliffe and Whatmore, 2006: 136), and although exceeding these things is very important, I am not convinced that 'intercorporeality', on its own, is the best vehicle for doing it. Intercorporeality is ultimately somewhat reductive, characterless and unatmospheric. I think that somehow, the ideas of assemblages, and intercorporeality, along with conviviality, although pointing us to a useful ecological liveliness, nevertheless in themselves lack the charisma and charge that spark affinities, as well as an openness to other elements in the mix that do not reduce to them.

Some approaches do help to address this, however. In particular, Ash Amin has developed the idea of *animated spaces*. His approach builds on the idea of conviviality that I have already discussed, but focuses on 'a something' that happens to create a charge, a tension, a spark in the atmospherics of animated spaces, or what he calls a 'charismatic crossing' (Amin, 2015: 255). He argues thus:

> to stand in a busy city anywhere in the world is to be surrounded by so much *that might turn out to be formative*: the private mingling with the public and the commercial with the noncommercial; *the rub* of humans, technologies, buildings, infrastructures, animals, and nature; the many

human acts of preying, praying, lingering, passing through, watching, and listening; the *amplifications* of intersecting bodies, objects, matter, symbols, smells, and sounds; the *rhythms* set by callers, clocks, codes, timetables, technologies, and official and unofficial guardians of a public space; and the *asynchrony* of repetition, emergence, and novelty following from the latter *impulses* and combinations. The busy street or mall presents as a space of multiple happenings, influences from near and afar, continuous ebb and flow, more than human resonances. (Amin, 2015: 242, my emphasis)

This description is consistent with a convivialities approach, but the words I have highlighted suggest something more – tensions, charges and relationalities that might lead *to something*, or to borrow Amin's phrase *be formative in something*, and this is more conducive to the idea of affinities as potent and charged connections. This is a view of the goings on and the charge of place that fits better with my discussion in the facets of the pulsing and singing cities of Murakami and McGregor for example; these are charged spaces that can engender a sense of vital precariousness and an almost random potency in city relationships. Amin is still a cultural geographer and he thus keeps the focus firmly on the concept of animated *space* – he is especially interested in the idea of emergent or animated 'public space' as 'a force field in its own right in which the play between bodies, objects, and matter, between divergent patterns of use, occupancy, and demand, and between many time-space conjunctions *acquires agency*' (Amin, 2015: 243, my emphasis).

This is intriguing, and at the beginning of his argument for animated space, he documents a personal story of an encounter on a train, where another passenger had some kind of convulsive episode and collapsed. He describes how this punctured the atmosphere of 'ambient togetherness and individual separateness' on the train: the emergency did something to and with the space, making it animated. People turned to look, volunteers tried to resuscitate the man, train staff talked urgently on the phone. 'The public space had become an event, its atmosphere and its new body/space rituals displacing earlier ones around a shared ethic of care' (Amin, 2015: 240).

I love the almost onomatopoeic cleverness in the way Amin's argument does what it describes: he tells of the electrifying and 'beckoning' capacity of a moment in place, by using a story to inject a charge that disrupts the flow of unimaginative and traditional discourses of place. This is convincing because it sparks the reader's imagination, attunes their senses to the argument he is going to make, and gathers their empathy for it through a strong resonance and recognisability with things that the reader knows do happen in real life (indeed they may have experienced a moment in place like this). In this way he animates his argument just as he would have us animate our understandings of space. His account deals with the multi-sensory and more-than-human sway and fold of his train event, and others, and uses this to make the reader acknowledge what they know already – the often overlooked richness, enigmatic temporalities, ineffable atmospherics and dynamics of places, and their multidimensional qualities, and the way an event like this can create a 'singular space, *its charged atmosphere a beckoning,* suspending private interests, forming a public of shared concern' (Amin, 2015: 240, my emphasis). Again, I think the directional force and energy in the idea of 'a beckoning' is useful here and connects with the facets and with my arguments about affinities.

Useful too is the idea that places are not inevitably static and fixed (either territorially or temporally). As we have seen in the facets, places can be formed through happenings and the mobilities of trains and cars – the we-ness as we travel, threading place through place. Places can be 'ways' and 'wayfarings' (Ingold, 2011) as well – including journeys through paths, routes, roads and rivers. As Dalakoglou and Harvey argue, 'non-places' such as roads are just as significant as 'material-cultural formations' with 'always interesting and creative relations to be explored' (Dalakoglou and Harvey, 2012: 463). But of course in talking of animated *spaces,* Amin is bringing to bear ideas of temporality, event, interaction, happening, sensation, affect and atmospherics into the frame of what we might think of as a place. Amin's interest, as with other cultural geographers, is in the qualities, nature and entanglements of (urban) spaces themselves, and with the collective animations they make possible. With animated space he is especially interested in places that become public and eventful spaces, sometimes charismatic, in *charged moments and configurations,* political or otherwise, and with how, when and why this happens, and this is useful perhaps in understanding 'the time of the floods' discussed in one of the facets. He is less interested than I am in affinities though, and although he speculates that such events might 'linger in the unconscious' of witnesses and participants, he is more focused on how *places/spaces* can become charged as public space, and then return 'to themselves' (Amin, 2015: 252). But it is not difficult to see that out of such moments/times/spaces/places/interactions – such 'charismatic crossings', such animated ecologies – affinities can be born.

One thing that is interesting though in all of these otherwise useful approaches to understanding the ecologies and animatedness of our involvements in and with places, technologies, journeys, things, non-human lives and so on, is the almost complete absence of weather – even though Amin at least is interested in atmospheres. The facets provided some illumination of how we live the weather, how weather is ingrained in the ecologies of which we are a part, and how it is in the socio-atmospherics. And Tim Ingold's ecological anthropology argues for the importance of weather not simply as an object of perception, but 'what we perceive *in*' (Ingold, 2011: 130). But the relative absence of weather from many theorisations of situated liveliness and experiences of places and things is interesting because it tells us something about the nature of the theoretical gaze and what it edits in and out. This provides another clue as to why we need to think differently if we are to apprehend affinities; I shall return to this point.

The feel of places, things, journeys and technologies

Amin's work helps us in understanding the kinds of 'charismatic crossings' that might lend something to the analysis of affinities. But there are other approaches, again largely inspired by cultural geography, that add a dimension by helping us to focus on the *experience and feel* of places, things and surroundings, and the sensations of them. Tuan (1977), for example, argues convincingly for the importance of regular and routine sensory engagement with places in constituting our intimate knowledge of them, but equally we know from Amin's train example that spaces can have searing or charismatic presences and atmospherics, even where we do not know them well. What both of these point to though is the importance of the experience or the 'feeling' of places (just like Sheller's 'feeling the car'). Degen and Rose's work is important here. They argue that the feel of a place is central in what place is, and that it depends on multiple senses (Degen and Rose, 2012). Reacting against the assumption in urban design that the design of buildings, and the spaces in between them, pretty much determines how humans experience them, they show that sensory engagement is much more active than this rather passive-recipient model suggests. They argue that this becomes very clear if we are attentive to people's experiences of journeying (and especially walking) through towns. Their research in the UK towns of Bedford and Milton Keynes used 'walk-alongs' with locals and elicited how they experienced these places, for example:

Milton Keynes town centre was uniform, grey/ivory, hot and angular, punctuated in specific places with bird song and the smell of doughnuts and soap; one walk-along participant said being there was 'like stroking a tile'. Bedford, meanwhile, was brown, a bit tatty and smelt of hamburgers, and was more 'like brushing your hand over a brick, not smooth at all', according to another participant. (Degen and Rose, 2012: 3276)

This short extract gives an insight into the multi-sensory experience of place, and interestingly highlights the importance of the sometimes underplayed sense of touch. Walking is not only part of people's sensory engagement with cities, as they make habitual or novel, accompanied or sole, brisk or ambling journeys through them, but of course movements of pedestrians, as well as flows of traffic, and of 'lively infrastructures' (Amin, 2014), and more-than-human lives (Whatmore, 2006), constitute some of the arteries, pulses and convivialities of urban life. Experience and sensory engagement are fundamental here and we have seen this too in the facets that explored other forms of journeying – in trains and cars.

What is also important about Degen and Rose's approach, however, is that it is not preoccupied only with happenings, convivialities or even sensory experiences in the 'presentist' sense, in the way that some of the other approaches can be argued to be. Their work on the feel of cities is central here (Degen and Rose, 2012; see also Degen, 2008; Rodaway, 2011). They write very convincingly about the role of 'perceptual memory' in our encounters with cities, in two ways that are particularly relevant. First they argue that people's sensory experience and perception of cities in the present are always layered with their memories of those places in the past. This, they point out, is something that urban designers tend to remain blissfully unaware of, in their assumption that sensory experience is entirely and directly a contemporaneous consequence of what is currently there in the built environment. Second, they argue that encounters of one urban environment will stimulate sensory memories of and comparisons with others that people have known and experienced. This requires that we blend an appreciation of the perception of 'territory' and the temporal, in ways reminiscent of a study by May and Muir of older people's sense of belonging to place. May and Muir draw on Fields's notion of 'belonging from afar' or 'distanciated belonging' (Fields, 2011: 265, cited in May and Muir, 2015: 5.4) to argue that older people experience belonging to place in ways that are 'not merely territorial but also temporal'. Belonging from afar is 'a sense of greater connection to a place where they no longer live' or 'a (nostalgic) sense of belonging from afar towards a neighbourhood lost in time' (May and Muir, 2015: 5.3). As Degen and Rose suggest, citing Bergson: 'There is no perception which is not full of memories' (Bergson, 1911: 24, in Degen and Rose, 2012: 3282).

The anthropologist Henrietta L. Moore has made some important arguments about the salience of *memory and history* in the experience of places and things which are helpful here. She too suggests that a presentist and generative concept of assemblage – which she associated particularly with affect theory – somewhat deflects us from this. She draws interestingly on the work of Navaro-Yashin who researched how Turkish-Cypriots have lived with the land and possessions they took from Greek-Cypriots during the 1974 war. Moore asks, 'What is it like to live on someone else's land, to equip your house with furniture acquired on looting expeditions?' (Moore, 2011: 183). That is a compelling thought. Moore argues that Navaro-Yashin's work makes clear that the answers to such questions mean recognising that people's relationships with land and things have specific histories and in this case have resulted in a ruined landscape and appropriated things that are then lived with. Navaro-Yashin's work, argues Moore, shows that the concept of assemblage is problematic because its presentist, generative and non-agentic emphasis on 'coalescing intensities', together with a tendency in some affect theory to dismiss other arguments rather than to coexist and collaborate with them, inevitably leads it to disregard key specificities, historical and political *legacies*, projections and so on. However, 'the "assemblage" of subjects and objects that Navaro-Yashin has studied in Cyprus has been created through acts of violence, the erection of a border and the exclusion of specific persons and things . . . these ruins of human agency can be "kept, lamented, cherished" and they leave marks on the memory and on the unconscious' (Moore, 2011: 184–5, citing Navaro-Yashin, 2009: 14). Affect, argues Moore:

> is not just a series of intensities and differentiating impulses that coalesce at certain moments into singularities – people, objects, landscape – because the relations and encounters in the specific environment are taken up and spun out in discourse – symbolized, politicized and projected forward as well as back in time, impacting on the processes and experiences of subjectification. (Moore, 2011: 184–5)

Moore wants us to take on board how affect is 're-energised' in the collective efforts of human agency, memory and history, rather than being viewed entirely as an 'autonomous energy' or a presentist one (Moore, 2011: 186).

And indeed, how could we forget memory and legacies? The facets I have written about are full not only of the feel of places and things for example, but of their memories, legacies and provenances – in Pearce's autopia of driving for example, or the teenager's city. Indeed these have been crucial in the whole book, for example in the in/tangible absent presences of the no-longer living in the lives of those in which they are conjured; through the sensations of characters and sensory-kinaesthetic memories that feel like encounters; and the lurking threat of a gamete donor playing a genetic trump card; or the idea that forms a hook which, when tugged, reveals ecological layers and atmospheres of provenance; to the text messages preserved on a phone as a reminder of those times; to the many faceted legacies and narratives of the time of a flood. There is always a temporal layering going on – a 'laying down of memories' (Smart, 2007: 105), or a less tidy entanglement of capricious connections, asymmetries and coincidences in time and space, or a sedimenting of traces – in the creation of the histories and affinities that characterise our lives (see, for example, Bertauz and Thompson, 2005; Mason and Muir, 2013; Misztal, 2003; Smart, 2007).

Enigmatic ecologies and the socio-atmospherics of living

So far in the argument I have drawn on a range of approaches to consider how places, things, journeys, technologies and lives are made of more-than-human energies, forces, flows, convivialities, happenings (assemblages if you like), animations and multidimensionalities, and that the boundaries between them are porous, or are not necessarily as we had conventionally thought. This seems crucial in an ecological and atmospheric attunement of the kind that I want to suggest is vital if we are to apprehend affinities. But we need to do more than to adopt the kind of stock ecological orientation which primarily says that everything is connected to everything else and that, as long as we try hard enough and scientifically enough, we can identify and document all the components in ecologies. A preoccupation with categorising all the components would be an unhelpful distraction for two reasons; the first is that it would ironically have the effect of reifying and accentuating the *elements that are thought to be in connection*, rather than focusing on the connections themselves, and I shall come back to a discussion of this in the next section. The second is that it assumes that it is possible to produce a typology of ecological elements, and that each element is somehow *unitary and categorisable*. But we have already seen that ecologies will not be so easily contained – places, for example, are not ever 'only' places, and 'material' things are animated and lively. Where do we put 'worlding' and 'bodying forth' in such an orientation and, crucially, what about those ineffable and enigmatic but nonetheless powerful and pervasive *socio-atmospherics*?

Atmospheres and atmospherics have been very important in this book, surfacing again and again, in all the parts. Indeed atmospheres have become quite fashionable in some social scientific circles of late, and I do see this as a good thing. We are now gaining an attunement to atmospheres. We are exploring how they might be understood as relational sensations and auras of things and situations and gatherings, as infectious, as rhythms, as affective, and more recently as weathery (see, for example, Anderson, 2009; Böhme, 1993; Brennan, 2004; Ingold, 2015; Mason, 2015). And crucially we are recognising that atmospheres are powerful and that they matter.

But with the concept of 'socio-atmospherics' that I have introduced in this part of the book, I want to push further than the idea of 'atmospheres' for several reasons. First I think the concept of atmosphere risks being downplayed as an embellishment or a quality or 'merely' a sense of other things (by implication, the main things); second I prefer the term atmos*pherics,* to appreciate the liveliness and relationality of the ecological (in the radical sense of the term) energies, effervescence and 'goings on' that are simultaneously tangible and intangible; and third I want to introduce the 'socio' to make it clear that socio-atmospherics are not somehow divisible from forces that we might think of as to do with 'the social' or 'the cultural' or indeed 'the historical'. Of course at the same time they are experienced in sometimes searingly personal, sometimes collective and public, and often in uncannily ethereal ways. Socio-atmospherics, I suggest, are not only an aura or feeling of what is going on, but the goings on themselves; the living in the world and the liveliness of the world including those ineffable and enigmatic things and forces that are part of that world. Socio-atmospherics are not just 'in the mix' – they *are* the mix, the soup, the weave, the dynamics from which affinities rise up, take shape and become potent.

So, in using the concept of *socio-atmospherics* I want to convey a sense of the enigmatic, complex, felt-experienced and emanating effervescence that seems to me to be the stuff of personal life and living and that can come into play so powerfully in affinities. Yet this of course could create an irony in itself, because of the almost irre-sistible impulse to try to pin it down, whilst knowing that part of the very essence of socio-atmospherics is that they are enigmatic. In an attempt to avoid that irony, I want to argue that socio-atmospherics are not simply the product of supposedly identifiable elements in an ecology, but emanate enigmatically in encounters and worldings, forces and flows, that rub shoulders, entangle, cling, effervesce, eva-nesce, coalesce, linger, haunt, and spark ineffably off each other. They can be manifest in a pervading yet enigmatic sense of 'the times', the place and of course the atmospherics, as we saw in the 'time of the floods' facet. Indeed we can say that affinities articulate and resonate with their times. Or they can be manifest in other ways. But socio-atmospherics are not amenable to scientific classification because they take shape in an altogether different register, expressing different ontologies. Socio-atmospherics will not be pinned down for formal categorisation as *types* of ecological or social or even more-than-social entity, but I suggest that we need an orientation that is open to perceiving them.

From what is connected to the dynamics of connection

Socio-atmospherics therefore challenge a conventional orientation to the idea of ecologies as categorisable elements in relation, but I now want to come back to the related problem that arises if we focus on *the ecological entities that are theorised to be in connection*, rather than exploring *the dynamics of the connections themselves*. Instead, my argu-ment centres on those dynamics, and I suggest that an ecological and atmospheric attunement should encourage us to focus on *the con-necting* more than what is connected. I am thus drawn to approaches that help us to understand the connecting, or the betweenness, the emanations and flows, that creates a charge, a potency, in what is undoubtedly a multi-sensory and dynamic set of circuitry, relations, convivialities, co-minglings or assemblages – whatever we want to call them. And the approach needs to be able to apprehend the in/tangibles, socio-atmospherics, forces and energies, and not to find itself ignoring ecological fundamentals like the weather, or the con-stitutive and creative role of memory and imagination. What I am looking for is something of the order of Stewart's ideas in her book *Ordinary Affects* of surging capacities to affect and be affected, but translated into an ecological sensibility, and uncoupled from any necessary association with 'affect' (Stewart, 2007). In this context it becomes clear that concepts like assemblage or co-mingling will only take us so far, because they do not have enough charismatic, ethereal and directional force to be able to evoke affinities that are felt and experienced as a searing, or a frisson, in a life.

Once again, I find the work of Tim Ingold very insightful in this respect. Ingold describes a revelatory moment in his thinking about the relationship between human beings as 'constituted both as organisms within systems of ecological relations, and as persons within systems of social relations' (Ingold, 2000: 3). Interestingly enough his revelation came whilst on his way to catch a bus on a grey and drizzly day in Manchester, and the salience of place and weather in this epiphanal moment is part of the point:

> it suddenly dawned on me that the organism and the person could be one and the same. Instead of trying to reconstruct the complete human being from two separate but complementary components, respectively biological and sociocultural, held together with a film of psychological cement, it struck me that we should be trying to find a way of talking about human life that eliminates the need to slice it up into these different layers. (Ingold, 2000: 3)

In pursuing this agenda, one of his first moves was to reach for James Gibson's 'ecological psychology'. More than a 'film of psychological cement', Ingold recognised something radical and important in ecological psychology whose proposition is that 'perceptual activity consists not in the operation of the mind upon the bodily data of sense, but in the intentional movement of the whole being (indissolubly body and mind) in its environment' (Ingold, 2000: 166). Ingold was influenced by Gibson's concept of 'affordances' for understanding the ecological relationship between organisms (animals, in Gibson's work) and environment, and this is important for my discussion because 'affordances' is potentially a concept that can help us understand the *connecting* that I am interested in. Gibson used the term 'affordance' to understand how animals (this can include humans) move in, perceive and gain knowledge of their environments in a direct and inherently relational way:

> The affordances of the environment are what it *offers* the animal, what it *provides* or *furnishes*, either for good or ill. The verb *afford* . . . refers to both the environment and the animal. . . . An affordance cuts across the dichotomy of subjective-objective and helps us to understand its inadequacy. . . . An affordance points both ways, to the environment and to the observer. (Gibson, 1979: 127–9, emphasis in original)

Unfortunately, the term 'affordances' has fallen into more everyday social science use as meaning 'attributes', or even usefulness, which removes the ecological mutuality from the idea. But what I find radical and interesting about Gibson, and what Ingold likes about him too, is the idea of an affordance as a movement that points *both ways*. An affordance implies a specific and particular kind of connecting takes place (implying an offer, an acceptance; or a practical idea and correspondence/use value). Gibson sees this as happening directly with and in environments, as humans dwell and gain skills, but in ways not necessarily mediated through symbols, cultures, cognition, representation. Both of these points are helpful in that they suggest the possibility of ecological emanation, circulation and flow. I like the suggestion of a world where things, humans and non-humans, or whatever, are directly 'speaking' to each other in an environment, and indeed it is this more than one-direction 'speaking' that constitutes the ecology. However, Gibson's notion of objects in the environment was somewhat static and rigid, and I think also his emphasis on skills of dwelling makes the idea of affordance somewhat human driven and utilitarian and, ultimately, somewhat characterless and lacking in an appreciation of ecological forces and flows emanating from outside the human–object relationship. Ingold in the end prefers Merleau-Ponty's 'Phenomenology of Perception', as do I, because, although both Gibson and Merleau-Ponty reject the mind–body Cartesian dualism, Merleau-Ponty concludes that 'since the living body is primordially and irrevocably stitched into the fabric of the world, our perception of the world is no more, and no less, than the world's perception of itself – in and through us' (Ingold, 2011: 12).

So Ingold moves beyond Gibson, and he does more than refusing to slice life up in traditional academic disciplinary ways. I think what is really important in his work is less in establishing the *premise* of ecological connection, and more in what he says about entang*ling*, or what we might think of as connective forces and energies. He sees entangling not simply as a static schema of how things *are* (for example such that people, organisms, non-humans, things, cultures are entangled, or indeed convivial), but as a vitality of channels, flows, forces, and energies of *being*, of *living*. Instead of, for example, seeing objects as mere materialities, he wants instead to focus on *things*: to 'bring things back to life' as the currents, forces and flows that sweep through them and constitute them. This, he says, is life. A kite is not just a kite but a 'kite-in-the-air'. A tree is a certain gathering of the threads of life. He takes issue with the ways in which we imbue the world with 'surfaces' – like the ground:

> What we vaguely call the ground is not, in truth, a coherent surface at all but a zone in which the air and moisture of the sky combine with substances whose source lies in the earth in the ongoing formation of living things. (Ingold, 2010: 9)

Living in the world and involvement in the world – ecology – argues Ingold, is about the live entanglement of these phenomena or zones, not the connection between so-say fixed points or solid objects. I think his work implies that experience is vital – because life is *lived* – but that it and indeed ecologies and atmospherics are not entirely conjured through or even always involved with human perception or agency or practices. There are forces and flows and 'worldings' – including the 'weather world' – that are not reducible to, for example, bodies, or assemblages. In his earlier work he calls this vitality of entangling a 'meshwork' (Ingold, 2000): the ontological point being that this is what *life is*, and not how life relates to a context. But this is both subtly and radically different from the more usual idea that life is in the supposed objects, units, organisms, things that are entangled (even where they are considered to be ecologically entangled), or even in the 'network', which concept Ingold is at pains to distance himself from. Life for Ingold is the meshwork, the entangling.

In his later work, he develops his thinking using the concept of 'lines', which he uses both literally and metaphorically (Ingold, 2007, 2015). With *lines* he argues that people or things should not be seen merely as *blobs* which can be isolated, or aggregated, and which are thought to have distinct surfaces and boundaries between their insides and their outsides. Instead people and things (and blobs) throw out lines. We can see the connection with the idea of affordances here and its implication of offers and acceptances, practical ideas and correspondence – lines and channels. But there is also a connection with the ideas discussed in part 2 of this book about ineffable kinship, and what such connectings are. Blobs, says Ingold, 'have volume, mass, density: they give us materials. Lines have none of these. What they have, which blobs do not, is *torsion, flexion and vivacity*' (Ingold, 2015: 4, my emphasis). Needless to say, Ingold favours lines over blobs.

For Ingold, what is distinctive about lines that are thrown out is that they *cling*:

> what happens when people or things cling to one another? There is an entwining of lines. They must bind in some way such that the tension that would tear them apart actually holds them fast. Nothing can hold on unless it puts out a line, and unless that line can tangle with others.

When everything tangles with everything else, the result is what I call a
meshwork. (Ingold, 2015: 3)

Ultimately, although his ideas are so important, his term 'meshwork', for me, connotes something too schematic to do full justice
to his effervescent argument and its potential, and the concept of
'lines' is too tidy and literally draw-able to capture the charge and
ethereality, the anarchic frisson, of atmospherics and affinities. But
his idea of life (organisms-things-environments-atmospheres) being
such a lively tangle is compatible with the notion of affinities, and his
insistence that we stop focusing on what we might think of as static
or unitary categories or inanimate objects (what he calls blobs), and
instead look at the lives and liveliness of entanglements and clingings
(what he calls lines), is exactly where I want to be as I move on to the
closing section of the argument in this part of the book.

Ecological poetics

We now have a sense of an ecological orientation that is sensitive to
the socio-atmospherics of living and the dynamics of connection, but
something is still missing, and it is crucial. Still we need to understand that *charge* in the connecting, the emanating and the flow (or
the clingings, or the affordances, or the beckonings, or the memories
and legacies for that matter) that constitute affinities, and that make
them feel so potent.

And this is where I think we need a different kind of sensibility if
we are going to be ready to perceive it: a poetic orientation that is
more artistic and imaginative, less scientific, less in search of evidence
and confirmation, less doggedly empiricist. I have already made an
argument for poetics in part 2 of the book, and we have seen the significance of poetics in this part as well, for example in Kingsolver's
'attendance in my soul', and Shepherd's *'something that moves between
me and it'*. Also, this has emerged in the natural poetics and lyricism with which my study participants lived and evoked weather. All
of those authors, professional and otherwise, had needed a poetic
sensibility to speak of ecological affinities in ways that did not kill
or drag them down with heavy technical terms, or (borrowing from
Wordsworth, 1999 [1888]) murder them to dissect.

Shepherd did not fully understand and could not fully describe
(and certainly not categorise or analyse) what moved between her
and her mountain, but she felt its power and she knew she was part

of the ecology of it as it was part of the ecology of her. Her lyrical and evocative accounts of her affinities with and immersion in (by walking, lying, breathing, touching, smelling, looking, sleeping) the water, air, ground, birds, animals, plants and spirit of the Cairngorms conjure channels of affinity that are vital and electric, and that any number of assemblages-based approaches, or formal analyses of affect, or even multispecies ethnographies, would be likely to miss, just like they miss the weather. And then consider Kingsolver's character Orleanna, whose cells had been divided so her 'body can never be free of the small parts of Africa it consumed' (Kingsolver, 1998: 99), and who was attended in her very soul by the atmospherics, the 'dank red earth', and the sensations of her time in Africa.

In conclusion then, we have added an ecological layering to the argument about affinities. We have seen that places are never 'just' places, things are never 'just' things, surroundings are never 'just' materialities or built environments or nature, and socio-atmospherics are powerful because they are enigmatic, ecological and hauntingly resonant for us. For sure, all of these things have fleshy, tangible textures and qualities, but in our affinities with them we experience and are often beguiled by their in/tangibilities, their enigma, their poetics. Sometimes, in revelatory moments, or in half-sleep and dreams, or in the intimacy of familiarity, we can glimpse and feel the poetics of the ecological weave of which we are a part, and feel the potent atmospherics of a world of lyrical association and suggestion.

Conclusion: Affinities in Time

I have argued from the start of this book that affinities are sparks or charges of connection that intensify, enchant or indeed toxify personal life and the experience of living. They are the revelation or charisma of potent connections that feel kindred in some way and in that sense they are fundamentally relational. To say they are affinities and feel kindred is not to say that are always inherently positive and enjoyable. They are connections that are searing and affecting, which means they can be toxic and fearful just as much as they can be enchanting and joyous. And they can be manifest as affinities of opposition and alterity just as much as of empathy and resemblance. What I have tried to do with the book is to understand something of their charge, their potency.

I have presented my argument in layers throughout the book and these use illustrations – facets – to try to flesh out the kinds of connection and association that affinities are. These do not in any sense represent the full range of possible affinities, and they are certainly not 'types' of affinity either. The facets are chosen and designed to give flashes of insight into the character of affinities, the kinds of charges and connections that affinities are, how they are lived, and what makes them potent. As such the facets are taken from a range of sources where I have been able to discern or write about sparks of affinity, including arts and literature, current affairs, poetry, music and academic research. The arguments at the end of each part of the book are designed to layer up the overall case for affinities, drawing the sometimes eclectic facets into a debate with existing thought. In the spirit of layers, the parts of the book segue, blend and fold into each other in more than one direction, and are not meant to stand alone. The argument about affinities needs them all, and still there is a final layer to add. This layer is crucial and has been present throughout, bubbling up in the argument as it has developed, but now I want to pull it out for discussion in this conclusion to the book. The layer in question is *time*. First let us consider the layers of the argument thus far, and then we will add in time. Finally, we will come back to my proposal at the start of the book that affinities constitute an invitation to think differently, and I will consider what it might mean for sociology to accept that invitation.

Three layers of the argument

In the first layer of the argument, developed with the help of the 'facets of sensation' in part 1 of the book, we saw that affinities come alive and take shape as sensations, and it is through encounters with emanating, circulating and reverberating sensations that we feel and know their potency. I used the 'sensations' part of the book to start to show that affinities, as I see them, are a core part of interpersonal relationships and the characterisations in our lives, but they are in no sense confined to these. Once we accept that affinities come alive as *sensations of potent connection, and of being kindred in some way*, then we will fail to grasp their essence and character if we confine our gaze to interpersonal relationships.

Part 2 of the book developed the second layer of the argument. It showed that people are fascinated by and fully involved in living ineffable kinship, and this is a kinship that has scant regard for social scientific ways of understanding and categorising relatedness or family. Instead, it involves live wires or charges of ineffable circuitry, or mysteriously connective auras, etherealities and in/tangibilities that dance to an altogether different tune, yet create the potent sensation of connections that are elementally kindred. I used examples of family resemblance, doppelgangers, organ transplant, heredity and offspring to help to make my arguments that what is at stake here is not actually a system of interpersonal kinship of unitary persons who are fixed in static relation to each other. Indeed, ineffable kinship can potentially come alive in other situations entirely, including for example in the intimacies of violence discussed in part 1 of the book, or the 'attendance in my soul' of Kingsolver's Africa in part 3. Instead of a formal interpersonal kinship, what I wished to illuminate in the argument in part 2 of the book is the *ineffable and fascinating circulations and relations themselves*. These constitute the charge of affinity, and the potent sense that some kind of elemental kinship is alive and kicking, somewhere.

The third part of the book introduced another layer into the argument. This time we explored ecologies and 'socio-atmospherics', in part so that we could look at affinities that might arise through some form of ecological connection, for example with places, things and environments. I quickly suggested however that we need a radical and open understanding of ecologies that moves beyond the descriptive and democratic idea that 'everything is connected to everything else' and then seeks to document the elements that are in connection, or indeed one that sees 'environment' simply as a backdrop to human existence. Places are never 'just' places, things are never 'just' things, surroundings are never 'just' landscapes or backdrops. Drawing on some exciting developments in cultural geography and ecological anthropology, as well as facets on animate places, things, journeys, memories and weather, I argued that affinities can arise in the dynamics of ecological connection, and in the socio-atmospherics of living. Socio-atmospherics are enigmatic, circulating, haunting, effervescent and involving auras and dynamics. They emanate in encounters and in 'worldings', as well as in forces, flows and energies, entanglements and evanescent coalescences. They can create a pervading and haunting sense of 'the times' for example, as an atmosphere that is in/tangible, that is knowable and recognisable yet ineffable, that is inherently personal yet open and public.

Taken together, these layers of argument tell us a lot about the character and nature of affinities through key themes and concepts that rise up again and again. I have suggested, for example, that affinities can be forces, flows, energies, and live wires of charismatic circuitry or effervescence. They are sensations and can be simultaneously tangible and intangible, as well as familiar yet ineffable, characterful, enigmatic, magical, ethereal, capricious and atmospheric. They are ecological and kindred, living somewhere beyond us and between us, and yet are part of us. They seem other-worldly and boundless yet we know, glimpse and touch them through the parochial aperture of our personal lives. They strike us or inscribe themselves into and through us as a 'frisson', a spark, a charge. They express themselves through a 'natural' poetics and a kind of philosophical wondering that lingers and fascinates.

Time: a final layering

Time is crucial in all of this, and has been lurking in all the dimensions of affinity that the book has addressed. Affinities articulate and resonate with their times. Now I am going to gather together key temporal threads in the various arguments I have been making, to start to explore explicitly the significance of time in the mix. It would be a truism to say that affinities are inflected by time, but it is also a cliché, because of course *everything* is inflected by time, for surely what time does is provide a sense, or a measure, or an experience, of change or happening or growth or duration or degradation or move-ment or reflection – a before and after – in things or situations and in us. In fact, the very idea of a situation as we know it, and quite pos-sibly a thing and us as well – relies on some kind of temporal register.

But quickly, if we follow this kind of logic, we reach a position where we understand time to be everything and nothing. It is *every-thing* because time as lived is never 'just' or 'purely' time – it is everything else as well that goes on in the living. And it is *nothing* because this makes it very hard for us to think and imagine 'time' outside of the things we experience or measure it in, whether that be measurement through 'clock time', a 'mathematically constituted *temps* of spatial time', or the more intuitive and experienced 'quali-tative temporality of the lived durée', where time is understood as processes of *becoming* and *duration* (Adam, 2004: 56; Bergson, 1960 [1889], 1991 [1896]).

Indeed, Adam points out that the answer to the question 'what is time?' is oddly elusive, having baffled and engaged philosophers for centuries, yet we experience time intimately *all of the time* (literally):

> We know that the clock tells us *the* time, but it does not tell us what time *is*. We live time, we experience it daily as an integral part of exist-ence. We know it intimately and yet the answer to this simple question seems extraordinarily difficult. (Adam, 2004: 3)

If we see 'time' as a broadly descriptive or abstract concept that applies to everything, or if we view it in the abstract sense as some-thing that just jogs along or passes in its own linear and exact rhythms and fashions, or in which life is located and charted, then it does not give us much analytical purchase specifically on affinities which are *felt as potent connections*. And yet some kind of quirk, or trick, or dis-cordance, or poetics of time is often part of that potency.

So, what I want to begin to understand here is some of the *ways in which time and affinities make each other potent, fascinating or intriguing*. I want to explore how time is an operator in the nexus of affinities, and not a mere descriptor, clock or locater. And I will not attempt to answer the question 'what is time?' because I think that time is nothing except the things it is measured or felt in (these ideas are familiar to philosophers of social time, but see Callender, 2010, for a fascinating discussion of the illusory nature of physical time). Some of those things are affinities – potent connections that rise up and matter in some way, and where it is possible to identify a spark or a charge or an association that intensifies or enchants relationalities and the everyday.

Affinities can be experienced through personal eras that connect people's own biographies with specific socio-cultural times, and particular sets of relationships which themselves have a history. Remembering (and forgetting) are part of how this takes shape. But equally, fleeting moments of association, realisation, rupture, discordance and connection can be highly significant for affinities. And how people negotiate change, and their relational pasts, presents and futures, as well as questions of lineage, roots, ancestry and progeniture and so on, all implicates particular understandings and experiences of time. The *experience* of time in its many guises is thus central to the discussion, and this will lead me to an argument about the importance of being attuned to 'the times' more than theorising 'time' as an abstract and singular concept, and in particular it will bring me back to the need for us to be fully tuned into the *socio-atmospherics of* living in the world. I shall aim to show that this is very different from simply arguing that time is important and affinities are inflected by time, but I am jumping ahead of myself here. First, let us consider what intriguing temporal morsels and questions arise from the discussions in different parts of the book – I shall select out some key examples of ways in which time and affinities make each other fascinating, intriguing or potent.

Time and sensations

I argued in part 1 that affinities are lived, made up of and made potent in and through sensations. I want now to tease out how time is implicated in this. Getting to know characters through sensations, for example, suggests an accumulation or duration of time. In some ways we could see this as the accrual and remembering and reanimating of multiple and incremental moments, encounters or situations of sensory-kinaesthetic relationality, as in children's accounts of the sensations of others for example, which were often based on specific anecdotes of encounters. What we see here on the face of it is the role of the accumulation of time in building relational sensory-kinaesthetic knowledge, and in that temporal frame of duration or accumulation we can conceive of ebbs and flows in relationships, for example as friends and close kin can become less or more close, and how significance may be judged in terms of duration and longevity – having 'always' known someone, or been close for a long time, or 'gone through' certain times and experiences together – including perhaps sensory and physical changes; or having been responsible for or supportive of someone over many years. There is a great deal of work that shows that cumulative relationships and commitments are highly valued and important (see, for example, Finch and Mason, 1993, on kinship; Mason and Tipper, 2008a, on children's kinship; Smart, 2007, on 'embeddedness'; Smart et al., 2012, on difficult friendships). Routine and non-routine interactions – with all their sensations – that take place over long periods of time undoubtedly construct a sense of relational history, commitment, tradition, narratives and memories. We also know that such relational biographies can even be 'borrowed' from others – and are therefore potentially transferable – to forge or account for a special 'like-family' relationship and sense of lineage with a non-kinsperson (Mason and Tipper, 2008a), or an affinity with a place lived in by one's ancestors but not oneself (Mason, 2008; May, 2016).

Yet time is a more enigmatic and lyrical player than that in some of the affinities I have discussed in relation to sensations. In particular, I want to talk about the charge or shock that comes about through certain quirks or 'tricks' of time, and that adds to the potency of the affinity. For example, we saw the potencies of sensory alignments and misalignments in time; the tantalising here-but-not-here of the 'sense of a presence'; the discordance between the dull and untrustworthy sensations of ashes and the sensory reanimations of earlier encounters with a living father.

This does not just say something about the emotive power of memory, but it takes shape in a *temporal discordance* – a multiply temporal time that can last a moment or much longer and that is highly charged precisely because it has no truck with linear time and allows people to glimpse past the confines of a linear framework into more fascinating and ineffable temporal dynamics. As I argued in part 1 of the book, it is not just (or even) that we have memories that are agile across the years, but it is because the sensory-kinaesthetic forces involved have their own temporal agilities and agendas so that these periods of temporal discordance feel more like encounters and experiences with 'times' (earlier, or other times) than memories of the past that we have conjured or invented; they assert themselves in/tangibly into our lives and sensations.

If these sensory-kinaesthetic forces are time-travellers, they make time-travellers of us as well. The feeling that I discussed of being *transported* to another time/place/situation/feeling, where some often tiny stimulus can almost literally *take us* there, is an experience of time-travel that is arresting, potent, usually unbidden and yet also a familiar and 'everyday' occurrence. But the clever bit is that we are not just or even travelling because we are *there-then-now*, as well as being *here-now* of course. What we encounter when we are *there-then-here-now*, is an immersion in the feelings, the multi-sensory atmospherics and the complete authenticity of *there-then* that we usually find impossible to describe, in words at least, but we know it and feel it. The *there-then* that we have been transported to is not easily defined 'simply' as place, nor a set of materialities or objects, nor a group of people, nor a set of relationships, nor even a set of sensations, although it may very well be all of these things. But I think instead it is better to see it as 'a time', or 'the times', knowing that all of those other dimensions are incorporated into that apparently simple temporal phrase, so that 'the times' are never 'just' time, were such a thing possible. When we are *there-then-here-now*, and because we are *there-then* but not literally *there-then*, we find it easier to perceive the multidimensionality of our lives and ecologies, because we are amazed at how authentically 'that or those *times*' have been reanimated, and the creative powers – surely not ours alone! – that achieved this incredible transportation. It is because such time-travelling atmospheric memory feels so deeply rooted in the specific entanglements of certain times, places, encounters, relationships and so on, and that these sensations are experienced as unbidden and non-contrived, that makes it feel very powerful and like a glimpse into other ways of the temporal world that we are simultaneously involved in, and yet strangers to. From our own parochiality, we have an aperture onto the temporally unbounded and ineffable. Like dreaming, when times can be simultaneously particular times and yet not those times, and places can be exact places except they are not those places ('it was my house, but it wasn't!'), and the atmospherics are utterly convincing and feel impossible to self-invent or conjure singlehandedly, time-travelling is a potent and absorbing experience of disjuncture and convergence; a beguiling discordance.

It is becoming clear also that 'moments' – of temporal transportation or otherwise – can play a profound role in making affinities what they are, and this somewhat pulls against the more familiar social scientific idea that it is *only* duration and longevity, or major events, that lead to or speak of significance. Moments are in themselves sensations of course. Moments that are electric, are highly charged, are revelatory, are epiphanal, have all figured strongly in all parts of the book. And yet moments are charismatic not because they are measurable fractions of clock time (which they are not), but because they are multi-sensory glimpses, windows, apertures or revelations into an intriguing and arresting discordance or conglomeration – an impossible holding in tension together of different 'times' and temporalities, a glimpse of coexisting and incompatible worlds, an insight into the layers and flows and forces that are ecologies. Moments are insights into the socio-atmospherics of life, and they are full of sensations.

Time and ineffable kinship

Charged moments play a key role in affinities of ineffable kinship, especially in relation to resemblances and the 'moment of perception', as we saw in part 2 of the book. A resemblance spotted by a stranger in the street; a chance encounter between lookalikes in a holiday village who share so much more; fleeting resemblances in looks, spirit or character that eerily come and go in an ethereal fashion, tantalisingly playing with our perceptions of what is tangible and what is intangible – these are all typical and familiar in the experience of resemblance. And yet again, what is intriguing about what is going on here has little or nothing to do with mathematical temporal measurement and what, in those terms, constitutes a moment.

I started to argue in part 2 that we could usefully draw on Barthes's notion of a 'punctum' – something that pricks and commands attention – in thinking about these moments, and that spotting resemblances makes us into witnesses and narrators of conjunctures and conjectures that are both new (in the impact of the moment, the punctum), and yet have the resonance and depth of time as duration; a resemblance seen, or a question posed about a resemblance, with someone else from a different time, known before or outside this one. Just think for a moment of some of the different elements of resemblance: resemblances that 'skip a generation'; or resemblances perceived fleetingly across longish periods of time; or resemblances only perceptible when someone is sleeping, or moving, or being spirited or stubborn; or resemblances only visible in 'real life' and not in photos, or the other way around; or a resemblance known to be passing 'along this side' of the family; or a resemblance perceived between someone living and present now, with an 'earlier version' of someone else stored in sensory memory, or with someone long dead, or far absent in time or place. I have given examples of all of these, and argued that they express something of the capricious nature of resemblance, as something – or a set of forces and energies – that is alive somewhere out there in the ether, somewhere mystical, somewhere that exists outside our notions of time, yet always connected to us or part of us. I shall expand on this briefly now.

I think what is interesting about these and other examples is that they trouble the idea of sequential or linear time. This is partly because they are incompatible with a unidirectional sequencing or flow, where resemblances are simply passed or echoed 'down' the generations. We can observe that echoes go in all directions, both genealogically and temporally speaking. There is something about perceiving or channelling the echoes that makes people feel connected to something ethereal, potent, ordinary but also out of the ordinary. A moment of perception can feel like a magical knot or crossing. Colloquially, we could say it adds a little spice to life. These observations do not suggest a steady and regular pace of change or evolution in resemblance (as in measured clock time), because of the different ways, for example, in which the perception of a resemblance can 'grow on you' and become relatively stable, so that it is gradually appreciated, or alternatively can appear and then disappear 'out of the blue', so that it is manifest in an instant and then gone.

Perhaps most importantly, these examples reveal an idea of resemblance as a relational something that *comes alive, or is living, in and across different eras and times.* Resemblance's natural temporal habitat, we might say, is in multiple times, memories, echoes, perceptions and connections. In trying to understand what 'it' is, resemblance requires us to re-envision what feels like a rather plodding and dull notion of linear or sequential time, or kinship as descendent generations, and to come up with something altogether more acrobatic and creative; a poetic more than a mathematical sensibility. In their different ways, these resemblance stories suggest that resemblances can be ephemeral and momentary, and yet are always there, somewhere, alive, ready to be activated – *ready to hit you, to beckon you, to pull you in* – possibly without warning.

Another way that ineffable kinship is entwined in charismatic ways with time is in relation to what it says about the mysterious relational processes and forces of connection and of life and of kinship. I suggested earlier that people know at some level that we are not all simply unitary and entirely separate persons, units or nodes (or blobs in Ingold's terms), fixed in static family-tree or network-diagram type relationship to each other, and I argued that people are enchanted, puzzled and sometimes scared by this. Family resemblances – those capricious, anarchic and haunting presences – put paid to the idea that we are entirely separate units related only through links that are socially or even genetically constructed. People *know* that the relational *connecting forces* at times are more potent, elemental, meaningful and durable or acrobatic across time, than the 'us' that they apparently connect. And I would argue people love to (or hate to) *wonder* about all of this.

The point I want to develop here is about what happens temporally speaking when we shift our focus from persons as units and individuals, to relational connecting forces and flows that may pass through, inhabit and characterise them, but do not exist simply to constitute them. We know for a start that these forces exist on a different time scale to individual persons, again as demonstrated by a family resemblance cropping up many years after a person who is resembled has died, sometimes raising a question about when it can be said a person begins and ends. The enthusiasm with which some of the sperm donors discussed in part 2 approach the task of populating the world with 'mini-mees', and the fears of parents of donor conceived children that a donor could be lurking with the trump card of genetic credentials that might turn out to matter more (or differently) than nurturing care, and the case of the still-beating heart, are all testimony to the idea that something passes in, through and beyond persons. But I have argued that that *something* is not readily or consensually defined as 'genes' even where people use that metaphor, and instead that the evidence points to something that is much more ineffable. So if we focus on ineffable relational forces and flows, we can see they exist outside of 'our' time, and quite possibly like Hardy's family face 'that heeds no call to die', they are eternal; certainly they are not mortal like us, but also they do not seem to inhabit a one-directional, linear version of time either.

Of course the very idea of *kinship* (or lineage or genealogy) makes sense only as we might say 'across time', although it is an idea that does not necessarily disrupt the idea of linear flow of time in the kinds of charismatic ways that we can see the forces and flows of ineffable kinship doing. Indeed, in many ways kinship props up the idea of linear time and organises itself accordingly. As Becky Tipper and I have argued, in negotiating their everyday family and kin relationships, people often know they are participating in a 'bigger kinship story' which both *has* and '*needs* a history' (Mason and Tipper, 2008b: 149). We suggested that:

> Kinship . . . is constituted in sets of relationships lived across time
> (Finch and Mason, 1993; Morgan, 1996). Events, practices, experi-
> ences, interactions and of course stories and narratives are *formative* in
> how kinship develops and changes in specific circumstances, and kin-
> ship is by necessity and definition a historically saturated state of affairs.
> There is a clear awareness in people's lived experience of kinship that
> relationships have a history and a future; that they are developing and
> becoming (Mason and Tipper, 2008b). Although kinship is always
> unfolding and in some senses has no finishing or starting point (because
> of the infinite nature of ancestry and descendancy), yet relationships
> can 'turn out' or end in particular ways, at particular times, just as there
> are births and beginnings. . . . Shifting and complex conceptualizations
> and understandings of being, becoming and *developing* are central in
> how kinship is understood and practised. (Mason and Tipper, 2014:
> 164–5, emphasis in original)

Kinship like this is mapped across linear time, and people know that
this is how it works. And yet their orientation to family resemblances,
and indeed to transilience and to wondering, shows that this apparently linear and formulaic framework is considered to coexist with a
much more effervescent, ethereal and temporally radical set of relational forces and flows. People do not seem to have much trouble in
living with the discordance between these approaches to time in their
personal lives. Indeed, as Adam has commented in relation to competing and different representations and features of time:

> In our everyday lives we weave in and out of this diversity of features
> without giving much thought to the matter. Without problem, we navi-
> gate through the inherent contradictions, knowing them as integral
> parts of the wider whole that constitutes time. In our social theories, in
> contrast, we seem to home in on certain aspects in preference to others,
> come down on the side of one pair of opposites, or choose one duality
> at the expense of all others. (Adam, 2004: 22)

Time, ecologies and socio-atmospherics

We have seen that encounters, perceptions and memories of places,
things, technologies, journeys and surroundings are multi-sensory and
are crucial in what those things are, and I want to argue now that time
is always implicated. And of course, it is to the sensations and atmospherics of places that we are often transported as time-travellers, and
such places are always place-times-worldings-atmospherics. Quite a
lot of the work that explores places and ecologies as convivialities and

assemblages has a somewhat 'presentist' or 'generative' and democratic orientation – all things comingled and playing a part in the here and now – and indeed that has been seen as a strength and also as a cause for criticism. It is a strength because it can help to express the more-than-human, more-than-material, more-than-nature livelinesses of places, things and surroundings that, when we really think about them, or when we are 'transported to them' as time-travellers, we fully recognise and experience. But it is a cause for criticism too because it does not handle well the dimensions of feeling, encountering and remembering, nor the charge or charismatic rising up that constitutes an affinity.

In my discussion of ecologies and socio-atmospherics I focused therefore not only on the convivialities, but also the animations that create a charge; the experiencing, feeling and remembering; the processes, mediums and atmospherics of connecting and betweenness more than the things that are connected; and, crucially, the ecological poetics in all of this. From this perspective, places, things and surroundings are not inert or static materialities, but neither do they simply house, corral or contain all of these elements either; they are more like conduits for them, entanglements of them (knots of lines as Ingold would have it), or channels for the energies involved, or focal points of the socio-atmospherics. Once again, intriguing temporal discordances are part of all of this.

For example, we have seen that different versions and experiences of a place can readily coexist, as people engage with places in both a here and now way, and a way that involves sensory-kinaesthetic memories and provenances of previous encounters there and in similar or contrasting places. In the same way places that are no longer 'there' can nevertheless be present, not least because multi-sensory perception is crucial in what places or things are when they are 'there' as well as when they are animated in memory. In this way places can become what Kingsolver's character Orleanna described as 'an attendance in her soul', and affinities and connections with them can feel timeless or somehow floating in an alternative (non-linear) time dimension. The mystique of that can be further enhanced when people have the sensation of an ineffable kinship with a place, a kind of inexplicable rootedness, when they first visit it, as though they have been there before or have some deeper connection to it. May has noted how the people in her study connected their haunting and ethereal sense of connection with place to ancestral links – ancestors who had lived in the place – many generations previously:

they use their genetic links to place as a 'folk theory' that helps to
explain the seemingly inexplicable. Such a fundamental connection to
place that is part of one's genetic make-up is timeless because it has no
clear temporal point of origin and cannot be touched by time – it exists
there always, even if at times dormant, for as long as the genetic line
survives. (May, 2016)

Anthropologists have noted mystical or potent feelings of connection
between lands, places and ancestors, such that it might be argued in
some 'primitive' societies 'the land has certain intersubjective relations with its human possessors, or indeed a certain kinship with the
people' (Sahlins, 2013: 6). Not only 'primitive' societies, I would
suggest. For May, the belonging to ancestral places she witnessed in
her study is a 'timeless belonging', or a 'belonging that "endures out
of time"', and we can see that it has an inherent fascination precisely
because it involves something of a trick of time, as well as an interweaving of the mysteries and interdependencies of place (in all its
non-humanness), people and kinship.

Just as places and things can seem to float in an alternative time
dimension, not following the rules of linear time, so too can we see how
our experiences with them can generate particular kinds of time – take
for example the time spent on car or train journeys discussed in part 3,
in driving through, in looking, and so on – that can feel weighty, light,
harried, significant, pregnant, atmospheric, philosophical, poetic, full
of appreciation and openness, or can become memorable (as Amin
put it, can turn out to be formative), in unexpected ways. Or consider the time Shepherd spent on her mountain, sometimes walking,
sometimes sitting, sometimes lying, sometimes sleeping and losing
track of time. These kinds of place-time-encounters can summon
something up in us that is significant, that can feel like an aperture
onto a temporal ecological weave of which we are a part without fully
understanding it, where we feel the poetics or power of it without conjuring them, and which makes an affinity.

And finally, weather and our affinities with and in 'it' have many
interesting associations with time. The concept of 'changeable' and
capriciously malevolent weather, so characteristic of the UK, itself
suggests a certain sense of how weather and time should go together.
Living the weather is certainly a way that people live and feel time
as duration, including many references to feeling ground down by
'never ending' rain for example. Weather also figures interestingly
in memory, both saturating our animated memories of place-times
for example, and yet being easily forgotten or made nostalgia of.

But weather is a fundamental part of and can trigger sensory and atmospheric memories, unlocking all those things that we live in the process of weather, just like Proust's madeleine cake. Weather is undoubtedly right there in the socio-atmospherics.

Some of those things are seasonal, and the return or turn of a season transports us to how we lived those times last time, or the time before. And despite popular wisdom that modern Western societies have no need to notice the seasons any more, actually the changing seasons and accompanying rhythms are experienced quite profoundly, and poetically too, as we saw in some of the weather poetry in part 3. The seasons, and the changing amounts of light and dark, and changing weather conditions, do not of course fit neatly with clock time (or the 'management' of the seasons through putting the clocks forward or back for example) and are suggestive of something that is temporally more cyclical than linear, and more ecologically and poetically than mathematically attuned or synchronised. People recognise a force in the weather and the seasons that has its own elemental agenda and temporality, irrespective of the attempts to impose human clock time, or efficiently calendar coordinated seasons, upon it.

But we saw also that there is anxiety about ways in which human damage and disregard might be injuring the weather's temporal-ity, and hastening climate change. Although for the most part such change is considered so abstract and 'slow' as not to be noticeable and thus is hardly quite believed (and some politicians and global corporate interests encourage that view), lived ecological events like a major flood in the area where you live, with so many multidi-mensional legacies, can give people a jolt and can be scary, as the temporal pace of climate change suddenly seems to be upon them (see also Bastian, 2012). At these points a strong and ambivalent affinity creates a point of connection between different temporalities, with the sense of foreboding that the weather – that most powerful force in our everyday lives – will pay no heed to our attempts to call it to time. This can contribute to a socio-atmospherics from which 'the times' emerge as a simultaneously personal and public, social and ecological, ephemeral yet enduring and era defining, set of haunting evanescences. These are beguilingly discordant and irrepressibly in/tangible and shape shifting, and show that socio-atmospherics go way beyond our attempts to categorise them into what social scientists can 'know' and evidence.

Coming back to Adam's comment that ordinary people – unlike theorists and philosophers – have no problem in 'weaving in and out of' diverse features of time, I think I would go further to say that the facets and the arguments in this book have indicated that actually people may be positively thrilled and engaged by (in positive or negative ways) witnessing apertures onto apparent diversities, contradictions and ineffabilities in the workings of time. These are alluring and fascinating, and can be a source of wonder, fear and intrigue. Certainly they are sources of potency, and they play a central part in affinities.

Accepting the invitation of affinities

Affinities, then, come alive in sensations. They are energies, forces and flows that can take shape in an ineffable kinship as well as in ecologies and in the socio-atmospherics of life, and they articulate and resonate with time and with their times. Their potency can come from the frissons, charges, alluring discordances and poetics that animate and enliven everyday personal lives.

I have written this book in a somewhat unconventional way because I wanted it to be an invitation – perhaps even an inspiration – to others to create new ways of seeing that can apprehend the kinds of energies that I have suggested affinities are. I wanted to open possibilities for others to do what they will with these insights, rather than to set out a doctrine of affinities, with exact rules, definitions and orthodoxies for others to follow. I fear that would deaden the very concepts and attunements I am trying to coax into the light of day. Instead I want to suggest a kind of 'affinities orientation' as a way of seeing, apprehending and asking questions. Although I see my approach as deeply sociological, I think an affinities orientation suggests some divergence with more conventional sociological approaches – and thus some opportunities for thinking differently. I started this book by suggesting that affinities represent an invitation to think differently, and I want to finish by considering what it might mean for sociology, in particular, to accept that invitation. This is not to start an argument with existing branches of sociology, but to encourage a move towards a more open, attentive (see Back, 2007; Smart, 2014) and poetic orientation.

Firstly, where conventional sociology has wanted to split and categorise human activity, individuals, groups and society into variables, typologies, structures, systems, processes, discourses, practices, or whatever, an affinities approach seeks out and explores connections, entanglements, energies, forces and flows involved in living in the world.

Secondly, and to extend that point, where conventional sociology has often focused on populations, social activity or social groupings, an affinities approach pursues an orientation that is attuned to the sensory-kinaesthetics, the ineffabilities, the ecologies and the socio-atmospherics of living in the world. This means an affinities approach can tune into emanating forces, energies, potencies, mysteries and atmospherics. It also means that where conventional sociology has wanted to own the 'social' as its disciplinary domain and sphere of expertise, and not always wanted to extend beyond it or to see the world in a way that challenges the concept of the social and social construction, an affinities approach pursues a more open ecological-relational dynamic. Here the aim is to understand the meld of human lives with animate things, places, environments, weather, other (non-human) lives, and so on, but without shying away from atmospherics, auras, ineffabilities and in/tangibilities or phenomena and forces that would otherwise have to be shoehorned into the concept of 'the social'. In some ways sociology is stuck on 'the social' with some wanting to bring everything back to social construction, and others wanting a radical disassembly of 'the social'. But both approaches still situate 'the social' as a central problematic, and neither leaves much room for what we might think of as in/tangible, atmospheric, ineffable or extra-sensory. An affinities approach and in particular the concept of socio-atmospherics, along with the kinds of attunement it suggests, could be very fruitful here. Where conventional sociology has certain blind spots (perhaps because they do not fit with current sociological sensibilities or rationalist forms of social science), an affinities approach argues that sociologists should be astute in sidestepping or moving beyond these, and should be ready to adopt a different – and more poetic – sensibility.

Finally, where conventional sociology has sometimes tended to be inward looking in a disciplinary sense, defining itself in opposition to other disciplines, an affinities approach seeks to expand and enliven sociology with a willingness to embrace and incorporate insights and ways of seeing from other disciplines, for example, cultural geography, ecological anthropology and the arts, and indeed from outside of traditional disciplinary orientations. I believe that apprehending something as multiple, as beguilingly and effervescently discordant, as irrepressibly in/tangible and shape shifting, as affinities, moves us beyond our attempts to categorise them using conventional social science tools. However, we should not ignore affinities and their like just because we cannot comfortably categorise and organise them. Instead, I argue that we should embrace ideas such as those that have been so central in this book, whether or not we can pin them down 'scientifically' – I am thinking of, for example, potency, charisma, poetics, in/tangibility, atmospherics. If these are important, and I argue that they are crucial, then it is not them, but our modes of appreciation and attunement, that we need to transform.

Notes

1. 'Children Creating Kinship', Jennifer Mason, Becky Tipper and Jennifer Flowerdew, ESRC, 2004–2007, RES-000-23-0271-A.
2. The 'Living Resemblances' project was part of the ESRC National Centre for Research Methods 'Node' 'Real Life Methods', 2005–2009, RES-576-25-5017. Other project team members were: Jon Prosser, Lynne Cameron, Josephine Green and Brendan Gough.
3. The photographer was Ed Swinden and the researchers were part of the 'Living Resemblances' team. The researcher asking the questions was me. See Mason and Davies (2011) for further information.
4. All names are pseudonyms.
5. All names are pseudonyms.
6. 'Living the Weather: a study in the socio-atmospherics of everyday life', Jennifer Mason, the Leverhulme Trust, 2015–2016, RF-2015-480.
7. A collection of the poems, and some pieces of prose, have been published in Mason (2016).

References

Abram, D. (1997) *The Spell of the Sensuous*, New York: Vintage Books.

Acampora, R. (2006) *Corporal Compassion: animal ethics and philosophy of body*, Pittsburgh: University of Pittsburgh Press.

Adam, B. (2004) *Time*, Cambridge: Polity.

Almeling, R. (2014) 'Defining connections: gender and perceptions of relatedness in egg and sperm donation', in T. Freeman, S. Graham, F. Ebtehaj and M. Richards (eds.) *Relatedness in Assisted Reproduction: families, origins and identities*, Cambridge: Cambridge University Press.

Amin, A. (2014) 'Lively infrastructure', *Theory Culture and Society*, 31(7/8): 137–61.

Amin, A. (2015) 'Animated space', *Public Culture*, 27(2): 239–58.

Anderson, B. (2009) 'Affective atmospheres', *Emotion, Space and Society*, 2(2): 77–81.

Arluke, A. and Sanders, C. (1996) *Regarding Animals*, Philadelphia: Temple University Press.

Back, L. (2007) *The Art of Listening*, Oxford: Berg.

Bahari, M., with Molloy, A. (2011) *Then They Came for Me: a story of injustice and survival in Iran's most notorious prison*, Oxford: Oneworld.

Barthes, R. (2000 [1980]) *Camera Lucida: reflections on photography*, London: Vintage.

Bastian, M. (2012) 'Fatally confused: telling the time in the midst of ecological crises', *Journal of Environmental Philosophy*, 9(1): 23–48.

Bay, B., Larsen, P. B., Kesmodel, U. S. and Ingerslev, H. J. (2013) 'Danish sperm donors across three decades: motivations and attitudes', *Fertility and Sterility*, 101(1): 252–7.

Benjamin, W. (1999) *Selected Writings* (vol. 2), Cambridge, MA: Harvard University Press.

Bennett, G. and Bennett, K. M. (2000) 'The presence of the dead: an empirical study', *Mortality*, 3(2): 139–57.

Bergson, H. (1960 [1889]) *Time and Free Will* (translated by F. L. Pogson), New York: Harper and Row.

Bergson, H. (1991 [1896]) *Matter and Memory* (translated by N. M. Paul and W. S. Palmer), New York: Zone Books .

Bertaux, D. and Thompson, P. (eds.) (2005) *Between Generations: family models, myths and memories*, London: Transaction.

Böhme, G. (1993) 'Atmosphere as the fundamental concept of a new aesthetics', *Thesis Eleven*, 36: 113–26.

Brennan, T. (2004) *The Transmission of Affect*, Ithaca, NY and London: Cornell University Press.

Brighenti, A. M. (2010) *Visibility in Social Theory and Social Research*, Basingstoke: Palgrave Macmillan.

Brown, R. H. (1977) *A Poetic for Sociology: toward a logic of discovery for the human sciences*, Chicago: University of Chicago Press.

Bull, M. (2001) 'Soundscapes of the car: a critical ethnography of automobile habitation', in D. Miller (ed.) *Car Cultures*, Oxford: Berg.

Bulwer-Lytton, E. (2010 [1830]) *Paul Clifford*, London: Penguin Classics.

Burkitt, I. (2010) 'Dialogues with self and others: communication, miscommunication, and the dialogical unconscious', *Theory and Psychology*, 20(3): 305–21.

Buscha, F. (2016) 'Does sunshine make you happy? Subjective measures of well-being and the weather', *The Manchester School*, 84(5): 642–63.

Callender, C. (2010) 'Is time an illusion?', *Scientific American*, 302: 58–65.

Cameron, L. (2011) *Metaphor and Reconciliation: the discourse dynamics of empathy in post-conflict conversations*, New York: Routledge.

Cappello, M. (2007) *Awkward: a detour*, New York: Bellevue Literary Press.

Carey, N. (2012) *The Epigenetics Revolution: how modern biology is rewriting our understanding of genetics, disease and inheritance*, London: Icon Books.

Carsten, J. (2004) *After Kinship*, Cambridge: Cambridge University Press.

Chalfen, R. (2010) 'Looking two ways: mapping the social scientific study of visual culture', in E. Margolis and L. Pauwels (eds.) *The Sage Handbook of Visual Research Methods*, London: Sage.

Charles, N. and Davies, C. A. (2008) 'My family and other animals: pets as kin', *Sociological Research Online*, 13(5): 4, http://www.socresonline.org.uk/13/5/4.html (consulted 11 June 2017).

Chu, S. and Downes, J. (2000) 'Odour evoked autobiographical memories: psychological investigations of Proustian phenomena', *Chemical Senses*, 25(1): 111–16.

Classen, C. (1992) 'The odor of the other: olfactory symbolism and cultural categories', *Ethos*, 20(2): 133–66.

Classen, C. (2012) *The Deepest Sense: a cultural history of touch*, Chicago: University of Illinois Press.

Clough, P. T. and Halley, J. (2007) *The Affective Turn: theorizing the social*, Durham, NC and London: Duke University Press.

Crossley, N. (2006) *Reflexive Embodiment in Contemporary Society: the body in late modern society*, Milton Keynes: Open University Press.

Cusk, R. (2014) *Outline*, London: Faber and Faber.

Dalakoglou, D. and Harvey, P. (2012) 'Roads and anthropology: ethnographic perspectives on space, time and (im)mobility', *Mobilities*, 7(4): 459–65.

Davies, H. (2015) *Understanding Children's Personal Lives and Relationships*, Basingstoke: Palgrave Macmillan.

Davies, K. (2012) *Turning Out: young people, being and becoming*, unpublished PhD thesis, University of Manchester.

Dawkins, R. (1986) *The Blind Watchmaker*, London: Longman.

Degen, M. (2008) *Sensing Cities: regenerating public life in Barcelona and Manchester*, London: Routledge.

Degen, M. and Rose, G. (2012) 'The sensory experiencing of urban design: the role of walking and perceptual memory', *Urban Studies*, 49(15): 3271–87.

DeNora, T. (2000) *Music in Everyday Life*, Cambridge: Cambridge University Press.

Doward, J. (2015) 'Rain or shine, it makes no difference to how happy most Britons feel', *The Guardian*, 14 March, https://www.theguardian.com/uk-news/2015/mar/14/sunny-days-no-difference-mental-wellbeing (consulted 4 July 2016).

Edwards, J. (2014) 'Undoing kinship', in T. Freeman, S. Graham, F. Ebtehaj and M. Richards (eds.) *Relatedness in Assisted Reproduction: families, origins and identities*, Cambridge: Cambridge University Press.

Fields, D. (2011) 'Emotional refuge? Dynamics of place and belonging among formerly homeless individuals with mental illness', *Emotion, Space and Society*, 4(4): 258–67.

Finch, J. and Mason, J. (1993) *Negotiating Family Responsibilities*, London: Routledge.

Finch, J. and Mason, J. (2000) *Passing On: kinship and inheritance in England*, London: Routledge.

Fortunati, L. (2002) 'The mobile phone: towards new categories and social relations', *Information, Communication and Society*, 5(4): 513–28.

Fox, K. (2014) *Watching the English: the hidden rules of English behaviour*, London: Hodder and Stoughton.

Freeman, T., Bourne, K., Jadva, V. and Smith, V. (2014) 'Making connections: contact between sperm donor relations', in T. Freeman, S. Graham, F. Ebtehaj and M. Richards (eds.) *Relatedness in Assisted Reproduction: families, origins and identities*, Cambridge: Cambridge University Press.

Gabb, J. (2008) *Researching Intimacy in Families*, Basingstoke: Palgrave Macmillan.

Gibson, J. J. (1979) *The Ecological Approach to Visual Perception*, Boston: Houghton Mifflin.

Gillis, J. R. (1997) *A World of Their Own Making: myth, ritual, and the quest for family values*, Cambridge, MA: Harvard University Press.

Gilroy, P. (2001) 'Driving while black', in D. Miller (ed.) *Car Cultures*, Oxford: Berg.

Gordon, A. (1996) *Ghostly Matters: haunting and the sociological imagination*, Minneapolis: University of Minnesota Press.

Gregg, M. and Seigworth, G. J. (eds.) (2010) *The Affect Theory Reader*, Durham, NC and London: Duke University Press.

Grosz, E. (1994) *Volatile Bodies: toward a corporeal feminism*, London: Wiley.

Guy, S. and Karvonen, A. (2011) 'Using sociotechnical methods: researching human-technical dynamics in the city', in J. Mason and A. Dale (eds.) *Understanding Social Research: thinking creatively about method*, London: Sage.

Haimes, E. (1992) 'Gamete donation and the social management of genetic origins', in M. Stacey (ed.) *Changing Human Reproduction: social science perspectives*, London: Sage.

Hallam, E. and Hockey, J. (2001) *Death, Memory and Material Culture*, Oxford: Berg.

Hallam, E., Hockey, J. and Howarth, G. (1999) *Beyond the Body: death and social identity*, London: Routledge.

Hardy, T. (2007 [1917]) *Moments of Vision and Miscellaneous Verses*, Gloucester: Dodo Press.

Harris, A. (2014) 'Drip, drip, drip, by day and night', *The Guardian*, 14 February, https://www.theguardian.com/books/2014/feb/14/english-literature-rain-flooding (consulted 4 July 2016).

Harris, A. (2015) *Weatherland: writers and artists under English skies*, London: Thames and Hudson.

Hecht, A. (2001) 'Home sweet home: tangible memories of an uprooted childhood', in D. Miller (ed.) *Home Possessions*, Oxford: Berg.

Heidegger, M. (1971) *Poetry, Language, Thought* (translated by A. Hofstadter), New York: Harper and Row.

Hinchliffe, S. and Whatmore, S. (2006) 'Living cities: towards a politics of conviviality', *Science as Culture*, 15(2): 123–38.

Hinchliffe, S., Kearnes, M. B., Degen, M. and Whatmore, S. (2005) 'Urban wild things: a cosmopolitical experiment', *Environment and Planning D: Society and Space*, 23(5): 643–58.

Howell, S. (2006) *The Kinning of Foreigners: transnational adoption in a global perspective*, Oxford: Berghahn Books.

Howes, D. (1991) *Varieties of Sensory Experience: a sourcebook in the anthropology of the senses*, Toronto: University of Toronto Press.

Howes, D. and Classen, C. (2014) *Ways of Sensing: understanding the senses in society*, London: Routledge.

Hull, J. (1997) *On Sight and Insight: a journey into the world of blindness*, Oxford: Oneworld Publications.

Hudson, N. and Culley, L. (2014) 'Infertility, gamete donation and relatedness in British South Asian communities', in T. Freeman, S. Graham,

F. Ebtehaj and M. Richards (eds.) *Relatedness in Assisted Reproduction: families, origins and identities*, Cambridge: Cambridge University Press.

Ingold, T. (2000) *The Perception of the Environment: essays in livelihood, dwelling and skill*, London: Routledge.

Ingold, T. (2007) *Lines: a brief history*, Abingdon: Routledge.

Ingold, T. (2010) *Bringing Things to Life: creative entanglements in a world of materials*, Realities, Morgan Centre Working Paper No. 15, University of Manchester, http://eprints.ncrm.ac.uk/1306/1/0510_creative_entanglements.pdf

Ingold, T. (2011) *Being Alive: essays on movement, knowledge and description*, London: Routledge.

Ingold, T. (2013) 'Prospect', in T. Ingold and G. Palsson (eds.) *Biosocial Becomings: integrating social and biological anthropology*, Cambridge: Cambridge University Press.

Ingold, T. (2015) *The Life of Lines*, London: Routledge.

Ingold, T. and Vergunst, J. L. (2008) *Ways of Walking: ethnography and practice on foot*, London: Routledge.

James, A. (2013) *Socialising Children*, Basingstoke: Palgrave Macmillan.

Jamieson, L. (2013) 'Personal relationships, intimacy and the self in a mediated and global digital age', in K. Orton-Johnson and N. Prior (eds.) *Digital Sociology: critical perspectives*, Basingstoke: Palgrave Macmillan.

Johnston, J. (2014) 'Electrifying moment mother felt dead son's heart beating', *Mail Online*, http://www.dailymail.co.uk/fcmail/article-2703417/Electrifying-moment-mother-felt-dead-sons-heart-beating-A-donor-heart-saved-Scott-death-And-incredibly-soon-Freda-set-eyes-sensed-shared-extraordinary-bond.html (consulted 28 August 2014).

Kay, J. (2010) *Red Dust Road*, London: Picador.

Kay, J. (2011) *Fiere*, London: Picador.

Kent, J. (2016) 'Ontological security and private car use in Sydney, Australia', *Sociological Research Online*, 21(3): 3, http://www.socresearchonline.org.uk/21/2/3 (consulted 25 June 2016).

Kingsolver, B. (1998) *The Poisonwood Bible*, London: Faber and Faber.

Kinsley, S. (2014) 'The matter of "virtual" geographies', *Progress in Human Geography*, 38(3): 364–84.

Konrad, M. (2005) *Nameless Relations: anonymity, Melanesia and reproductive gift exchange between British ova donors and recipients*, New York and Oxford: Berghahn Books.

Kramer, A.-M. (2011) 'Kinship, affinity and connectedness: exploring the role of genealogy in personal lives', *Sociology*, 45(3): 379–95.

Kuhn, A. (1995) *Family Secrets: acts of memory and imagination*, London: Verso.

Lawler, S. (2014) *Identity: sociological perspectives*, 2nd edition, Cambridge: Polity.

Leedham, R. (2013) 'How clean is your iPad? A Which investigation', http://blogs.which.co.uk/technology/news/how-clean-is-your-mobile-a-which-

hygiene-investigation/?intcmp=HP.hero.large.1.wcutechdaily.tablethygi
ene.sept17 (consulted 17 December 2015) .

Lyon, D. and Back, L. (2012) 'Fishmongers in a global economy: craft and social relations on a London market', *Sociological Research Online*, 17(2): 23, http://www.socresonline.org.uk/17/2/23.html (consulted 11 June 2017).

McCandless, J. and Sheldon, S. (2014) 'Genetically challenged: the determination of legal parenthood in assisted reproduction', in T. Freeman, S. Graham, F. Ebtehaj and M. Richards (eds.) *Relatedness in Assisted Reproduction: families, origins and identities*, Cambridge: Cambridge University Press.

Macfarlane, R. (2011) 'Introduction', in N. Shepherd, *The Living Mountain: a celebration of the Cairngorm Mountains of Scotland*, Edinburgh: Canongate.

McGregor, J. (2002) *If Nobody Speaks of Remarkable Things*, London: Bloomsbury.

MacKian, S. (2012) *Everyday Spirituality: social and spatial worlds of enchantment*, Basingstoke: Palgrave Macmillan.

McQuoid, C. (2015) Research Briefing: *Unregulated Internet 'Sperm Donors' and Violence Against Women*, https://clairemcquoid.files.wordpress. com/2015/02/research-briefing-project-internet-sperm-donors-and-vio lence-against-women.pdf (consulted 17 June 2016).

Mabey, R. (2013) *Turned out Nice Again: on living with the weather*, London: Profile Books.

Madianou, M. and Miller, D. (2012) 'Polymedia: towards a new theory of digital media in interpersonal communication', *International Journal of Cultural Studies*, 16(2): 169–87.

Mason, J. (2008) 'Tangible affinities and the real life fascination of kinship', *Sociology*, 42(1): 29–45.

Mason, J. (2011) 'Facet methodology: the case for an inventive research orientation', *Methodological Innovations Online*, 6(3): 75–92.

Mason, J. (2015) 'The socio-atmospherics of weather', plenary address, Atmospheres, Morgan Centre for Research into Everyday Lives International Conference, 1–2 July, University of Manchester.

Mason, J. (2016) *Living the Weather: voices from the Calder Valley*, Manchester: Morgan Centre for Research into Everyday Lives, University of Manchester.

Mason, J. and Davies, K. (2009) 'Coming to our senses? A critical approach to sensory methodology', *Qualitative Research*, 9(5): 587–603.

Mason, J. and Davies, K. (2011) 'Experimenting with qualitative methods: researching family resemblance', in J. Mason and A. Dale (eds.) *Understanding Social Research: thinking creatively about method*, London: Sage.

Mason, J. and Muir, S. (2013) 'Conjuring up traditions: atmospheres, eras and family Christmases', *The Sociological Review*, 61(3): 607–29.

Mason, J. and Tipper, B. (2008a) 'Being related: how children define and create kinship', *Childhood*, 15(4): 441–60.

Mason, J. and Tipper, B. (2008b) 'Children and the making of kinship configurations', in E. Widmer and R. Jallinoja (eds.) *Beyond the Nuclear Family: families in a configurational perspective*, Berlin: Peter Lang.

Mason, J. and Tipper, B. (2014) 'Children as family members', in G. B. Melton, A. Ben-Arieh, J. Cashmore, G. Goodman and N. K. Worley (eds.) *Handbook of Child Research*, London: Sage.

Mason, J., May, V. and Clarke, L. (2007) 'Ambivalence and the paradoxes of grandparenting', *The Sociological Review*, 55(4): 687–706.

May, V. (2016) 'What does the duration of belonging tell us about the temporal self?', *Time and Society*, 25(3): 634–51.

May, V. and Muir, S. (2015) 'Everyday belonging and ageing: place and generational change', *Sociological Research Online*, 20(1): 8, http://www.socresonline.org.uk/20/1/8.html (consulted 19 July 2016).

Merleau-Ponty, M. (2002 [1945]) *The Phenomenology of Perception* (translated by C. Smith), London: Routledge and Kegan Paul.

Merleau-Ponty, M. (2004 [1948]) *The World of Perception* (translated by O. Davis), London: Routledge.

Milgram, S. (1974) *Obedience to Authority*, New York: Harper and Row.

Misztal, B. (2003) *Theories of Social Remembering*, Milton Keynes: Open University Press.

Mohr, S. (2014) 'Beyond motivation: on what it means to be a sperm donor in Denmark', *Anthropology and Medicine*, 21(2): 162–73.

Moore, H. (2011) *Still Life: hopes, desires and satisfactions*, Cambridge: Polity.

Morgan, D. H. J. (1996) *Family Connections*, Cambridge: Polity.

Morgan, D. H. J. (2009) *Acquaintances: the space between intimates and strangers*, Maidenhead: Open University Press/McGraw Hill.

Murakami, H. (2008) *After Dark*, London: Vintage.

Navaro-Yashin, Y. (2009) 'Affective spaces, melancholic objects: ruination and the production of anthropological knowledge', *Journal of the Royal Anthropological Institute*, 15(1): 1–18.

Navarrete, C. D., McDonald, M. M., Mott, M. L. and Asher, B. (2012) 'Virtual morality: emotion and action in a simulated three-dimensional "trolley problem"', *Emotion*, 12(2): 364–70.

Nordqvist, P. (2010) 'Out of sight, out of mind: family resemblances in lesbian donor conception', *Sociology*, 44(6): 1128–44.

Nordqvist, P. and Smart, C. (2014) *Relative Strangers: family life, genes and donor conception*, Basingstoke: Palgrave Macmillan.

O'Farrell, M. (2006) *The Vanishing Act of Esme Lennox*, London: Headline Review.

Oxford Dictionary of English (2005) 2nd edition, Oxford: Oxford University Press.

Pearce, L. (2000) 'Driving north/driving south: reflections upon the spatial/temporal co-ordinates of "home"', in L. Pearce (ed.) *Devolving Identities: feminist readings in home and belonging*, Aldershot: Ashgate.

Pearce, L. (2013) 'Autopia: in search of what we're thinking when we're driving', in J. Stacey and J. Wolff (eds.) *Writing Otherwise: experiments in cultural criticism*, Manchester: Manchester University Press.

Philpott, C. M. and Boak, D. (2014) 'The impact of olfactory disorders in the United Kingdom', *Chemical Senses*, Advance access published 8 September.

Pink, S. (2015) *Doing Sensory Ethnography*, 2nd edition, London: Sage.

Proust, M. (1996) *In Search of Lost Time Vol 1: Swann's way* (translated by C. K. Scott Moncrieff, D. J. Enright and T. Kilmartin), London: Vintage.

Rapport, N. (1997) 'The "contrarieties" of Israel: an essay on the cognitive importance and the creative promise of both/and', *Journal of the Royal Anthropological Institute*, 3(4): 653–72.

Riach, K. and Warren, S. (2015) 'Smell organization: bodies and corporeal porosity in office work', *Human Relations*, 68(5): 789–809.

Richards, M. (2014) 'A British history of collaborative reproduction and the rise of the genetic connection', in T. Freeman, S. Graham, F. Ebtehaj and M. Richards (eds.) *Relatedness in Assisted Reproduction: families, origins and identities*, Cambridge: Cambridge University Press.

Ricoeur, P. (1991) 'Narrative identity', *Philosophy Today*, 35(1): 73–81.

Rodaway, P. (2011) *Sensuous Geographies: body, sense and place*, London: Routledge.

Rose, S. (2005) *Lifelines: life beyond the gene*, London: Vintage.

Rose, H. and Rose, S. (2012) *Genes, Cells and Brains: the Promethean promises of the new biology*, London: Verso.

Sahlins, M. (2013) *What Kinship Is – And Is Not*, Chicago and London: University of Chicago Press.

Schillmeier, M. (2006) 'Othering blindness – on modern epistemological politics', *Disability and Society*, 21(5): 471–84.

Scott, L. (2015) *The Four-Dimensional Human: ways of being in a digital world*, London: William Heinemann.

Sheller, M. (2004) 'Automotive emotions: feeling the car', *Theory, Culture and Society*, 21(4/5): 221–41.

Shepherd, N. (2011) *The Living Mountain: a celebration of the Cairngorm Mountains of Scotland*, Edinburgh: Canongate.

Shields, C. (2003) *Duet*, London and New York: Fourth Estate.

Slovo, G. (2000) *Red Dust*, London: Virago.

Smart, C. (2007) *Personal Life*, Cambridge: Polity.

Smart, C. (2011) 'Families, secrets and memories', *Sociology*, 45(4): 539–53.

Smart, C. (2014) 'Fragments: living with other people's lives as an analytic practice', in C. Smart, J. Hockey and A. James (eds.) *The Craft of Knowledge: experiences of living with data*, Basingstoke: Palgrave Macmillan.

Smart, C., Davies, K., Heaphy, B. and Mason, J. (2012) 'Difficult friendships and ontological insecurity', *The Sociological Review*, 60(1): 99–109.

Sopory, P. (2005) 'Metaphor and affect', *Poetics Today*, 26(3): 433–58.

Stacey, J. (1997) *Teratologies: a cultural study of cancer*, London: Routledge.

Stacey, J. (2010) *The Cinematic Life of the Gene*, Durham, NC and London: Duke University Press.

Stewart, K. (2007) *Ordinary Affects*, Durham, NC and London: Duke University Press.

Synnott, A. (1993) *The Body Social*, London: Routledge.

Tallis, R. (2013) *Reflections of a Metaphysical Flaneur: and other essays*, London: Routledge.

Taussig, M. (1993) *Mimesis and Alterity: a particular history of the senses*, New York and London: Routledge/Taylor Francis.

Thorn, P., Katzorke, T. and Daniels, K. (2008) 'Semen donors in Germany: a study exploring motivations and attitudes', *Human Reproduction*, 23(11): 2415–20.

Thrift, N. (2001) 'Still life in the nearly present time: the object of nature', in P. Macnaghten and J. Urry (eds.) *Bodies of Nature*, London: Sage.

Thrift, N. (2004) 'Driving in the city', *Theory, Culture and Society*, 20(4/5): 25–39.

Tipper, B. (2011) '"A dog who I know quite well": everyday relationships between children and animals', *Children's Geographies*, 9(20): 145–65.

Tipper, B. (2012) *Creaturely Encounters: an ethnographic study of human–animal relations in a British suburban neighbourhood*, unpublished PhD thesis, University of Manchester.

Tipper, B. (2013) 'Moments of being and ordinary human–animal encounters', *Virginia Woolf Miscellany* (Special Issue on Woolf and Animals), 84: 14–16.

Tuan, Y. F. (1977) *Space and Place: the perspective of experience*, Minneapolis: University of Minnesota Press.

Vannini, P., Waskul, D. and Gottschalk, S. (2011) *The Senses in Self, Society, and Culture: a sociology of the senses*, London: Routledge.

Vincent, J. (2006) 'Emotional attachment and mobile phones', *Knowledge, Technology, and Policy*, 19(1): 39–44.

Wetherell, M. (2012) *Affect and Emotion: a new social science understanding*, London: Sage.

Whatmore, S. (2006) 'Materialist returns: practising cultural geography in and for a more-than-human world', *Cultural Geographies*, 13(4): 600–9.

Widerberg, K. (2010) 'In the homes of others: exploring new sites and methods when investigating the doings of gender, class and ethnicity', *Sociology*, 44(6): 1181–96.

Wilding, R. (2006) '"Virtual" intimacies? Families communicating across transnational contexts', *Global Networks*, 6(2): 125–42.

Wilkie, R. (2010) *Livestock/Deadstock: working with farm animals from birth to slaughter*, Philadelphia: Temple University Press.

Wilson, S., Houmøller, K. and Bernays, S. (2012) '"Home and not some house": young people's sensory construction of family relationships in domestic spaces', *Children's Geographies*, 10(1): 95–107.

Winterson, J. (1997) *Gut Symmetries*, New York: Knopf.

Woolf, J. (1985) 'The invisible flâneuse: women and the literature of modernity', *Theory, Culture and Society*, 2(3): 37–46.

Wordsworth, W. (1999 [1888]) *The Complete Poetical Works*, London: Macmillan and Co., Bartleby.com, 1999, www.bartleby.com/145/ (consulted 11 October 2011).

Wright, D. (1990) *Deafness: a personal account*, London: Faber and Faber.

Index